Spirituality, Religion, and Education

This series publishes books that examine fundamental questions of life, touching on the meaning, purpose, and mission of education from a variety of spiritual and religious perspectives. The series provides a forum for scholars to explore how to engage learners spiritually and holistically. It studies how spirituality, religion, and education intertwine with the learning of wisdom, peacebuilding, cultural and interfaith dialogues, and the integration of learners' body, mind, emotions, and spirit. Commonalities and differences among spiritual and religious traditions are explored alongside new developments from science that bridge the spirit and the mind. The series especially pays attention to the educational initiatives, outcomes, and programs that simultaneously engage the cognitive, affective, and spiritual dimensions of both students and educators. The world we live in focuses mostly on education for the intellect, thus restricting our ability to explore and understand deeply the nature of the cosmos and the meaning of our life. Although education is accessible to more people than ever before in human history, the dominant paradigm focuses solely on knowledge, skill, and material acquisition that neglects the meaning and purpose of life. This creates a huge void in learners and produces a huge number of people who are unhappy, unfulfilled, restless, lost, or desperate. An education that distills and recovers wisdom from spiritual and religious traditions can fill the void and help cultivate citizens who have love, compassion, knowledge, and the capacities for enlightened action. Books in the series address these age-old pursuits of inquiry, meaning, purpose, growth, transformation, and change. To submit proposals to the series for consideration please contact Jing Lin at jinglin@umd.edu.

More information about this series at
http://www.palgrave.com/gp/series/15331

Njoki Nathani Wane · Miglena S. Todorova ·
Kimberly L. Todd
Editors

# Decolonizing the Spirit in Education and Beyond

## Resistance and Solidarity

palgrave
macmillan

*Editors*
Njoki Nathani Wane
University of Toronto
Toronto, ON, Canada

Miglena S. Todorova
University of Toronto
Toronto, ON, Canada

Kimberly L. Todd
University of Toronto
Toronto, ON, Canada

Spirituality, Religion, and Education
ISBN 978-3-030-25319-6 ISBN 978-3-030-25320-2 (eBook)
https://doi.org/10.1007/978-3-030-25320-2



This Palgrave Macmillan imprint is published by the registered company Springer Nature Switzerland AG
The registered company address is: Gewerbestrasse 11, 6330 Cham, Switzerland

*We dedicate this work to a vision of new decolonial futures that are steeped in love of the Earth, the reawakening of Spirit in all that we do and the collective movement towards justice and healing. Moreover, this work is our prayer for the regeneration, renewal and rebirth of the spirit within each of us, and so we also dedicate this work to the labour, the struggle and the courage it takes to walk such a path. Collectively we can do the work that needs to be done in order to heal our planet in the wake of climate change, to upend and dismantle colonial systems and structures and to center the work of Spirit once again.*

# Foreword

This book is a prayer and celebration of the distance we have traveled and the travails we have endured. Our journeys have left their marks and throughout it all Spirit is immutable and cannot be contained, diminished, and is ever present. Spirit is our breath. Every author in this book has their own dance and their own wisdom. Each brings their knowledge, and they are also in the process of regaining their ancestral knowledge and the centrality of Spirit in that knowledge as they reclaim their voices. We share this process with everyone included here. The process of our reconstitution and our reconnection to the Sacred (Spirit) is the central project of our Indigenous selves.

The ongoing process of colonization attempts to separate Indigeneity, Land, and Spirit, continually obscuring the pathways and connections that make their relationship evident. Indigeneity, Land, and Spirit are all one. They are intertwined. They are not separate parts of something. Indigeneity is bestowed upon us by the Land, in its deepest expression and culturally by people who are part of ancestral lineages connected to the Land. The Land is Spirit-made manifest. Spirit, Land, and Indigeneity are all ephemeral and abundant. They are not defined by human constructs of oppression or liberation. *Decolonizing the Spirit in Education and Beyond—Resistance and Solidarity* grapples with the contradictions and paradoxes of our relationship to Indigeneity, and with the contradictions and paradoxes of our relationship to Indigeneity, Land, and Spirit. It offers a landscape of interdisciplinary theories, practices, and approaches for decolonization and resistance. Its basic premise is that Spirit cannot be colonized. This book is an enactment of solidarity as we stand together in the effort to see clearly and reclaim our birthright. We are different from each other in keeping with our hard-won expressions of our Indigeneity in the midst of this continuing experience of oppression. Because each of our voices is unique and distinct, we are choosing to be in appreciation with each expression of sovereign logic. Therefore, we will highlight text directly from each chapter that we believe demonstrates each of our unique perspectives. This book is organized into four parts: Soul, Body, Mind, and the Re-centering of Spirit. Each part reveals the multiplicity of ways in which we are working diligently to make evident the richness of our lived, observed, and embodied manifestations. The following are highlights from each chapter in each contributor's own voice:

## Part I: Soul

### *Spirituality*

In Chapter 2, Njoki Nathani Wane asks "Is Decolonizing the Spirit Possible?" She poignantly points out that spiritual knowledges remain an essential part of self and resurfaces even in the face of oppression and colonization.

> What has amazed me, however, is how members of the colonized people held on to certain knowledges that they pushed to their sub-consciousness and whenever the environment was clear, they would pass on this knowledge to their children or their neighbors. This is particularly true when it comes to African Indigenous healing and spiritual practices. It's very liberating to be able to freely articulate your inner self, your spiritual self and not shy away from lifting the lid to let your light shine as you embrace your total self.

### *Land*

In Chapter 3, "Spirituality and a Search for Home: The Complexities of Practising Sikhism on Indigenous Land," Mandeep Kaur Mucina adds,

> I have searched for a place called home for much of my life, but I find I am more settled in my contention with it and with the notion that this will be a perpetual search. At times it may be satisfied and I may feel at home;

> at other times I may feel at a loss for home. However, I am okay with this never-ending search and believe in the notion of searching. I will find peace and comfort in living in the present dailyness of breathing and being respectful to all the beings, the places and the stories that live around me. Home is in my spirit and I am happy to have had the Gurudwara to heal my past spiritual injuries and move forward, toward a new vision and way of being "Indigenous to place."

In Chapter 4, Wambui Karanja, Land and Healing: A Decolonizing Inquiry for Centering Land as the Site of Indigenous Medicine and Healing, speaks of her own sense of healing and connection through land,

> In my travels back and forth from my country of residence to my country of birth, I can also testify to the euphoric spiritual connection I feel with my country of birth and the wholeness and connectedness I experience when I visit, a form of overwhelming peacefulness that makes me feel spiritually connected to my ancestral homeland. I conceptualize this feeling as healing from the land through my spiritual and indigenous connection to it. It speaks to the centrality of the physical and spiritual relationship and connectedness I have with the land in my motherland.

We think it is apropos to say that each contribution made in these first three chapters seeks to resituate our experiences of the Sacred within the Soul through our embodiment of Indigeneity, our relationship with Land and our relationship with Spirit.

## Part II: Body

### *Healing*

In Chapter 5, "Healing and Well-Being as Tools of Decolonization and Social Justice: Anti-Colonial Praxis of Indigenous Women in the Philippines," Rose Ann Torres shares her learning from healer women of the Aeta people in the Philippines,

> In the course of many honest exchanges and the simple, but powerful, act of listening, the Aeta healers in the Circle taught me that I should always be ready to reference the ultimate library of knowledge: what our Mother Nature is willing to give to us. These are lessons in limits and possibilities, and truths such as that we are made from nature and neither the controller

> nor arbiter of the possible. These ecological, biological, physical and emotional truths are ones Western science and ecology are only now rediscovering. When I met them, this set of caring women taught me how to pay attention to their way of life and practices.

In Chapter 6, "Decolonizing Western Medicine and Systems of Care: Implications for Education," Jacqueline Benn-John explains the impact of colonization on her own understanding the value of her people's traditional healing practices while reclaiming a new understanding and appreciation for her own traditions,

> Until recently, my narrow definition of health and healing—mind, body and spirit—reflected Western hegemonic notions of health and healing. In my colonized understanding of health and healing, there is an erasure of where and how humans are situated within space and community, and what our relationship with this space/community is. As part of my decolonizing journey, I developed an understanding of Indigenous health that challenged normative perceptions about Indigenous health. I was able to empathize with marginalized traditional healers and I developed a deeper appreciation for my cultural knowledge of traditional healing.

In Chapter 7, "BLOOD-ANGER: The Spirituality of Anti-Colonial Blood-Anger for Self-Defense" Stanley Doyle-Wood brings us to the state of re-membering as an anti-colonial act,

> The word re-*membering* [my italics] plays on the image of reordering the members (as in bodily members), creating a counter [embodied] memory or refraining in the body of goodness, spirit and interconnection. It involves both affirming sacred moments in one's past and acknowledging the sacredness of the self in the present. It includes reconnecting with spiritual and cultural traditions that have meaning for one's life now and re-membering the body's connection with the Earth (pp94). Active re-membering as relational to untying and therefore anti-colonial blood-anger are all of this and more. It is constant, reflexive, ongoing and active. Active re-membering is an epistemological position that is lived/alive. It is tactile. It burns. It breathes. It screams. It whispers. Active re-membering requires that our blood-anger as the body-tongue of our blood-memory talks with and back to our bodies; that our blood-anger engages in conversation with our blood-memories which at this point has become radically politicized and de-victimized. This talking,

> this conversation, this dialogue [with-and-by blood-anger to-and-from blood-memory and the whole of the self] are a whole-bodied listening, hearing, feeling, re-connecting, re-membering, anti-colonial blood-anger talk.

### *Food*

In Chapter 8, Janelle Brady's poem, "In my Mother's Kitchen: Spirituality and Decolonization," confronts us with the following moment,

> I remembered her words to me in the kitchen to "Move yuh hand fast" and how we would laugh | We would laugh because it was comical, but true, no time to delay, and as she would say, you | need to "cut n go tru"

In Chapter 9, "Reclaiming Cultural Identity Through Decolonization of Food Habits," Suleyman M. Demi shares the following memory connecting food, land and embodied indigenous knowledge,

> I vividly remember my grandmother used to prepare a meal consisting of leaves called "Zoogala gandi" (in Hausa language) mixed with "gari" and oil. After boiling the leaves, she sieved the leaves to separate the solid part from the liquid. As children, we sipped the leftover liquid, an action that received no reprimands from my grandmother because she knew its medicinal value as according to her, she inherited it from her great-grandparents. About ten years later, after I had graduated from the university and was teaching in the city, I heard of a wonder plant called "moringa" which according to scientists cured several diseases. The leaves were dried, grinded and the powdered form sold to schools, corporate organizations, as well as individuals in Ghana to incorporate in their food. Our school decided to purchase the seedlings to plant on our school compound. To my utmost surprise, the wonder plant is no other plant than "Zoogala gandi" that we were exposed to several years earlier. This encouraged me to value our food cultures bequeathed to us by our ancestors.

## Part III: Mind

### *Consciousness*

In Chapter 10, "A Journal on Ubuntu Spirituality," Devi Mucina reveals the complexities and gifts to be found in the relationships indigenous people living on Turtle Island successfully make with Indigenous peoples from the Americas,

> As I locate myself in southern Africa among the Ubuntu, while living here on Turtle Island, I am cognizant that I am a visitor and an unwelcome settler on Indigenous territories. Colonial governance structures and other settlers welcomed me to these Indigenous territories. I also acknowledge our ancestors that were brought here forcibly, those that lost their lives in the middle passage and our relatives that continue to leave their territories due to war and political prosecution. I raise my hands to you in recognitions of the tensions you experience about being here, but I particularly want to acknowledge that as I speak about Ubuntu spirituality, I am cognizant that I am privileging a particular Indigenous spirituality while being in the spiritual context of Turtle Island and its Indigenous peoples. The friendships and familial bonds I have developed with Indigenous peoples on these territories are saving me from colonial amnesia and trickery. I know home physically and spiritually because you have welcomed me into your colonial struggle. Our engagements about Indigenous resurgence shape my everyday actions. Through our relational bonds, I am learning to walk, play, live and work.

Chapters 5 through 9 focus on the exploration of embodied domination and resilience, on engaging with Indigeneity, Land and Spirit to fully embody ourselves in our bodies.

In Chapter 11, "Shedding of the Colonial Skin: The Decolonial Potentialities of Dreaming," Kimberly L. Todd shows us how dreaming connects us to Spirit,

> Dreaming has taught me the language of spirit. It has taught me to read dreams. It literally initiated me into the realm of spirit through the course of a reoccurring dream.
>
> Through this year of the Sea Turtle, I was birthed anew and it took me the full year to determine the meaning behind Her symbolism. I can now in hindsight understand that this process was actually the shedding of my colonial conditioning and is still continually decolonizing me. After that year I could no longer adhere to the worldview I had been born into. The dream process completely ruptured that worldview; it was as if I had undergone a radical re-membering of who I was. Perhaps, not unlike a soul retrieval, I experienced the great power inherent in dreaming and realized that it should be valued because it provides a gateway into the sacred that can help initiate and facilitate the decolonizing process.

## Part IV: The Re-centering of Spirit

In Chapter 12, "Critical Spirituality: Decolonizing the Self," Josue Tario speaks from the voice of *latinidad* and expounds on the idea of *critical spirituality* and its potential role of advancing the agenda of decolonization,

> I believe that death to the self/ego is the closest thing to nirvana/heaven/higher form of existence. The temporality of life will always include movement, uncertainty, fear, insecurity and pain. The best way to deal with this is to try to surrender the ego, realize the interconnectedness of the universe and love. I would like to conclude by recognizing the amount of privilege I have, sitting here in a nice office, writing about the decolonization of the self and spiritual transcendence when many of our Indigenous and African descendant brothers and sisters are fighting for material decolonization of the land. Decolonization cannot only be about theory or pontifications, it must be about praxis and tangible action. Many are literally fighting to survive and dying daily because of colonization. However, I do believe that decolonization of both the land and the self must be done for true decolonization to take place one day. The self has colonized this earth. The spirit cannot be colonized because it is what decolonizes the self.

In Chapter 13, Kaylynn Sullivan TwoTrees and Sayra Pinto: "A Landscape of Sacred Regeneration and Resilience," we speak to the centrality of connecting to the Sacred and the need to be driven and guided by faith,

> Our individual journeys have guided us to choose to expend our energy dreaming into the future from a foundation of the Sacred. We will not attempt to define the Sacred since we see defining the Sacred in itself as a reductive act and a replay of colonization. At best, we can attempt to point toward the Sacred, an act that is never to be mistaken for the Sacred itself. Although we will not offer a definition, we affirm that when one encounters the Sacred, one knows one has done so. The Sacred has many names and faces all over the world. All of these point to the ineffable, the Great Mystery, and all the names given to the Sacred Source. The turn toward the Sacred means the turn toward faith even in the heart of rationality. We affirm that faith is driving the car, not rationality. Faith is an expression of our intimate, dynamic relationship with the Unknown and Unknowable.

Lastly, an interview by Kimberly L. Todd of Njoki Nathani Wane serves as the closing dialogue for this book. Miglena S. Todorova's conclusion helps us all bring this experience to a close. We hope that the chorus of voices included in this book offers you ways to support, affirm and enhance your own ideas on your own journey relating to Indigeneity, Land, Spirit and decolonization. We believe it is an important gift to maintain our unique and earnest voices that we may be able to connect and meet other ones who also yearn and courageously live lives that unapologetically connect to that which is Sacred.

Burlington, USA

Kaylynn Sullivan TwoTrees
Sayra Pinto

# Acknowledgements

We would like to acknowledge the incredible work of our contributors. Their work is honest, poignant and inspiring. We thank them for the patience they have had with us throughout this process. We would also like to thank our publishers for the labour they have put into this project. We would also like to thank our ancestors (parents, grandparents, great-grandparents moving backwards through time). We can always feel their love and presence guiding us when we need it most. Their spirits led to this project—out of one, many have joined to reignite a re-centering of Spirit.

# Contents

## Part II Body



## Part III Mind



## Part IV The Re-centering of Spirit

# Notes on Contributors

**Jacqueline Benn-John** is a Ph.D. candidate in the Department of Social Justice Education at Ontario Institute for Studies in Education, University of Toronto. Jacqueline's research interests are in the area of Indigenous knowledges, decolonizing healing, feminist counselling and Black women's resistance.

**Janelle Brady** is an activist and scholar, and her work looks at Black and African feminist mothering practices as forms of resistance. She is currently a doctoral candidate at OISE and has published in a number of peer-reviewed journals and books on the topics of anti-racism, Black feminism, spirituality and progressive educational policies. Janelle is also involved in political activism and women's organizing and has been an active voice and advocate for meaningful equitable policies and outcomes.

**Suleyman M. Demi** is a Ph.D. candidate at OISE and the School of the Environment and Senior Doctoral Fellow at New College of the University of Toronto. His scholarly interests are multidisciplinary and include environmental justice and sustainability, social justice and food systems analysis. He uses Indigenous knowledge and philosophical frameworks in his research. His research focuses on the impact of climate change on Indigenous food systems and its implications on livelihoods and health of smallholder farmers.

**Stanley Doyle-Wood** is an Assistant Professor cross-appointed in the Equity Studies Department at New College, University of Toronto, and in the Transitional Year Program at the University of Toronto, Canada. Doyle-Wood is an artist, poet, writer, scholar and educator in the areas of critical anti-racism, equity, anti-colonial studies and grass-roots community engagement. Doyle-Wood's scholarly work and practice lie in an analysis and contestation of structural and accumulative forms of racialized violence and spirit-injury and the possibilities and praxis of resistance as embodied spiritual acts of pedagogy, survival and liberation from the standpoint of the historically oppressed.

**Wambui Karanja** is a Ph.D. student at the Ontario Institute for Studies in Education of the University of Toronto, Canada. Her research interests lie in anti-colonial thought, anti-racism theories and frameworks, decolonizing theories, Indigenous knowledges and land rights, development and modernization theories, Afrocentric frameworks and gender issues. Her current research explores Indigenous conceptions of land at the nexus of colonial/neo-colonial encounters. Wambui has published on African Women's land rights, Indigenous knowledges and the coloniality of Western research practices in developing countries. She has a bachelor of laws degree from the University of Nairobi, Kenya, and a master's degree in law from the University of Toronto, Canada, and has recently completed extensive research on the role of Elders' cultural knowledges in schools. She has a passion for community development, equity and social justice issues.

**Devi Mucina** is an Assistant Professor in the Indigenous Governance Program at the University of Victoria. His academic interests are Indigenous African philosophies, decolonizing Indigenous masculinities, Indigenous fathering and other-fathering while using Ubuntu oratures as entrance points to international Indigenous convergence and collaborative dialogues.

**Mandeep Kaur Mucina** is an Assistant Professor at the University of Victoria with over 15 years of frontline experience as a child and youth care practitioner and social worker. Mandeep's research and social justice work focuses on family violence, gender-based violence, understanding the role of trauma in migration and exploring second-generation immigrant youth's stories of resistance, identity and encounters with racism in the diaspora, all from a feminist critical race and anti-colonial lens. Mandeep has in-depth experience conducting life histories with racialized women and girls. Mandeep's current research explores the intersections between migration, trauma and refugee and immigrant children, youth and families' encounters with child welfare and the criminal justice systems. Furthermore, she will be expanding her research on violence in South Asian communities in British Columbia.

**Sayra Pinto** leads change processes that support the transformation of nonprofits, schools, colleges, city governments, hospitals, police departments, neighborhoods and communities. She has an undergraduate degree from Middlebury College, an MFA from Goddard College and a Ph.D. from the Union Institute and University. Her work is informed, inspired and fueled by the trajectory of struggle and transcendence of Indigenous peoples and our collective obligation to strengthen communities. As an immigrant from Honduras who is a naturalized citizen, Sayra builds connections and collaborations that create profound systems change and that engage individuals in deeply transformational experiences. She is currently working on a book on leadership, is a Leadership Team member of the University of Vermont's Master's in Leadership for Sustainability and does freelance consulting with organizations and institutions seeking to create cultures of connection, belonging, well-being, innovation and excellence.

**Rose Ann Torres** has a Ph.D. in Sociology and Equity Studies in Education and Women and Gender Studies from the Ontario Institute for Studies in Education (OISE) of the University of Toronto (U of T). She is a Lecturer in the Social Justice Education Department of OISE/U of T. Her teaching and research interests are in the areas of: critical race and gender studies, transnational feminisms, queer studies, global health, Indigenous epistemologies and Asian/ African/studies.

**Josue Tario** is an Equity Program Advisor for the Toronto District School Board. His work is focused on providing educators with equitable pedagogies using an anti-oppressive framework. He also does work with students around equity, human rights issues and leadership capacity. Josue has an honors bachelor's degree in sociology and a master's degree in education. Most importantly, he is a proud father to an amazing fourteen-year-old son and loves to spend time with him.

**Kimberly L. Todd** is a fourth year Ph.D. candidate in the Department of Social Justice Education. Her research interests include education, decolonization, spirituality, dreaming and teacher praxis. She is a certified educator who has taught in South Korea, in the United Arab Emirates and in a First Nations community in North West Saskatchewan. She has also designed curricular resources for the David Suzuki Foundation and Amazon Watch.

**Miglena S. Todorova** is an Assistant Professor in the Department of Social Justice Education at the Ontario Institute for Studies in Education (OISE), University of Toronto. She is also the Director of the Centre for Media, Culture and Education at OISE. Her research and teaching are in the areas of racial formation, transnational feminism(s) and post-socialist studies, focusing especially on social relations and knowledge/cultural production. Dr. Todorova is an international scholar whose work advances feminist, intersectional and relational paradigms linking local and global sites and issues.

**Kaylynn Sullivan TwoTrees** is an artist/catalyst. She has spent a life at the crossroads where species, cultures, beliefs and the unknown collide and find both dissonance and resonance. Her work helps humans re-orient to our Indigenous mind and regenerate our essential relationship with the Earth's wisdom. She is part recipient of the Lila Wallace International Artist Award and has held positions as Academic Challenge Scholar in Interdisciplinary Studies at Miami University and Scholar in Residence in the schools of Business and Fine Arts at Miami University and at the Cleveland Institute of Art. She is currently on the faculty of the Master's in Leadership for Sustainability Program at the University of Vermont's Rubenstein School of Environment and Natural Resources.

**Njoki Nathani Wane** is a recognized scholar in the areas of Black feminisms in Canada & Africa, African Indigenous knowledges, African women and spirituality. Dr. Wane is currently the Chair of the Department of Social Justice Education at the Ontario Institute for Studies in Education (OISE). One of her most recent publications is *Indigenous African Knowledge Production: Food Processing Practices Among Kenyan Rural Women*. She has co-authored an Anti-racist training manual, *Equity in Practice: Transformational Training Resource*, with Larissa Cairncross, *Ruptures: Anti-Colonial & Anti-Racist Feminist Theorizing* with Jennifer Jagire & Zahra Murad, *A Handbook on African Traditional Healing*

*Approaches & Research Practices* with Erica Neeganagwedin. She has also co-edited *Spirituality, Education & Society: An Integrated Approach* with Energy Manyimo & Eric Ritskes and *The Politics of Cultural Knowledge* with Arlo Kempf and Marlon Simmons. Prof. Wane headed the Office of Teaching Support in 2009–2012. She has been nominated TVO Best Lecturer and is the recipient of the Harry Jerome Professional Excellence Award (2008) and of the African Women Achievement Award (2007). She is also a recipient of the prestigious David E. Hunt Award for Excellence in Graduate Education for 2016, University of Toronto and the President of Toronto Teaching Award, 2017.

CHAPTER 1

# Introduction

*Miglena S. Todorova, Njoki Nathani Wane and Kimberly L. Todd*

*Decolonizing the Spirit* signifies two related epistemological and political practices simultaneously. It stands for the relationship between colonialism, oppression and racial violence, and the human aspirations, higher consciousness, and connection to the mysterious and the universal of the colonized, racialized, and oppressed. While the term and rhetoric of *spirit* suggests notions of religion and faith, the questions, as well as acts and attempts at resolution, articulated in *Decolonizing the Spirit*, query myriad informal iterations of spiritual life and understanding. The heart of *Decolonizing the Spirit* is the idea that the spirit cannot be colonized. Certainly, the spirit can go into hibernation for its own protection; however, we posit that a people's spirituality re-emerges at appropriate, safe, and growth times

M. S. Todorova (✉) · N. N. Wane · K. L. Todd
University of Toronto, Toronto, ON, Canada
e-mail: miglena.todorova@utoronto.ca

N. N. Wane
e-mail: njoki.wane@utoronto.ca

K. L. Todd
e-mail: k.todd@mail.utoronto.ca



N. N. Wane et al. (eds.), *Decolonizing the Spirit in Education and Beyond*, Spirituality, Religion, and Education,
https://doi.org/10.1007/978-3-030-25320-2_1

during and after colonization. While imperial projects, domination, and racial violence have aimed to break and destroy the spirit, the spirituality of colonial subjects not only has survived but it has been re-activated across national borders to claim social justice and equality for those whose lands were stolen and their bodies murdered and wounded.

*Decolonizing the Spirit* also captures a myriad of contemporary 'decolonizing' intellectual and political activities especially intense in North American academies as intellectuals, activists, and communities identify, disrupt, and dismantle material and symbolic structures extending and supporting violence against racialized and Indigenous peoples after the formal disintegration of empires. The essays included in this collection enact these projects, albeit differently, from diverse standpoints in Africa, Asia, and South and North America. These individual enactments, however, seek to reach others in a shared space. That space was first forged by women, especially Black academic women of African descent whose activism over a decade ago created a conference called 'Decolonizing the Spirit' at the University of Toronto in Toronto, Canada. Over the years, Indigenous in North America, Latina, Black Canadian, African American, Caribbean diaspora, Southeast Asian, and White women, men and non-binary people have joined this conversation about decolonization and the spirit. Questions pertaining to resistance, political alliances, togetherness, and difference centered the debates, showcasing the political power of knowledge exchanges blessed with love, respect, and spiritual mutuality amid cultural and historical difference.

The political and intellectual collaborations initiated at the conference over the years have opened important spaces and critical conversations about the Euro-centric and neoliberal nature of scientific research, knowledge production, and teaching. Questions about the role of these colonizing practices in dividing individuals and communities, normalizing land theft, extraction of natural resources, and related immigration policies, and justifying state violence against differently racialized, gendered, and sexed bodies have anchored our decolonization conversations over the years. Yet explicit analytical frameworks regarding spirituality seem to have alluded us, leaving a gap in the decolonization literature.

This book addresses the gap, offering multiple points of entry to perceive the relationship between (de)colonization and spirituality locally and globally. The authors whose voices grace the collection are not necessarily in agreement about the various polemics of decolonization or the spirit. Rather, the chapters share unique spiritual views and perform decolonization differently through multiple epistemologies and fields of practice. Together, the chapters illuminate spiritual and political resurgences among many communities across the world. The Indigenous communities of North and South America, Africa, and Asia are revisiting their ways of knowing and insisting that their knowledges be honored and included in public education and schooling in meaningful ways. They have indicated in more ways than one that they will not be idle any more. This reawakening is not unique to Indigenous peoples. Rather, resurgence or political and cultural energies evident in communities around the globe beg the question about the source of such raising and strength. Throughout the various keynotes, panels, and paper presentations delivered at the *Decolonizing the Spirit* conferences over the years, it was clear that intellectuals, activists, and community members were evoking theories of resistance rooted in their communities, as well as deep desire for solidarity and connections between struggles and communities. The presenters were no longer speaking from that position of a spirit that has gone into hibernation, but from a political stance evoking the spirituality of their ancestors. Hence, the emphasis of this anthology is the importance of theorizing the spirit and better understanding moments and processes of spiritual emergence/re-emergence. *Decolonizing the Spirit* attempts such theorizing without claiming to exhaust the multiple methodological and epistemological angles that could anchor a theoretical framework of spirituality and de/colonization.

Furthermore, this anthology is an attempt to truly value spirit and its capacity for individual and collective decolonial transformation. Educational spaces and institutions have been and are currently a site of ongoing colonial violence. They need to be revolutionized. It is necessary to begin actively dreaming, visioning, and building toward a spiritual and political decolonial future. Classrooms can potentially provide the spaces for this incubation. We hope that this anthology will enter these spaces as a catalyst among many other wonderful works for decolonial resistance and renewal. We are dreaming of a world that values spirit and spiritual technologies and their individual, communal, and political implications for the benefit of all sentient life on this planet and this anthology is a glimpse into that/this world.

The collection is organized by themes, each addressing spiritual resurgence and decolonizing practice related to *Soul, Body, Mind and the Recentering of Spirit*. The chapters speak to these themes from within distinct geographical, cultural, and social locations, fostering understanding of spiritual and decolonizing practices that are present in Canada and the United States but do not originate in these nation-states. In her chapter, Njoki Nathani Wane attempts defining of 'spirituality' only to embrace the perpetuity of meanings and practices signified by the term in diverse cultural, historical, and linguistic contexts. Wane also asserts that the spirit cannot be colonized thus laying the foundations of a theoretical paradigm of spirituality that anchors this collection. Mandeep Kaur Mucina complicates the issue of healing and well-being by posing important questions about the South Asian diaspora in North America, decolonial resistance, and the contestation of practicing spirituality on stolen Indigenous lands in Canada.

Wambui Karanja extends the paradigm to Indigenous land and traditions, focusing on how spirituality emerges out of the unique connection that Indigenous peoples have with land and cosmos. In that connection, Karanja also finds healing and centered existence that is key to Indigenous and postcolonial personal and social well-being.

Rose Ann Torres writes about healing and well-being through centering the voices of Indigenous Aeta women healers from the Philippines. Their struggles against colonial violence are a testament to the work of resistance grounded in spirituality as site for transformation and justice. Jacqueline Benn-John critiques the current models of healing and medicine and troubles Canada's Western hegemonic colonial narratives surrounding health care. She discusses anti-racist and anti-colonial frameworks that could serve as decolonizing solutions. Stanley Doyle-Wood's chapter pushes the issue of health and prosperity further by connecting the spiritual to the political directly and by calling for re-articulation and re-assertion of the anger of the oppressed. Doyle-Wood theorizes anger as the body's organizing language of/for self-defense; a language manifested in what the author calls 'blood-anger.'

Janelle Brady utilizes the medium of poetry to conjure resistance, spiritual connection, and decolonization through the act of cooking in her mother's kitchen. Through this poem, Brady charts generations of resistance to patriarchy, colonial violence, and anti-Blackness. Brady's poem reveals how the act of cooking is a spiritual and decolonial praxis connecting her to her ancestors. It is a powerful reminder of how resistance, spirituality, and decoloniality can be enacted in many forms that honor our ancestral ties. Suleyman M. Demi argues the case for the revival of Indigenous eating habits in Africa. Demi writes about the colonial degradation of eating habits utilizing his own experience as a centerpiece in the unravelling of this chapter. He explores the connection between food, culture, and African spirituality. Demi unpacks the devastation that colonial farming and diets have wrought on African bodies and land and the imperative for the decolonization and revival of Indigenous food practices on African soil.

Devi Mucina elaborates on the links between spirituality and politics amid difference by activating an Indigenous decolonizing tradition of Ubuntu dialogue so that he may speak truthfully about Ubuntu spirit while honoring and respecting his relationships with other Indigenous peoples, especially the Lekwungen-speaking peoples on whose traditional territory he and his family live. Likewise, Kimberly L. Todd in her chapter seeks political connections to others by exploring how dreaming and dreams can reconnect people by coalescing around deep remembering of ancestry, myth, landscapes, and animal symbolism that heals and strengthens colonized and racialized minds and bodies.

Josue Tario interweaves his narrative of resistance, movement, and belonging alongside the primary research he has conducted with Latin American Canadians. Spirituality, specifically critical spirituality, is unpacked and so is its capacity for empowerment, interconnection, and love in the lives of both the author and the young individuals whose experiences he studies. Tario posits the power inherent in critical spirituality to rupture bonds of internal oppression. Likewise, in their chapter, Kaylynn Sullivan TwoTrees and Sayra Pinto examine in depth our unbroken connection to spirit in the face of colonization and Euro-centricity. They argue that by choosing the framework of decolonization and spirituality, we could examine the sources of our survival thus preventing distancing of Indigenous peoples from each other and the strength of spirit. Conversations about decolonization and the spirit link us to our ancestors allowing for deep remembering that re-enlivens our ability to dream a shared future of courage, resilience, and hope.

The dialogue chapter is a snapshot of a moment in time between Njoki Nathani Wane and Kimberly L. Todd. The dialogue unravels around the destruction of colonial violence materially and internally and the role of spirit from its state of dormancy to its full-fledged emergence. This theoretical discussion of spirit is punctured by storytelling, dream narratives, and laughter.

The concluding chapter by Miglena S. Todorova takes on a postsocialist view to address critically the intersections between socialism/Marxism, colonization, and spirituality. The author argues that decolonization theories and practice in Western academies have failed to recognize Indigenous struggles in the former Soviet Union. By recognizing such violence specifically within the context of Northern Russia and highlighting the resurgence of Indigenous spirituality in Russia and Siberia, Todorova reminds us of the importance of material, spiritual and global efforts towards decolonization. The conclusion addresses this gap and extends the discourse on the broader epistemological, material, geographical and political contexts within which the authors contributing to this collection address spirituality, decolonization(s), and the future.

PART I

# Soul

CHAPTER 2

# Is Decolonizing the Spirit Possible?

*Njoki Nathani Wane*

## Introduction

There is no universal definition for spirituality since it implies a relationship with what people variously refer to as the life force, God, Creator, the higher self or purpose, or the Great Mystery. What is essential, however, is how one defines their own spirituality and spiritual practices. The context of spirituality differs from individual to individual and from group to group. For many people, it encompasses a sense of wholeness, healing and the interconnectedness of all things. In this paper, I reflect on different notions of spirituality. In particular, I look back to the time I became aware of my spirituality as an academic and in particular how I decided to evoke spirituality in my teaching, researching and writing. I situate the paper on the following questions: What do we need to decolonize from? What are the tools of colonization? How can spirituality be a decolonizing tool? What can we learn from the past to guide our education endeavours for the future? Why has it been important to emphasize spirituality as a pedagogical tool in teaching and learning? Why do we need to reconnect the intellect with the spirit? What are the implications of our spiritual

N. N. Wane (✉)
University of Toronto, Toronto, ON, Canada
e-mail: njoki.wane@utoronto.ca



N. N. Wane et al. (eds.), *Decolonizing the Spirit in Education and Beyond*, Spirituality, Religion, and Education,
https://doi.org/10.1007/978-3-030-25320-2_2

ways of knowing in terms of knowledge dissemination and in this particular time when almost every other person I meet talks about decolonization, decolonial or re-colonization? Are these new debates or a resurgence of old debates more acceptable now in our everyday conversation in our colonial institutions than they were a number of decades ago? What should teaching that embraces spirituality look like? How would you define teaching pedagogy that is spiritually driven? What has been the impact of separating the spiritual aspect of our teaching and learning from the intellectual development? How do we define spirituality? How can we create an inclusive space using spiritual lens? In this chapter, I argue that the spirit has never been colonized, will never be colonized and that the spirit is always there, in either an active or dormant mode. I will draw from the African people's spirituals to show when the spirit becomes subsumed in everyday experiences through either activism, resistance or emotional sustainability. I situate this chapter on anti-colonial and African Indigenous theoretical frameworks. I reflect on my own spirituality as I locate myself as a woman of African ancestry who believes the spirit is alive and well.

## Locating Myself

I am an African woman living in North America. As I enter in this discourse of spirituality and spiritual ways of knowing, I must state first and foremost the tendency for many of us who are schooled within the western canon to assume we are a tabula rasa until we were steeped in foreign beliefs. I am here to tell you that, growing up in a small African village, my parents filled my every cell with spiritual ways of knowing. In our waking up, my parents' ritual was to commune with the spirit, the giver of everything, the living and the dead. The morning devotion started with evocation of the mighty Ngai (Creator), who granted us another day, another chance to perfect our relation with the seen and unseen; another chance to give thanks for the gifts Creator had given us, the moon, the sun, the rivers, the trees, the air, the stays, our neighbours, our beautiful environment, the foods, our joys and sorrows of life. This morning devotion awoke the spirit and provided enough energy to go throughout the day. This ritual was repeated at the end of the day, as members of the family prepared to go and rest. My parents gave thanks and asked for rejuvenation of our every dimension of our bodies, lives and relationships. Looking back, it was every word that was spoken in thanksgiving, added a layer of warmth around our bodies, our homes and our relationships. There was comfort in knowing that, we were not alone, we had the living and the departed ancestors all forming a fortified war that nothing could go through it. This was my daily routine. All this was scripted in my consciousness and safely locked up somewhere in my sub-consciousness. I strongly believe that, no matter the amount of brainwashing and colonization, the sacredness of my parents' inculcation of spiritualism could not be erased even with the indoctrination of the foreign religious spiritual practices. This early spiritual grounding is what makes me the person I am today—an African woman warrior who will always be a spiritual being having a human experience. In this paper, I therefore argue that, based on the relationship that people have with their spirit, the spirit cannot be colonized. The spirit may stay in what might appear a "dormant" state ready to spring to action at an appropriate time and moment. The paper will show how the spirit becomes an invisible inner strength that many hold on when the physical body has been subjected to different types of oppressions. My working definition in this paper is that spirituality is a way of living, a method and a practice through which one lives and aspires towards his or her goals and ambitions and their connection to the collective well-being of society.

The above reflection is ground on African ways of knowing and will be explored under the African Indigenous theoretical framework.

## Theoretical Framework

Theorizing decolonization as a way of eradicating colonization is an elusion exercise. Colonization was crafted in such a way that it found mechanisms of regulating itself as well as reproducing and fortifying its structures. That is why, when we hold a dialogue of the mechanics of colonization, we need to go back to our source, our past and our Indigeneity. We also need to have a thorough understanding of the totality of colonization. Colonization is not just economics and political control, it was total consumption of a society with everything visible and invisible. The aim of colonization was to have a type of social control that had been derived from a Eurocentric school of thought. As Fanon aptly states, the idea was to create a Black person, who was alien to himself/herself. In other words, he/she was going to be "uprooted, dispersed, dazed and doomed to watch as the truths he/she had elaborated vanish one by one…" (2007, p. xii). Kipusi (2018) quoted Mazama who argues that "colonization was not simply an enterprise of economic exploitation and political control, as it was commonly held, but also an on-going enterprise of conceptual distortion and invasion, leading to widespread confusion and ultimately, mental incarceration" (Mazama, 2003, p. 3). The conceptual distortion and mental incarceration are concealed as a wholesome and "normal" way of life because colonialism came as an enveloping and interlocking social order that dominated and cut across the spirit, mind, intellect, knowledge, social life, subjectivity, economics, social and politics of life towards imperial expansion and a Eurocentric governed world (Kipusi, 2018). That is why an African Indigenous theoretical framework is suitable to interrogate the alienation of the colonized African so as to make sense of what needs to be done to *decolonize* the spirit.

African Indigenous theoretical framework is a particular type of knowledge system that can be understood as a collective consciousness, as embodied through a shared epistemology and ontology rooted in the collective ethic of people of African ancestry. An African Indigenous theoretical framework, according to Odora-Hoppers (2009), is systems of knowledge in philosophy or science, education, etc., that are grounded in the totality of a community's culture and have been maintained over centuries. Mbiti (1969) states that, "… culture covers many things, such as the way people live, behave and act, and their physical as well as their intellectual achievements. Culture shows itself in … dance, music and drama, ….in social organizations and political systems, in religion, ethics, morals and philosophy, in the customs and institutions of the people, in their values and laws, and in their economic life" (1969, p. 7). Also Mbiti eloquently stated in his 1969 book on *African Religions and Philosophy*, "I am, because we are; and since we are, therefore I am": individuals become part of a collective as they become conscious of their being and their responsibilities to their communities. This collective consciousness is rooted in a cultural philosophy that encompasses a shared historical consciousness, collective experiences of marginalization, oppression and resistance, and, therefore, a collective vision of justice that is anti-colonial. African Indigenous theoretical framework therefore is a philosophy that is rooted in the spirit of African worldview that wholeness, community and harmony are deeply embedded in cultural values. Central to the African worldview is the strong orientation to collective values and harmony rooted in a collective sense of responsibility which acknowledges that survival of the group derives from harmony through interdependence and interconnectedness (Mkabela, 2005). That is what becomes the cultural philosophy and collective consciousness of a people. If that is the case, can the spirit be colonized? As I have stated elsewhere (Wane, 2009), Indigenous knowledges are lived experiences and they are ways and systems of being and seeing. In these knowledges, we ground our experiential practices and our theoretical systems. In other words, African ways of knowing, informs their practice and vice versa. These Indigenous and traditional knowledges are transmitted through unique and multiple ways of being, seeing and knowing, through acts and practices, dreams and visions, passed down over generations and from elders to subsequent generations (Castellano, 2000; Ray, 2012). These knowledges are not linked to individuals or even to a particular historical period or place, but link multiple generations (McGadney-Douglass & Douglass, 2008), transmitting knowledges on culture, economics, social histories, education and governance (to name a few). These knowledges, in the form of memories, often passed down in oral traditions, can be a tool to rectify distortions in history and to produce new understandings of the ways in which communities thrive.

For instance, Michael Dantley (2005) argues that spirituality, with components of critical reflection, has been one of the main pillars of the African American experience. "Our spirit", he writes, "enables us to connect with other human beings" (p. 654). Spirituality, therefore, is about meaning making—it is about how people construct knowledge through largely unconscious and symbolic processes manifested through image, symbol, ritual and music. Spirituality is about the ongoing development of identity or moving towards what many refer to as their greater authentic self. It is simultaneously collective and personal (Wane, 2007, 2011). Derezotes defines spirituality as "a complex, intrapsychic dimension of human development" (1995, p. 1), while Bullis argues that spirituality is "the relationship of the human person to something or someone who transcends themselves" (1996, p. 2). Mazama, writing from an Afrocentric perspective, states that spirituality is "cosmic energy that permeates and lives within all that is", which "confers a common sense to everything in the world, and thus ensures the fundamental unity of all that exists" (2002, pp. 219–221). In short, spirituality has been defined as "a complex, intrapsychic dimension of human development" (Derezotes, 1995, p. 1), or "the relationship of the human person to something or someone who transcends themselves" (Bullis, 1996, p. 2). Many people include spirituality in a search for meaning that shapes their identities, which enables them to cope with everyday challenges (Watt, 2003). I would say that spirituality is about inner strength, faith and groundedness; it facilitates networking, survival and collectivity; it connects the personal to larger social systems and meaning-making (Wane, 2007). Spirituality has been a contentious topic in education, let alone as a philosophy or teaching tool. In recent times, different authors have examined different ways that spirituality may be incorporated in education (Elton-Chalcraft 2002). Others have pointed the silencing of spirituality in higher education and, in particular, its absence as a research tool (Dillard 2000; hooks, 2003). Moreover, each one of us needs to make sense of our spirituality in order to create balance and maintain connectedness with the self and the world at large.

## Situating Spirituality

Spirituality is a collective experience and an intricate interplay between the inner self and the social world; consequently, some studies suggest that spirituality can be used to mobilize women who are subjected to injustice and oppression (Dantley, 2006; Odora-Hoppers, 2005; Wane, 2007). Pratt and Ashforth (2003) proposed three dimensions to spirituality in a workplace context: connections with something greater than the self (transcendence), an integration of the various aspects of the self (holism) and realization of one's potential (growth). Fry (2003), Miller (2005), Phipps (2012) and Polat (2011) have also suggested that spirituality is essential to an organization's creativity, commitment and productivity. For Miller, when leadership is grounded in spiritual principles, business skills are applied with excellence, and people strive for high values in productivity, communications and management practices (also see Neal & Biberman, 2003; Phipps, 2012; Polat, 2011; Reave, 2005; Shahjahan, 2010). Gallagher and Golant (2000), Hayward (2005), Hyman, Scholarios and Baldry (2005), Delgado and Canabal (2006), and Carli and Eagly (2007) have also observed that many women draw on families, peers/friends, neighbours and social networks to deal with the everyday stress situations at workplace in a manner similar to relying on spirituality. Spirituality is about a sense of wholeness, healing and the interconnectedness of all things…related to a connection to what many refer to as the life force, God, Creator, a higher self or purpose, Great Mystery or Buddha (Tisdell and Tolliver, 2003 p. 374). Spirituality is a way of being in the world where one is connected to one's cultural knowledge and/or other beings (Shahjahan, 2009, p. 122). Moreover, it connects humanity to the life force and the sacredness of life through our relationships with ourselves and the world around us (Pulido, 1998, p. 721).

## Tools of Colonization

Colonialism is not satisfied merely by hiding people in its grip and emptying the native's brain of all form and content. By a kind of perverted logic, it turns to the past of the oppressed people and distorts, disfigures and destroys it. This work of devaluing pre-colonial history takes a dialectical significance today (Fanon, 1994, p. 37). Fanon's (1994) article, *A Dying Colonialism*, captures the insidiousness of colonization. The colonizers were determined to ensure that, by the time their work was done with the colonized, they would not recognize themselves, nor would they believe in themselves. They would be looking up to the settler who supposedly provided the "ingredients" of a subdued colonized subject whose knowledge and ways of knowing were "not good enough", not equal to the standard of the colonial master. The above train of argument is captured by what Fanon (1994) stated: "When we consider the efforts made to carry out the cultural estrangement so characteristic of the colonial epoch, we realize that nothing has been left to chance and that the total result looked for by colonial domination was indeed to convince the natives that colonialism came to lighten their darkness" (p. 37). What this means is that colonialism was a calculated, well-orchestrated project, with a clear road map on how to achieve the colonizing of the mind of the natives. Fanon further advances: "The effect consciously sought by colonialism was to drive into the natives' head the idea that if the settlers were to leave, they would at once fall back into barbarism, degradation and hostility" (Fanon, 1994: p. 37). There was an assumption from the colonizer's standpoint that once their colonizing tools were applied, that is, colonial education, religions (spirituality) or medicine, the colonized subjects would have been enlightened and no longer barbaric. What an arrogant preposition! The colonial master thought it would be a clean sweep—one of emptying the natives head, and the second round, filling it with hatred of themselves, their ways of being and their inferior status within the classification humans. How mistaken they were! The colonizer thought they could colonize the spirit (African Indigenous religions in my case), Indigenous knowledges and ways of healing. This notion of the spirit cannot be colonized made me therefore engage in this conversation of whether the spirit can be colonized. The section below engages with different aspects of the spirituality as a tool, theory and methodology, just to advance my argument that the spirit cannot be colonized.

Spirituality can be a tool or methodology that can enable one to navigate through life after their complete life has been distorted, fragmented and many times destroyed. Through contemplation, one can bring depth to their thought process and be in a position to reach into their past and surpass the colonial history. By doing this, one can start making sense of purpose in life. It is important to note, however, that spirituality can be a tool of colonization. In this section, I will briefly discuss three tools of colonization, mainly education, religion and medicine, in order to provide the basis for my discussion of anti-colonial thought.

As I have said in many of my publications, I cannot imagine the amount of energy and effort that the colonizers put in their planning, execution and implementation of their colonial project. In the case of Africa, Europeans had traded with people from the continent of Africa for centuries. What I have never found out was when did the tide change? How long did it take for the Europeans to decide to create loopholes for chaos and fragmentation for African or Aboriginal societies? At what point did the European rulers decide to be exploiters and control the lives of non-Europeans mentally, physically and spiritually? When did they decide to sit at the main dining table, throw the owners out of their homes into the streets sometimes with no clothes and no foods? What blinders did they employ to confuse thousands and thousands of people that they needed rescue by the very people who threw them out? I have no answers to all these questions, but they can create a dialogue among and between both the colonizer and the colonized. Throughout my academic career, I have been searching for answers and the closest I have come to making sense of taking over other people's mind, body, spirit and all their possessions is through controlling of particular aspects of their lives. Namely, destruction of people's educational, spiritual and medicinal systems and creation of desperation as the fragmentation of the total being are reduced to a state of self-doubt, self-hatred and great desire to be like your controller/rescuer. The destruction of personhood starts with creation of doubt of people's divine, creator, the Omni present. In the case of the African people, the population had been depleted through four hundred years of European and Arabic slave trade. Where was the African God when they were being dehumanized, led in chains and packed like sardines in cargo ships that took them to the Americas, to the people whom they had traded with for thousands of years. I do not even want to imagine the reaction of the Indigenous peoples of Turtle Island as they saw the Africans in chains and being auctioned like animals. I also want to believe; the Africans were shocked to see what had happened to the people they used to trade with. They had been pushed from their land to the reserves. Both populations were really at their lowest point in their history. Their spirit had been broken (so the Europeans thought) and this was the perfect moment to take over the control of their souls. Religion became therefore one of the colonizing tools. Then, of course, the Europeans came with the notion that if they believed in their God, they would be rescued.

The second colonizing tool was the need to take over the control of the colonized people's minds. In the case of Africans, education became the weapon with which to cultivate the intellect of the Africans and in particular the medium of instruction. The education was therefore to be delivered in a foreign language. In this way, the colonized would live their lives mimicking colonizer, desiring to be like their master (see Fanon 1994; Memmi 2013; Thiongo 1986). I still remember being beaten by my teachers (African and Europeans) for speaking my vernacular. The colonizers' mission of being schooled in a foreign language was not to give us the tools to learn about our history, our culture and our system of thought, but to ensure we could read only what they wrote—they were the producers of knowledge and they were the disseminators. They wrote what they wanted us to read, and that was about their history and a very distorted history of African people. The colonizers made sure whatever we read about ourselves would be so bad that we would strive to distance ourselves from it. They succeeded in creating alienation in us to the point where we hated anything that had any semblance of self, even our old age healing practices.

The third colonizing tool then was foreign medicine. As soon as colonizers had succeeded in making sure we despise our healing processing, just like the way we had done with our education and our spiritual practices, medicine in form of pills and injections was introduced to the community. What many community members did not know was the fact that the pills contained a diluted form of medicinal plants that had been harvested and shipped to Europe for processing. The colonizers had created disease in ourselves that resulted in sickness of both physical and mental bodies and interestingly, that could not be cured using the African Indigenous medicines. And again, who did we turn to for rescue, the oppressor, the destroyer and our controller. We despised our healing practices and called them backwards and primitive and we turned our backs to our spiritual rituals because we thought they were demonic and witchcraft.

What has amazed me, however, is how members of the colonized people held on to certain knowledges that they pushed to their sub-consciousness and whenever the environment was clear, they would pass on this knowledge to their children or their neighbours. This is particularly true when it comes to African Indigenous healing and spiritual practices. It's very liberating to be able to freely articulate your inner self, your spiritual self and not shy away from lifting the lid to let your light shine as you embrace your total self. For instance, when you think of the history of slavery, residential schools and holocaust, these bodies were literally in chains, visible and invisible. What made them hang in there? What made them survive to tell their horrible stories to their future generation? I believe the spirit took over when the physical body curved in and could not stand any more pain. In this chapter, therefore, my focus is spirituality; hence, I will dwell on it as one anti-colonial tool.

## Spirituality: Anti-colonial Tool for Decolonization

"Mother Africa blessed people with an everlasting love of the Eternal Spirit. Mother Africa taught her children to respect the earth and all that dwell on her. She taught them the laws of nature and helped them understand the cosmic rhythms" (Arewa, 1998, p. 38). The Earth holds every living and non-living beings. Africa, the cradle of civilization, has been constant with spirit of giving. Mother Africa has provided her children with teaching from the land and hence the importance of respecting what provides us with nutrients for living well. The four elements (earth, wind, fire and water) of the Eternal Spirit are given to all people equally. African rhythms are part and parcel of people of African ancestry. These can be found in music, the different drum bits and dance movement. This last insertion is expressed below by Arewa when she states: "Her (Africa) people, who created rituals to communicate with these forces, which they then deified and praised, knew the celestial realms and elements" (1998, p. 38). The above statement is an indication of the Eternal Spirit. We witness it in music, expressions through art and different rituals, such as pouring of liberation before a meeting or gathering, or a ceremony begins. Arewa confirms: "Belief in the Eternal Spirit and respect for our Ancestors is probably the world's oldest spiritual practice. Ancient Africans believed in the continuation of Spirit. For this reason, they returned the dead to the womb of the earth, ensuring a long lineage and unbroken cycle of life" (Arewa, 1998, pp. 38–49).

Cabral (1973) emphasized the importance of returning to the source—that is, going back to re-educate yourself in terms of your authentic self—your knowledge. I was tempted to do so as I prepared for this section. Mother Africa holds the hidden secrets of spirituality. However, in many conversations, Africa is never seen as a land that is spiritually vibrant or a continent that can offer people the essence of being whole again. In order for us as occupants of the planet to heal, and to employ spirituality as a decolonizing tool, we need to be open and authentic to ourselves. We need to develop certain skills such as deep listening to our inner self so as to have access to the talents and mental map that everyone is born with and from which most of us do not know it exists and we just need to retrieve it. The retrieval and the acknowledgement of our being will provide us with the tools we need to question universal standards by pointing out or recognizing their limited scope and perspective (Amadiume, 1987; Dei, 2000; Smith, 1999). We shall also engage in interrogating power colonial relations embedded in knowledge production and dissemination. To awaken our spirit for the purpose of decolonization is complex and multifaceted. However, "when soul is present ..., we listen with great care not only to what is spoken but also to the messages between the words-tones, gestures, the flicker of feeling across the face" (Kessler, 1998, 1999, p. 50). It is always important to remember that "Spirituality is nourished, not through formal rituals..., but by the quality of relationship that is developed between person and world. We can, and must cultivate an attitude of caring, respect, and contemplation to replace the narrow modernist view that the world is a resource to be exploited" (Kessler, 1998, 1999, p. 51). Kessler goes on to say, "Through deep connection to the self, [we] encounter a strength and richness within that is the basis for developing the autonomy central to ...discovering purpose, and for unlocking creativity" (Kessler, 1998, 1999, p. 51). Because our spirit "enables us to connect with other human beings; it underpins our ability to take steps to dismantle marginalizing conditions..." (Dantley 2005, p. 654), while decolonizing our mind, body and soul, not to mention our institutions and their Eurocentric system of thought.

## Conclusion

Is Decolonizing the Spirit possible? is a chapter that is reflective and that took a longtime to write as I had to really think through what I wanted to say. I do remember every time when one of my co-editors of this book would email me and ask me when the chapter would be ready, I had no definitive answer. It took many hours of contemplation to retrieve my inner thoughts in order to state that the spirit cannot be colonized, but can stay in a dormant state for years until it is awakened. The paper cannot be concluded as it is an ongoing dialogue as we search for our spiritual tools for the purpose of decolonization.

## References


Amadiume, I. (1987). *Male daughters, female husbands: Gender and sex in an African society*. London, UK: Zed Books.

Arewa, C. S. (1998). *Opening to spirit: Contacting the healing power of the chakras and honouring African spirituality*. London: Thorsons Publishers.

Bullis, R. K. (1996). *Spirituality in social work practice*. Washington, DC: Taylor & Francis.

Cabral, A. (1973). Identity and dignity in the context of the national liberation struggle. In Africa Information Service (Ed.), *Return to the source* (p. 60). New York: Monthly Review Press.

Carli, L. L., & Eagly, A. H. (2007). Overcoming resistance to women leaders: The importance of leadership style. In B. Kellerman & D. L. Rhode (Eds.), *Women and leadership: The state of play and strategies for change* (pp. 127–148). San Francisco: Jossey-Bass.

Castellano, M. B. (2000). Updating Aboriginal traditions of knowledge. In G. J. S. Dei, B. Hall, & D. Goldin-Rosenberg (Eds.), *Indigenous knowledges in global contexts: Multiple readings of our world* (pp. 21–36). Toronto: University of Toronto Press.

Dantley, M. E. (2005). Moral leadership: Shifting the management paradigm. In F. W. English (Ed.), *The sage handbook of educational leadership* (pp. 34–46). Thousand Oaks: Sage.

Dantley, M. E. (2006). African American spirituality and cornel west's notions of prophetic pragmatism: Restructuring educational leadership in American Urban Schools. *Educational Administration Quarterly, 41*(4), 651–674.

Dei, G. J. S. (2000). Rethinking the role of indigenous knowledges in the academy. *International Journal of Inclusive Education, 4*(2), 111–132.

Delgado, E. A., & Canabal, M. E. (2006). Factors associated with negative spillover from job to home among latinos in the United States. *Journal of Family and Economic Issues, 27*(1), 92–112.

Derezotes, D. S. (1995). Spirituality and religiosity: Neglected factors in social work practice. *Arete, 20*, 1–15.

Dillard, C. B. (2000). The substance of things hoped for, the evidence of things not seen: Examining an endarkened feminist epistemology in educational research and leadership. *International Journal of Qualitative Studies in Education, 13*(6), 661–681.

Elton-Chalcraft, S. (2002). Empty wells: How well are we doing at spiritual well-being? *International Journal of Children's Spirituality, 7*(3), 309–328.

Fanon, F. (1994). *A dying colonialism* (Vol. 430). New York: Grove/Atlantic.

Fanon, F. (2007). *The wretched of the earth.* New York: Grove/Atlantic.

Fry, L. W. (2003). Toward a theory of spiritual leadership. *The Leadership Quarterly, 14*(6), 693–727.

Gallagher, C., & Golant, S. K. (2000). *Going to the top: A road map for success from America's leading women executives.* New York: Viking Adult.

hooks, b. (2003). *Teaching community: A pedagogy of hope* (Vol. 36). New York: Psychology Press.

Hyman, J., Scholarios, D., & Baldry, C. (2005). Getting on or getting by? Employee flexibility and coping strategies for home and work. *Work, Employment & Society, 19*(4), 705–725.

Kessler, S. (1998). *Lessons from the intersexed.* Rutgers University Press.

Kessler, R. (1999). Nourishing students in secular schools. *Educational Leadership, 56,* 49–52.

Kipusi. (2018, June). *Experiences of Black entrepreneurs in Toronto.* Paper presented at Decolonizing Education Conference at the University of Embu, Kenya.

Mazama, M. A. (2002). Afrocentricity and African spirituality. *Journal of Black Studies, 33*(2), 218–234.

Mazama, A. (Ed.). (2003). *The Afrocentric paradigm.* Trenton: Africa World Press.

Mbiti, J. (1969). *African philosophy and religion.* Nairobi: African Educational Publishers.

McGadney-Douglass, B. F., & Douglass, R. L. (2008). Collective familial decision-making in times of trouble: Intergenerational solidarity in Ghana. *Journal of Cross-Cultural Gerontology, 23*(2), 147.

Memmi, A. (2013). *The colonizer and the colonized.* London: Routledge.

Miller, J. P. (2005). *Educating for wisdom and compassion: Creating conditions for timeless learning.* Thousand Oaks: Corwin Press.

Mkabela, Q. (2005). Using the afrocentric method in researching indigenous African culture. *The Qualitative Report, 10*(1), 178–189.

Neal, J., & Biberman, J. (2003). Introduction: The leading edge in research on spirituality and organizations. *Journal of Organizational Change Management, 16*(4), 363–366.

Odora-Hoppers, C. (2005). Between 'mainstreaming' and 'transformation': Lessons and challenges for institutional change. In L. Chisholm & J. September (Eds.), *Gender equity in South African education 1994–2004: Perspectives from research, government and unions* (pp. 55–73). Cape Town: HSRC Press.

Odora-Hoppers, C. A. (2009). Education, culture and society in a globalizing world: Implications for comparative and international education. *Compare, 39*(5), 601–614.

Phipps, K. A. (2012). Spirituality and strategic leadership: The influence of spiritual beliefs on strategic decision making. *Journal of Business Ethics, 106*(2), 177–189.

Polat, F. (2011). Inclusion in education: A step towards social justice. *International Journal of Educational Development, 31*(1), 50–58.

Pratt, M. G., & Ashforth, B. E. (2003). Fostering meaningfulness in working and at work. In K. S. Cameron, J. E. Dutton, & R. E. Quinn (Eds.), *Positive organizational scholarship: Foundations of a new discipline*. San Francisco: Berrett-Koehler Publishers.

Pulido, L. (1998). The sacredness of "Mother Earth": Spirituality, activism, and social justice. *Annals of the Association of American Geographers, 88*(4),719–723.

Ray, L. (2012). Deciphering the "Indigenous" in Indigenous methodologies. *Alternative: An International Journal of Indigenous Peoples, 8*(1), 85–98.

Reave, L. (2005). Spiritual values and practices related to leadership effectiveness. *The Leadership Quarterly, 16*(5), 655–687.

Shahjahan, R. A. (2009). The role of spirituality in the anti-oppressive higher-education classroom. *Teaching in Higher Education, 14*(2), 121–131.

Shahjahan, R. A. (2010). Toward a spiritual praxis: The role of spirituality among faculty of color teaching for social justice. *The Review of Higher Education, 33*(4), 473–512.

Smith, L. T. (1999). *Decolonizing methodologies: Research and indigenous peoples.* London: Zed Books.

Thiongo, N. W. (1986). *Decolonizing the mind: The politics of language in African literature.* Oxford: Heinemann.

Tisdell, E. J., & Tolliver, D. E. (2003). Claiming a sacred face: The role of spirituality and cultural identity in transformative adult higher education. *Journal of Transformative Education, 1*(4), 368–392.

Wane, N. N. (2007). African women and Canadian history: Demanding our place in the curriculum. In N. Massaquoi & N. N. Wane (Eds.), *Theorizing empowerment Canadian perspectives on Black feminist thought* (pp. 129–154). Toronto: Inanna Publications and Education.

Wane, N. N. (2009). Indigenous education and cultural resistance: A decolonizing project. *Curriculum Inquiry, 39*(1), 159–178.

Wane, N. N. (2011). Reclaiming our spirituality: A pedagogical tool for feminism and activism. *Canadian Woman Studies, 29*(1/2), 159.

Watt, S. K. (2003). Come to the river: Using spirituality to cope, resist, and develop identity. *New Directions for Student Services, 104*, 29–40.

CHAPTER 3

# Spirituality and a Search for Home: The Complexities of Practising Sikhism on Indigenous Land

*Mandeep Kaur Mucina*

## Introduction

It had been almost 10 years since I had entered the Sikh Temple, in the small village that I grew up in as one of the second generation of my family, the first to be born as a settler/occupier on the traditional land of the Quw'utsan (Cowichan Tribes). It had been one year since my grandmother's long beautiful life had come to an end, and based on Sikh tradition, we were marking this anniversary with a prayer and service for our community. It was a strange sensation to mark my grandmother's life here where she spent 35 years on land that she read as white man's territory and where she was marked as an outsider. My grandmother had intimate acts of resistance to whiteness, resistance to speaking any of the colonial languages she was expected to speak, resistance to ever wearing anything but her traditional

M. K. Mucina (✉)
School of Child and Youth Care, University of Victoria, Victoria, BC, Canada
e-mail: mmucina@uvic.ca



N. N. Wane et al. (eds.), *Decolonizing the Spirit in Education and Beyond*, Spirituality, Religion, and Education,
https://doi.org/10.1007/978-3-030-25320-2_3

clothing, and always reminding her grandchildren that this was not our home, that we are visitors here and will forever be treated that way, and that our true home was in India. Yet, when I think back now to how my grandmother understood her life on this foreign land, I wonder how colonization impacts her understanding and relationship to this land and to this nation. My grandmother never recognized herself in relationship to the Indigenous community that surrounded the town we were settled on and Indigenous communities that encountered active acts of violence and genocide before and after she came to Canada, in attempts to create a white Canada forever (Ward, 2002). I thought about my grandmother when I entered the doors of the Gurudwara that weekend, but I also thought about the hundreds of South Asian migrants that had come before my grandmother and after my grandmother, all of whom have very little understanding or recognition of Indigenous people and their history. There is a strong path of South Asians migrating to this part of Canada, a history that we talk about in our intimate spaces where we share and listen to stories of active racism that our ancestors have encountered over the decades, of our current encounters with gun violence, gangs, and domestic violence within our community. These conversations speak to what Celia Haig-Brown (2009) recognizes as a common struggle, as diasporic racialized communities we continuously ask ourselves "where do we come from?" within this question recognizing our homelands, what has been sacrificed to come here and what was left behind. However, a central question we in the diaspora rarely ask is "where have we come to?" and what does it mean to be settlers on the traditional land of Indigenous people. Celia Haig-Brown asks her readers to engage with these questions in hopes of theorizing diaspora studies from a decolonial lens that encourages racialized communities to consider the implications of living in a colonized country. Similarly, I ask the readers and communities of racialized migrants who come to Indigenous territories, what does it mean to practise our spiritualities on spaces that are stolen from Indigenous communities? How do we decolonize our spiritual communal spaces, while decolonizing our histories and recognizing how the colonial relations underpin the historical racism and oppression our community faces, is based on the colonization of this land and its first peoples. Gurudwaras across Canada are a symbol of the Sikh Punjabi community; they are a symbol of our resistance and are places of freedom. Like any other place of worship, what does it mean to practise collective notions of spirituality on unceded Indigenous land that has a history of displacing and exercising violent forms of colonial genocide on Indigenous people across this nation we call Canada? As racialized communities, who also have a history of violent racism enacted on our minds, bodies, and spaces since migration, how do we hold these contradictions? How do we begin decolonizing diasporic communities? This chapter is an attempt to start a conversation within South Asian communities across Canada to recognize and reconcile the role we play in the continued colonization of the Indigenous peoples and their territories. Finally, this chapter explores the complexities of practising spirituality, as a diasporic community, on sacred land that holds historical and spiritual significance for Indigenous communities.

In order to effectively share this story and begin addressing the above issues, I will be breaking this chapter into four main parts. In the first part, I will share the devastating history of genocide and colonization of the Hul'qumi'num language speakers and their land, which is where this story takes place. Parallel to the startling history of colonialism and ongoing genocide are the racism and contempt demonstrated towards the Punjabi Sikh community of British Columbia, by white settlers who advocated for a "White Canada forever" (Ward, 2002). Finally, I will conclude this part by speaking to the Sikh beliefs that centre around the Gurudwara and land as sacred places, by exploring the specific relationship that the Lake Cowichan Sikh community had to the Gurudwara and the land the Indigenous land it sits on. In the second part, I will expand on spirituality and wisdom that sits in places (Basso, 1996) and the meaning this has for both First Nations communities and my own Sikh community. Finally, I will end with the implications of practising Sikhism and holding land, space, and place as sacred in the diaspora, where our connection to this land is at the detriment and dispossession of Indigenous communities and how we as settlers can build reconciliation and collaboration in the call for action put forth by the Truth and Reconciliation Commission of 2015.

## Theorizing Diaspora and Spirituality

A community and its individuals are impacted by the time and space in which the formative events of their lives have occurred. The work of Vine Deloria (1994) and Keith Basso (1996) speaks poignantly to wisdom and knowledge that sits in places, the land of a community that has resided there for time in memorial. By utilizing an anti-colonial framework, I am interrogating the systems of power embedded in the history of this land and who has claims over it. George Dei (2002) suggests that "The anti-colonial discourse theorizes colonial and re-colonial relations and the implications of imperial structures on the processes of knowledge production and validation, the understanding of indigeneity, and the pursuit of agency, resistance and subjective politics" (p. 43). What do we do with knowledge once we have gained it? This question and the process of unpacking this are as important as is the pursuit of knowledge. As a practitioner, researcher, and academic, I have committed myself to carrying out work that is anti-oppressive, committed to social change and taking an active role in that change. This active role is about connecting the personal to the political and using my voice and my writing as a forum for resistance against those systems that have been created to oppress, marginalize, and racialize communities of people. Potts and Brown (2005) state that,

> Anti-oppressive research involves making explicit the political practices of creating knowledge. It means making a commitment to the people you are working with personally and professionally in order to mutually foster conditions for social justice and research. It is about paying attention to, and shifting, how power relations work in and through the processes of doing research. (p. 255)

This chapter is one step towards making explicit the knowledge that we have created and shifting that knowledge so that we are aware of our oppressive positions, and the positions of power that we may hold as immigrant communities settling on unceded Indigenous land.

The very terms that I have carefully chosen to use in this chapter are making the personal political, and the political personal, defining the underpinnings and assumptions that drive many feminist beliefs. Using my own narrative to a political place is one step towards making the personal political and the political personal. However, as Leela Fernandez (2003) suggests, "if, as feminism has rightly argued, the personal is the political, then social and political transformation requires a kind of practice that is linked to a sense of personal, everyday ethical practice" (p. 56). Therefore, much of the latter half of my chapter will focus on what we can do in our everyday lives in order to materialize the true essence of this statement. We have a responsibility to strategize decolonizing practices in the diaspora, and these strategies require a detailed examination of our steps towards creating an anti-oppressive, anti-colonial, and anti-racist knowledge in the academy, in systems of power, and in the everyday practices of individuals and communities.

Conclusively, these overarching frameworks will be weaved throughout the narrative and analysis informing the argument and setting the stage for how we can begin speaking to the complexities of practising spirituality, as immigrant communities, and decolonizing our practices to become good allies to Indigenous communities fighting for sovereignty and governance.

## Part I: A Short History of the Hul'qumi'num Speaking People

### *The Quw'utsun First Nation*

Lake Cowichan is the English phonetic name for a small town of 3000 people, located in South Central Vancouver Island, British Columbia. The Cowichan people of the Coast Salish Nation called this area Quw'utsun, which means "basking in the sun". The story that white settlers record in text states that the Hul'qumi'num First Nations, people of the Quw'utsun valley, took refuge from a rising flood on the top of Mt. Tzouhalem. When the water receded, the survivors found a giant frog warming itself on the side of the mountain, hence the word Quw'utsun (basking in the sun). When I began researching the history of the Hul'qumi'num (people of the land) who lived in that area, I found very little research or writing about this community which required deeper engagement and deconstructing what it means to write about an Indigenous community that has nearly been wiped from history.

The Hul'qumi'num used the area surrounding the lake and the river on a seasonal basis and would travel to these parts predominantly in the summer; however, there are records that one particular Hul'qumi'num community lived along the surrounding areas, which are now called Skutz Falls, on a more permanent basis. The white settlers, who stole the land that we now call Lake Cowichan, state that when they arrived in this area, there was evidence of a community wiped by disease (small pox), and those that survived were taken in by the surrounding Cowichan nation, which is in the nearest town now called Duncan (http://www.hulquminum.bc.ca/hulquminum_people/lake_cowichan). These same records suggest that the Quw'utsun First Nation had been killed off by rival warrior groups and by the time settlers came into the area they had all been decimated and so the land was theirs for the taking (http://en.wikipedia.org/wiki/Cowichan_Lake_First_Nation). This collective white knowledge of not only the Hul'qumi'num First Nations, but all First Nations communities of British Columbia, is best described by Arnett (1999) in his book *Terror on the Coast*, "there remains the colonial myth that, contrary to what happened south of the 49th parallel, the British resettlement of British Columbia was benign, bloodless and law-abiding" (p. 16). The myths that justify the trickery and hunger for land and resources are also the colonizers' tools for justifying their current and future aims for dispossessing Indigenous people, their land, and ultimately continuing the genocide of Indigenous people and their culture. Arnett's book begins the process of decolonizing the history of the Hul'qumi'num First Nations of Vancouver Island by shedding light on the Lamacha warriors fight with the British soldiers and the treaties that were signed thereafter, but never honoured by the British. A re-writing of this history is necessary and the voices of the Hul'qumi'num (people of the land) are central to this writing.

When I was growing up in Lake Cowichan, the Hul'qumi'num that were living in the community that I knew of were two families, and their daughters and sons went to school with me. They were the only Indigenous children in our school at the time and I was close friends with both of them. I have distinct memories of visiting their small reserve, which was set off on a hill away from the town centre. As a child, I did not realize what a reserve was, yet I understood that my friend lived in another part of Lake Cowichan that was segregated from the rest of the town, just like my community was segregated to a particular neighbourhood. My friend Mila[1] shared with pride that her father being the chief of their reserve, at the time I did not understand the significance of what she was sharing, since our education had not recognized the history of colonization on this land or across Canada. The education we were both receiving had systematically erased the history of Mila's father, her grandfather, and their ancestors, who fought against the British for their land and sovereignty. Our education system had not imagined Mila's story when they pushed a colonial history in the classroom, as a result I was ignorant to Mila's story even though I sat beside her in class every day from childhood to the end of secondary school. I did not know her history or how it may have felt for her to sit in a sea of settlers every day. Ignorance ran through my upbringing and our community, and this ignorance rendered the people who came from Quw'utsun land as non-existent; rendered the spirits that sit on the Quw'utsun land as invisible; and regarded Mila and her family as uneasy reminders of the people that they did not annihilate, and thus, they were pushed to a corner of the town where they could easily be forgotten.

The history of colonization on Quw'utsun land can be heard in the whispers of the trees, the river, and the lake; however, as in most of British Columbia, these natural resources encountered violent genocide along with their caretakers. By the time I was in the twelfth grade, the surrounding mountains that I grew up admiring, which had been lush and endless, were methodically cleared and cut down in order to reap the surrounding land of all its resources. This destructive history is the backdrop to the story of Lake Cowichan and the story of many Indigenous communities impacted by settler colonialism who only saw greed and a false sense of entitlement to the most sacred elements of the land and its people. As we carry on unraveling the history of Lake Cowichan from an anti-colonial lens, the introduction of cheap labourers to reap the land of these natural resources is established and my ancestors are introduced to this story.

## Part II: A Short History of the Sikh Punjabi People on Cowichan Territory

Whenever I tell people that I grew up in a small "blue collar" town on Vancouver Island, most people, especially other racialized people, will ask me how my family ended up there. This is such a complex question, with a simple, yet historically significant, answer. Our community, as well as other people from the East, including Chinese and Japanese migrants, were brought over and encouraged to come to British Columbia to be cheap labourers in the process of dispossessing Indigenous people from their land and extracting resources for the benefit of creating a settler society. There are various reasons that the Sikh Punjabis were some of the first to immigrate to Canada. Forces external to Punjab society played a role in the first waves, as is described by Ward (2002), who states "that they had frequently been lured to British Columbia by glowing propaganda from steamship lines, ticket agents, and fellow-countrymen who sought to exploit them" (p. 80). Other records state that the Punjab area of India was becoming overpopulated and the land, which we had farmed for generations, was being overtaxed and wage rates for labour were low due to inflation all remnants of the British colonialism. Hence, the need to make money abroad to send back to families was an incentive of those that were struggling to survive (Jagpal, 1994; Ward, 2002). As is the case even now, the colonial government saw the bodies of brown men as commodities for cheap labour. They saw these men fulfilling the difficult jobs that their white counterparts either refused or protested the menial wages. Canada did not have the manpower to achieve colonization of the land without these bodies and their labour. For many generations, migrant communities lived on bare minimum wages with very little incentive or encouragement to have women and children come to their "White Canada" in an effort to maintain a false homogeneity (see the work of Ali Kazmi on the Komagata Maru). However, as we see the waves of immigration began to change and more immigrants were "allowed" in, the face of British Columbia began to change with it. Many small mill towns began to see a strong contingent of Chinese, Japanese, and South Asian men working and being segregated to their own spaces. There were forms of resistance by these men with the desire to create a family and spaces where our people were visible and distinct, rather than invisible and segregated.

The animosity the white community had towards Asians and Indians was apparent and can be demonstrated most effectively in the example of the 1907 Asian riots. The riots started in Bellingham (USA), as a movement by the white community to drive Punjabi Sikhs out of the lumber industry. These sentiments eventually seeped across the border, and on September 7, a white supremacist group marched to Vancouver city hall to demand a white Canada. Many proceeded to attack Chinatown, the Japanese and Sikh businesses around Powell Street, in Vancouver. The riots were not only a landmark in the rise of racism in Canada, they also signalled the beginning of systematic federal intervention to prohibit Asian immigration to Canada through the imposition of quotas on Japanese emigration, continuous voyage regulations and a $200 landing fee to exclude those from India, and the enforcement of head-tax laws against the Chinese; when that proved ineffective, the passage of the Chinese Exclusion Act in the year 1923 (Ward, 2002). Despite Asian Canadian efforts to fight these measures, this period was marked by escalating injustices, including the infamous Komagata Maru[2] case of 1914 and the uprooting, dispossession, and dispersal of Japanese Canadians during and after World War II[3] (Ward, 2002).

My father's maternal aunt had come to this land as a young woman in 1920, to meet her husband who had migrated in 1904 by boat that set sail from India and took months to reach the shores of Vancouver. Years later, she sponsored her brothers in the 1960s. Many immigrants were encouraged by their relatives to take advantage of the labour jobs that needed to be filled. My uncles witnessed the poverty and struggles my father was encountering in India and encouraged him to come as a young adult, thinking they could get him a job in the Youbou lumber mill they were working in. At the time, this position was considered prosperous to have amongst our community, a union job with full benefits, most importantly it was stable and guaranteed a secure living. The colonial mentality had convinced our community that these natural resources would never run out and they would have steady jobs for not only their selves but also their children, which as we will see later on was not the case.

My father was a "midnight child" born during the 1947 partition of India and Pakistan and suffered poverty, loss, and intergenerational trauma from the moment he was born in an Independent India. Coming to Canada was not a choice that he took lightly, it was something that he described as a necessity, and for the rest of his life, my father was described as one of the lucky ones expected to give back to his sisters and brothers back home who did not have the same privilege. It took my father almost ten years before he was hired at the Youbou lumber mill. During this time, he worked on the E&N Rail across Canada, breaking his body down in the process and coming close to death a number of times. My family and father's story is not unique to the Punjabi Sikh community of Lake Cowichan, or British Columbia. As a child, the community elders would share their stories of racism they experienced in the workplace, racial slurs they encountered when they would walk in town, and the limits placed on them for practising a way of life that was culturally and spiritually unique to our community. As a result, the Punjabi Sikhs of Lake Cowichan were also segregated to one particular area of the town. As brown bodies, we were daily reminders of a community who refused to assimilate to whiteness; the only ones that did share this space with us were the lower socio-economic class families that could not afford to live near the lake and river.

Growing up as a child of this community and as one of the few racialized kids in our school, I understood oppression from a subversive sense, where the insidious nature of racism played a strong role in my life. We, myself and the 5 other brown bodies in my grade, were called all sorts of names, but even those were tolerable because they were overt. It was the everyday experiences of being ignored, forgotten, misunderstood, and invisible that were difficult. It was the sense that we would never be as good as them and as fortunate as them, which we were reminded of every day. It was the gaze that they cast on us, the gaze of being an "other", a part of a community that they understood as savage, backwards, and only worthy of labour. It was these daily messages that we, the second generation, experienced alongside our parents.

### *The Gurudwara*

The literal translation of Gurudwara is the gateway or door to the teacher/guru, and most of the Gurudwaras built in Canada were designed like a home, with two levels and four doors on each floor that represent the four corners of the world and the diverse people that inhabit it. No one is ever denied entry into the Gurudwara based on their identity, and the significance of this has allowed for these spaces to be temporary homes for many people who seek shelter and food. Langar is a large part of the Gurudwara space and process, which is the process of sharing food with all people who come to the Gurudwara. In the process of sharing food, made by our community members, our Sikh gurus (spiritual teachers) imagined communities coming together to fight against oppression against any marginalized people. Sikhism was built as a social justice movement that fights against the status quo. The Langar and Gurudwara are institutions that are meant to foster that energy and strength amongst Sikhs so they can do the work of fighting against oppressive powers. The following excerpt speaks volumes to the social justice nature of the Gurudwara and the process of engaging in Langar:

> Langar is the foundational Sikh revolutionary space. It's where Sikhs come together to discuss the revolutionary ideas of the house of Nanak; it's a safe space for all the oppressed people of the world, to share a meal with the Khalsa and learn about our revolutionary struggle so that they too can take part; it's not a passive space where you come to observe and have a free meal. (https://naujawani.com/blog/langar-is-not-free/)

As a community, we learned to create a very strong shield around ourselves, to not let very many people into our inner circles, and to not venture too far out of that circle of safety. My family practised this the best; very rarely were we allowed to spend time at the homes of white children and if we did, we had to travel in pairs. From my earliest memories, the one place and space where we did not experience this racism and oppression was in our local Sikh Temple, our Gurudwara. The Gurudwara became a safe place for the community to gather, worship, and be free. It was the only place that our community felt safe, outside of the home. It is here that we shared our history, stories of resistance and survival, and shared in a collective. It was in this space and place that we would meet regularly to tend to the spiritual injuries that we experienced in our everyday lives and the history of our struggles were reflected in an almost archival sense in the Gurudwara. The physical space itself had pictures of the history of Sikhism, but also was where we displayed our history as an immigrant community in Lake Cowichan. There were medals of awards won by children and adults in local sports games, pictures of the Gurudwara in the earlier days when it was being built, pictures of men who worked in the forests and in the mills. When visitors from the urban areas would come to the Gurudwara, they would ask us why the women in the temple would sit with blankets covering their legs during the service, which our elders explained was symbolic of a time when women in our community were forbidden to wear our traditional clothes in public, and expected to wear skirts, like white women. The Sikh tradition is to sit on the floor cross-legged, so Punjabi women needed blankets to cover their legs and keep them warm. This story was a part of community's experience and was memorialized through the blankets, which we continue to use even today.

The story of the physical building that we call Gurudwara went through a similar history of displacement and oppression. During the 30s and 40s, the Punjabi Sikh community was growing to the point where we became a distinct group of people in the area. We first held services in people's homes, since there was no physical space created for the Guru Granth Sahib, which is the holy text that we believe is our living Guru and we treat it like we would a human being (Jagpal, 1994). The term Gurudwara itself translates into the "home of the Guru" and the belief is that we should treat our scriptures and teachings that are compiled in a book we call the Guru Granth Sahib, as we would our teacher or Guru (Singh, 2002). Thus, we build it a home, and we gather to that home when we want to sing the hymns, to do a reading from the Guru Granth Sahib, and to learn from this living text. As the Sikh community grew, they could not sustain the practice of the religion in people's homes, the Gurudwara was relocated three times, as were the Punjabi Sikh community based on where the sawmill was built. Eventually, one family donated a plot of land for our community and the community pooled money to start the construction of the Gurudwara. The final settlement is where it currently sits in Lake Cowichan (Jagpal, 1994).

As I look back on my upbringing in the Gurudwara and think about the significance of this place, I am reminded of how the second generation connected to the Gurudwara, as opposed to the first generation. I recall a deep connection and faith from the first generation, but for the second generation, we developed a sense of entitlement to this place and the land, and we saw it as our home and our only connection to something called home, which was supported by our Punjabi spirituality and worldview. The Gurudwara was created by the generations that migrated before us for our community's needs, and so the land and the building itself are considered sacred—physical space and place where our spirits can be in harmony with the land, the spirit world, and the community. So, if this connection to land and spirit is so essential to our cultural knowledges, what happens when we are living away from our ancestral land? What happens when land is so essential to our cultural knowledges? Yet our Gurudwaras are on the land of Indigenous peoples of other places. These questions lead me to the next part of this chapter, where I will begin addressing the complexities and contradictions of these knowledges.

## Part III: When Spirituality and Wisdom Sits in Places

When I was seven years old, my family made a trip back to our village in India for the first time since my parents got married. This was a significant trip for all of us; it had been almost 10 years since my parents had returned, as children my siblings and I were going "home" for the first time. From the moment my feet touched India's soil I remember feeling different about myself and my family. There was a connection between the land and my soul, something I would dream about for years upon returning. A connection to land and place was a major part of my teachings, and my grandmother would say that our connection to land has lived through generations and is a part of our identity and livelihood, in India.

Yet, as much as there was a connection between the land and my spirit when I went to India, there was also a disconnection that was very apparent and continued each time I went back. My siblings and I were considered outsiders to our family in India, we are the family that made it out, and we were the children born on another nation. Each time we went there, we were told we were home, but we were also given contradictory messages that we do not know what it means to be Indian, which was demonstrated in their reaction to our "white accents" when we spoke Punjabi, to the way we carried ourselves, the way we ate, and even how much we weighed. As much as we tried to fit in, we could not and were always considered visitors to our family and village. This became such a large part of our reality that my siblings and I hated leaving the village to venture into the nearest town with the fear of being called "farangi" (foreigner) by the locals. We found ourselves asking where is home? Where were we truly accepted? These multiple encounters of not belonging in our ancestral land and in the land where we were born lead to a sense of displacement and disconnection.

In *God Is Red* (1994), Vine Deloria quotes Chief Luther Standing Bear of the Sioux tribe:

> The man from Europe is still a foreigner and an alien. And he still hates the man who questioned his oath across the continent...But in the Indian spirit of the land is still vested; it will be until other men are able to divine and meet its rhythm. Men must be born and reborn to belong. Their bodies must be formed of the dust of their forefather's bones. (p. 60)

Deloria speaks to the difference between those who are Indigenous to land and those who are intruders and have the "psychological burden of establishing his or her right to the land in the deep emotional sense of knowing that he or she belongs there" (p. 60), such as the generations of settlers who have continued to exploit the land and its people for generations. Through the stories of Apache Tribe, Basso created Apache maps, solely through wisdom that the community has carried through the generations. Basso demonstrates that the "constructions of place reach deeply into other cultural spheres, including conceptions of wisdom, notions of morality, politeness and tact in forms of spoken discourse, and certain conventional ways of imagining and interpreting the Apache tribal past" (1996, p. xv). Furthermore, these scholars, as well as a host of others (Arnett, 1999; Deloria & Wildcat, 2001; Pearkes, 2002), reveal the power associated with place, space, and land, a power that is not only material, but also profoundly spiritual.

The words of Chief Luther Standing Bear speak to the spiritual connection that lives in the soil of Indigenous lands, purely by the generations of remains that have been buried there, which creates a link to the spirits or souls of many generations. The above quote by Vine Deloria reminds me of being a child and having arguments with my father about my sense of belonging. My siblings and I would speak to Lake Cowichan as our home, and when we would proudly suggest to my father that we were "Canadian", he would correct us by stating: "You are a visitor here. Your home is and always will be in Guluwa, Una (India), where my father and his father and his father built their home, where we have towed the dirt of the land on which we earned our living, for generations" (personal communication). This connection to home in Guluwa, Una, is contested by our family and the community and sense that we are "foreigners" or "visitors"; our connection to home in Canada is contested by white settlers whose micro aggressions remind us that we do not belong in their "White Canada" and would always be labourers; the only home that we did know as children was in the Gurudwara, within those four walls and in the place it sits.

Herein lies the contradiction, the Gurudwara is the physical place for community away from the pain and daily trauma of racism and oppression. Yet, we as children are told by our families that this is not where our spirits belong, particularly because white supremacy has not imagined us in this space, nor will they ever allow us in. However, this land is and always has been of the Hul'qumi'num people and if we are to honour the belief that land lives through generations, and if we truly honour what Sikhism pushes us to fight for the sovereignty of those who are encountering oppression, then how can we continue to demonstrate a sense of entitlement to this land?

Spirituality that is situated in a space and place called home, a belonging to people, land, and the spirit world, that is what the Gurudwara does for our community. Yet there is very little acknowledgement and discussion of our role as immigrant communities in the subjugation of Indigenous people. Through the medium of spirituality and religion, we further colonize the land and the caretakers of the land, as well as ignore the fact that we are playing an active role in the colonial project (Tuck & Yang, 2012). As a community, we have a history of being colonized and oppressed not only on this land but also on our ancestral land, with generations of blood, and bones of our ancestors who fought waves of colonialism in the north of India; nevertheless, we must also recognize the role that we play in keeping the wheels of colonialism turning, whether it is conscious or not.

For the second generation and the generations that will continue these stories and traditions in our Gurudwaras, this sense of home and entitlement to the land is all we have ever known and leaves us with a great conundrum. As a generation that sits in a chasm between many worlds and identities, our sense of home and connection is constantly contested by others; however, it is even more crucial that we move beyond this sense of entitlement and search for home, and for a place where deep respect for Indigenous communities is centred. We are the generation to start transforming our understanding of spiritual connection to land and moving towards a revolutionary understanding of our religion and spirituality.

## Part IV: Where Do We Go from Here?

My father has been reluctant to share his early stories of coming to Canada as a young man and any part of his difficult childhood with his children. I recognize this resistance now as an adult as his way of coping with the difficult parts of his past, keeping it silent. However, my mother does not have the same reluctance, has heard some of my father's stories of survival, and has since slowly begun to share them for him when he does not have the voice to do so himself. One particular story speaks to the complexities of being a migrant and Indigenous body in colonial space, where divide and conquer keep the layered systems of oppression together. I think about this story when I want to recognize how difficult it has been for my community to survive here, and any colonially constructed idea of success comes at the expense of the genocide of Indigenous communities. When my father came to Canada, he arrived as a visitor, and then overstaying his visitor status, as a result, my father moved around the country from labour job to labour job, much of which came as he worked on building and maintaining the E&N Railway. As a result, he found himself in remote parts of the country. On one particular morning while he was waiting for the train to take him to his next job, a group of men approached him shouting racial slurs and tossing his bags around. There was a moment where this encounter started to become violent and my father recognized these men as Indigenous, so he asked them to stop what they were doing by stating "we are brothers, they call us both Indian". At that moment, there was a recognition of what the colonial project had created, the anger and despair the Indigenous men may have felt seeing a foreign body working on the land of their ancestors and displacing their community. The fear and recognition that he was going to encounter violence by men that were oppressed themselves led my father to turn to what he knew best, to build a connection and relationship with the men by saying we are brothers. The "they" in his statement spoke to the common colonizer with a colonial project of dividing and conquering, and in moments like this, chalking up encounters of violence as individualized acts instigated by external factors. I turn to this story because it speaks volumes to the ways in which we have been separated and divided to believe we are not connected or impacted by the colonization of minds, bodies, land, and communities for generations. Can this story lead us to a path of reconciliation and in the true Sikh way, fighting for the oppression of our brothers and sisters? It is time we break down these colonial barriers and play a significant role of changing how we are going to become allyies to Indigenous communities.

The Gurudwaras in Canada have come a long way from their meagre beginnings; they now make millions entirely from donations, which come from the Sikh Punjabi community. These donations have been the primary source of revenue in the Gurudwara, here and across the world; however, they are intended to keep the goings of the temple funded and food available for daily *langar*. This reality has changed drastically from its humble beginnings and now those who are running the temples are doing so like a business. It is not rare to see temple leaders driving SUVs with the income they make from running the Gurudwara. Fernandez (2003) speaks to how spiritual leaders manipulate religion for other ends, and in the case of temple donations, our spiritual leaders are seeing this money and their personal gain "divinely" connected, so are using the name of religion to bring in these donations from community members. We are a community that has bought into the immigrant capitalist dream, whether by choice or by sheer desperation to survive. With the prosperity that emerges from labour, many contribute to the temples and community; however, we could use that money in ways that are a lot more effective than individual wealth. Setting up a foundation where money funds First Nations projects and programs that are contributing to their struggle for land and governance is one way our community could give back to First Nations whose land our Gurudwaras are sitting on. This is not a novel idea, in fact Khalsa Aid, a Sikh humanitarian agency run by Jatinder Singh, recently gifted the Ahousaht First Nation with money to right the wrongs of past colonial violence that has left ripples in both the Ahousaht community and the Sikh community. Jatinder Singh recognized a common encounter of colonial violence when he heard about the story of Maggie Sutlej, an Ahousaht child who was violently stolen from her mother and renamed Maggie. The Sutlej River in India, was also renamed by British colonizers to commemorate the British East India Company, it is a sacred site for Punjabi Sikhs as it is where many of our spiritual leaders' ashes are spread and our Gurudwars line the river's edge. This space is sacred for our community, the name given to the toddler stolen from her mother by colonialism and the river stolen from our community by similar colonizers, brought two communities together to build relationships built on reconciliation. This story is profound as it demonstrates a resistance to how colonialism continues to impact racialized and Indigenous communities in Canada, to divide us, and to conquer our spirits. Colonialism continues to convince racialized settlers that we are not connected to the struggles of Indigenous peoples and that our vision for freedom, happiness, and progress must be at the expense of each other and a perpetual pursuit of capitalism. What does it take for us to remove the colonial chatter and begin to see each other and our struggles, to find reconciliation beyond the political contexts that set out this vision without us?

Immigration trends have shifted a great deal since my father's generation and the generation of elders from my community. We see people coming to this nation with degrees in engineering, doctors, lawyers, and accountants, professional degrees that have actually facilitated their entry to the doors of Canada. This new face of immigration is very different than the farmer and labourer with very little education, who could only work in mills and do hard labour jobs. Yet, as much as the status of the immigrant has changed, we still see that the only jobs we are expected to take are in the labour and trade fields and that the education that immigrants come with is not recognized (Chatterjee, 2015). The education and information that is provided to immigrant communities before they arrive in Canada are becoming a big topic in South Asian communities, and many settlement non-profit organizations, such as Council of Agencies Serving South Asians (CASSA) and Ontario Council of Agencies Serving Immigrants (OCASI), are working towards changing what information immigrants are provided before they decide to immigrate. The history of colonization and the human rights violations that Canada has been recognized for violating towards Indigenous peoples of this land must be a part of that education and information session, so that we understand our relationship to First Nations people, and we understand how we are contributing to this colonial project.

This education should not only be incorporated in information sessions before deciding to come to Canada, but also within our Gurudwaras in the diaspora. Community discussions and information sharing are a large part of what happens in the temple. We need to begin incorporating our responsibility as immigrants to this land, to these discussions, and provide education on what this responsibility looks like and how we can begin taking action towards educating ourselves and other immigrant communities. This discussion should reflect the colonial history that has been erased from our daily understanding of First Nations peoples, since many people will have gone through life not truly understanding the history of colonization of this land and the genocide of Indigenous peoples.

During the process of writing this chapter, I came across a magazine article entitled, *The Rights of Land*, by Robin Kimmerer. In this article, the author is speaking about the Onondaga Nation of North America, who is proposing a radical new vision on property rights. They are asking for freedom to exercise their responsibility to their Indigenous land, which spans out to 2 million acres and much of this land is sacred to this nation. The vision is to fight for the right to be the active agents in any decision that is made on this land and to be given back responsibility to their land, rather than making claims for ownership of that land. The Onondaga are practising their Indigenous beliefs in making sure that the land to which they are the caretakers is respected and treated with the kindness it has not received from white settlers; thus, it is their responsibility to claim it back and make every decision they need to in order to exercise responsibility for it. The author makes provocative references to the offering of healing that the Onondaga nation is providing Indigenous and non-Indigenous peoples, since they are not looking to displace anyone from their homes, but are taking active action in healing the land, which contributes to the healing of their people and to the wider world. Kimmerer goes on to state that what the Onondaga Nation is offering is an invitation to all non-Indigenous people to becoming “Indigenous to place”, which she defines in the following words:

> No newcomer can ever match the Onondaga’s identity with these hills, but what does it mean for an immigrant culture to start thinking like a native one? Not to appropriate the culture of Indigenous people, not to take what is theirs, but to throw off the mindset of the frontier, the mindset that allows people to bury sacred sites under industrial waste, to fill a lake with mercury. Being Indigenous to place means to live as if we’ll be here for the long haul, to take care of the land as if our lives, both spiritual and material, depended on it. Because they do… Becoming Indigenous to place also means embracing its story, because the restoration of the land and the healing of our relationship mirror one another. Coming to terms with injustice is an act of liberation. By making the past visible, we can then see our way forward. (2008)

The concept or idea that Kimmerer is presenting here is profound in what it can achieve for Indigenous and racialized immigrants and white settlers that inhabit this land. Kimmerer offers us the chance to begin healing from the past and working towards sharing space, in a way that is respectful of the spirit that lives in the land and our relationship to it. Being “Indigenous to place” is about a way of life that sees the importance of bearing witness to stories of what has happened before us and what we need to think about for “seven generations” after us.

Moreover, the writing of this chapter is just the beginning of this spiritual journey for my community. In order to truly make the past visible, and move forward, we must bear witness to the story of the Hul'qumi'num and to how the Gurudwara in Lake Cowichan, which has become a forgotten site since our community dispersed, could be a site of true Sikhism. Fighting for the most oppressed in our community, we are warriors and our war is to fight for the rights of those who are displaced by a power over their land and minds.

In the beginning of this chapter, I started with some questions that spoke to the search for home and a connection to place, a safety in a sense of space. Much had shifted for me during my exploration of home. This final piece about the Onondaga Nation and the message they have facilitated in others, such as myself, about being Indigenous to place has shifted my spiritual search for a place called home and my relationship to this land. I have searched for a place called home for much of my life, but I find I am more settled in my contention with it and with the notion that this will be a perpetual circular search. At times, the search is satisfied and I may feel at home, and at other times I may feel at a loss for home; however, I am okay with this never-ending search and believe in the notion of searching. I will find peace and comfort in living in the present dailyness of breathing and being respectful to all the beings, the places, and the stories that live around me. Home is in my spirit, and I am happy to have had the Gurudwara to heal my past spiritual injuries and move forward, towards a new vision and way of being a good guest on the unceded land of Coast Salish people of Canada.

## Notes

1. Name has been changed for anonymity.
2. See the work of Ali Kazmi (2012) and R. Dhamoon, D. Bhandar, R. Mawani, and S. K. Bains (2019).
3. Following the attack on Pearl Harbour on December 7, 1941, the government of Canada, the United States, and Australia rounded up, removed, and incarcerated people of Japanese descent in the name of national security. The forced internment of 22,000 Japanese Canadians lasted until 1949. See the work of M. Oikawa (2012) for a deeper analysis.

## References

Arnett, C. (1999). *The terror of the coast: Land alienation and colonial war on Vancouver Island and the Gulf Islands, 1849–1863*. Burnaby, BC: Talonbooks.

Basso, K. H. (1996). *Wisdom sits in places: Landscape and language among the western apache*. Albuquerque: University of New Mexico Press.

Chatterjee, S. (2015). Skills to build the nation: The ideology of 'Canadian experience' and nationalism in global knowledge regime. *Ethnicities, 15*(4), 544–567.

Dei, G. (2002). Spirituality in African education: Issues contentions and contestations from a Ghanaian case study. *International Journal of Children's Spirituality, 7*(1), 37–56.

Deloria, V. (1994). *God is red: A native view of religion* (3rd ed.). Golden, CO: Fulcrum Publications.

Deloria, V., & Wildcat, D. R. (2001). *Power and place: Indian education in America*. Golden, CO: Fulcrum Resources.

Dhamoon, R., Bhandar, D., Mawani, R., & Bains, S. K. (2019). *Unmooring the Komagata Maru: Charting colonial trajectories*. Vancouver, BC: UBC Press.

Fernandes, L. (2003). *Transforming feminist practice: Non-violence, social justice and the possibilities of a spiritualized feminism*. San Francisco: Aunt Lute Books.

Haig-Brown. (2009). Decolonizing diaspora: Whose traditional land are we on? *Cultural and Pedagogical Inquiry, 1*(1), 4–21.

Hul'qumi'num—Lake Cowichan First Nation. Available from http://en.wikipedia.org/wiki/Cowichan_Lake_First_Nation and http://www.hulquminum.bc.ca/hulquminum_peopl/lake_cowichan. Accessed on December 13, 2008.

Jagpal, S. S. (1994). *Becoming Canadians: Pioneer Sikhs in their own words*. Madeira Park, BC: Harbour Pub.

Kazmi, A. (2012). *Undesirables: White Canada and the Komagata Maru—An illustrated history*. Vancouver, BC: Douglas & McIntyre.

Kimmerer, R. (2008, November/December). The rights of the land. *Orion Magazine*.

Oikawa, M. (2012). *Cartographies of violence: Japanese Canadian women, memory, and the subjects of the internment*. Toronto, ON: University of Toronto Press.

Pearkes, E. D. (2002). *The geography of memory: Recovering stories of a landscape's first people*. Nelson, BC: Kutenai House Press.

Potts, K., & Brown, L. A. (2005). Becoming an anti-oppressive researcher. In L. A. Brown & S. Strega (Eds.), *Research as resistance: Critical, Indigenous and anti-oppressive approaches*. Toronto: Canadian Scholars' Press.

Singh, S. (2002). *The Sikhs in history*. Amritsar, India: Singh Bros.

Tuck, E., & Yang, K. W. (2012). Decolonization is not a metaphor. *Decolonization: Indigeneity, Education & Society, 1*(1), 1–40.

Ward, W. P. (1978). *White Canada forever: Popular attitudes and public policy toward Orientals in British Columbia*. Montreal: McGill-Queen's University Press.

Ward, W. P. (2002). *White Canada forever: Popular attitudes and public policy toward Orientals in British Columbia* (3rd ed.). Montreal, QC: McGill-Queen's University Press.

CHAPTER 4

# Land and Healing: A Decolonizing Inquiry for Centering Land as the Site of Indigenous Medicine and Healing

*Wambui Karanja*

## Introduction

This chapter argues for the primacy of land in Indigenous medicine and healing practices and contends that colonial dispossession of Indigenous people of their lands disrupted the ability of indigenous people to practice their medicine and healing practices. It explores the interconnectedness of land and indigenous healing and argues that discourses that engage indigenous healing practices must contend with colonial settler land relationships. The chapter engages a decolonizing framework to center land as the site of indigenous healing and to problematize settler colonial policies that continue to deny indigenous people access to their medicines and healing practices and provides examples of approaches that can be applied to challenge colonial land relationships to reconnect Indigenous peoples with their lands and sources of healing knowledges and practices.

W. Karanja (✉)
Department of Social Justice Education, Ontario Institute for Studies in Education, University of Toronto, Toronto, ON, Canada



N. N. Wane et al. (eds.), *Decolonizing the Spirit in Education and Beyond*, Spirituality, Religion, and Education,
https://doi.org/10.1007/978-3-030-25320-2_4

## Indigenous People and the Land

The term, 'Indigenous People' has been used to include a diverse group of people defined by the criteria of ancestral territory, collective cultural configuration and historical location in relation to the expansion of Europe. As existing descendants of non-Western peoples, indigenous people have continued to occupy their ancestral lands after conquest by Westerners, and in some cases comprise people who have been relocated forcibly in the process of colonization (Purcell, 1998). Although diverse, Indigenous people share commonalities including existing as autonomous communities as original occupiers of their lands (Randall & Warner, 2013) who have always had their own Indigenous knowledges and healing systems that predate European contact. For Indigenous people, land is conceptualized beyond the physical space to include the universe, the sky, seas, water, rivers, plants, etc. It is a place of knowing and of experiencing everyday living, includes the living and non-living universe, and is interlinked with identity and self-hood (Dei, 2008). To Indigenous peoples, land, healing and spirituality are interconnected, and the maintenance and renewal of the relationship with their lands are critical to the practice and maintenance of Indigenous knowledges and healing (Robbins & Dewar, 2011).

## Conceptions of Indigenous Medicine and Healing in the Global Context

Different terminologies have been used to define Indigenous peoples. For example, in Africa, the term, 'traditional people,' has been used to refer to indigenous peoples of Africa while in Australia, the term 'Aboriginal' is applied to the original inhabitants of Australia and New Zealand. The terms 'Native American' and 'Indigenous' have been used to refer to North American Indigenous peoples and First Nations, Metis and Inuit peoples of Canada, respectively. It is also crucial to posit that the identity of being indigenous has only been relevant at the intersection with settler colonial encounters and indigenous is a binary that has been attributed to the 'Other.' I would argue that a more fitting descriptor is 'the original inhabitants of the land.' In this chapter, I reluctantly use the term 'indigenous' to refer the people whose knowledges and healing practices were and continue to be disrupted by settler-hood and colonialism, drawing references to the healing practices of the first peoples of Africa and Canada and other parts of the world. In Africa, the term indigenous is highly contested due to the binaries that exist between the tribes who continue to live very close to the land such as the Masai of Kenya and other tribes who are considered to be more Westernized. The chapter, however, applies the term 'indigenous' to all people of African ancestry irrespective of their degree of proximity to the state of being colonized as well as all the original inhabitants of lands in Canada.

It is argued that Indigenous medicine is the oldest form of medicine from which all later forms of medicine evolved. It is further argued that Indigenous healing and healing practices used by indigenous people before European contact survived colonization and continue to be practiced by indigenous communities all over the world (Wane, 2013). Different conceptualizations of Indigenous healing exist depending on the environment in which the medicine and healing are produced and practiced. In Canada, the Royal Commission for Aboriginal People refers to indigenous healing as traditional healing and has defined it as the 'practices designed to promote mental, emotional and spiritual wellbeing that are based on beliefs which go back to the time before the spread of western scientific bio-medicine' (Schiff & Moore, 2006, p. 49). It has also been defined as an indigenous way of restoring balance and homeostasis, a process that allows health and healing to occur, resulting in the restitution of the natural state of a human being—the state of being in balance with itself, its environment and its spirit (Ryan, 2014).

Healing practices differ between and among indigenous communities based on age-old healing practices informed by each community's conceptualization of healing and experiences of their natural environment and worldview. Among indigenous African people, healing systems address the pathology of the body and the social relations. The concerned is with healing the social body and repairing damage that might have been caused by different kinds of misfortunes (Vaughan, 1994). Wane has posited that the main purpose of indigenous African healing is to remove dissonance and distortions and to restore equilibrium or balance into one's life or environment (Wane, 2013). It is holistic, requiring consideration of the physical, emotional, psychological, social and spiritual engagements for healing to occur, and focusses on assisting the body to remove harm, rather than stopping the symptomatic expression of the harm. Indigenous African healing practices are diverse and include spiritual, herbal, community and ritual healing (Wane, 2013), ancestral reverence, use of spirits and spirit guides (Sangomas), re-incarnation, medicinal plants, dreams, divinations, etc. (Cumes, 2013). Among the Zulu of South Africa, ability to heal is a gift passed down from grandmothers to younger generations (Solomon & Wane, 2005).

Native American healing traditions operate in the context of the relationship with four constructs: Spirituality (Creator, Mother Earth, Great Father); Community (family, clan, tribe/nation); Environment (nature, balance, daily life); and Self (inner passions, peace, thoughts and values). Healing and wellness emphasize the necessity of seeking harmony with oneself, with others and with one's surroundings and also seeking an active relationship, harmony and balance with the physical and spirit world (Portman & Garrett, 2006). Wellness is connected with spirituality and considered to be life itself while spirituality is considered to be 'walking the path of Good Medicine' (living a good way of life) in harmony and balance (through the harmonious interaction of mind, body, spirit and natural environment) 'with all our relations' (Portman & Garrett, 2006, p. 457). Portman and Garrett continue to urge that to Native Americans, medicine refers to the 'essence of life' or inner power that creates every person's way of life and presence and can consist of physical remedies such as herbs and teas. The very essence of a person's inner being, medicine, experiences, events or memory all connect the body to the stream of life (Portman & Garrett, 2006, p. 459).

Indigenous people of Canada see healing as holistic with illness tied to the laws of the universe or natural law. There exists a strong connection with the planet and the universe through intricate relationships with the land, and healing may involve the use of traditional medicines, ceremonies, sweat lodges, smudges, quests, etc. (Robbins & Dewar, 2011). Healing practices are considered to go beyond limited notions of recovery and practice to offer profound and practical ways of addressing the physical, emotional, spiritual and mental health of Indigenous peoples (Lavallee, 2010). For others like the Maori of New Zealand, cultural perspectives influence their views of the healing of the mind, body and spirit. Fundamental to healing and a person's health are family/genealogy (whakapapa) and land (whenua) which are all considered interconnected aspects of health (Mark & Lyons, 2010). As well, healing among Indians in the Indian sub-continent can include practices such as Ayurveda and astrological methods that go back to more than ten thousand years (Valiathan, 2003).

Despite these variations, striking similarities in conceptions of healing exist across all Indigenous peoples globally to make Indigenous healing distinct from Western medicine (Robbins & Dewar, 2011). Examples include orality of transmission of indigenous healing knowledge from one generation to the next rooted in the culture of indigenous oral tradition, rootedness in the cultural practices of respective indigenous communities and the cultural specificity of each respective Indigenous community. Unlike Western medicine, Indigenous healing practices are holistic and are focused on addressing the physical, mental, spiritual and emotional aspects of the human being, operating interdependently to create balance in the person (Ermine, 2009). Healing emphasizes a deep connection between human beings and the forces of nature, the universe, the planet, land and sea. In all Indigenous healing practices, the earth's health is believed to be intrinsically connected to human health within a relational interconnectedness of the body, mind, spirit, land, the universe, ancestors and all living and non-living things (Martin-Hill, 2003).

## Medicine and Healing: A Personal Introspective

I come to this topic implicated as a guest of settler government on Indigenous lands. As a diasporic African woman living in the West, I have benefitted from Western medicine and continue to benefit from its conveniences and abilities to treat diseases. But as a young girl growing up in rural Africa, I also remember my mother using traditional medicines to treat our stomach aches, headaches, measles, skin rashes and colds when I or one of my siblings fell sick and when Western medicine was unavailable. In my travels back and forth from my country of residence to my country of birth, I can also testify to the euphoric spiritual connection I feel with my country of birth and the wholeness and connectedness I experience when I visit, a form of overwhelming peacefulness that makes me feel spiritually connected to my ancestral homeland. I conceptualize this feeling as healing from the land through my spiritual and indigenous connection to it. It speaks to the centrality of the physical and spiritual relationship and connectedness I have with the land in my motherland. My conflicting identities, complicities and implications in relation to the healing forms I have experienced vest me with responsibility to attest to the healing truths of the land not just for the body but for the soul and spirit as well, a responsibility that has led me to this chapter.

## Indigenous Peoples' Conceptions of Their Lands

Globally, Indigenous peoples conceptualize their land as counter to Western conceptions of land. In Eurocentric thought, land is a physical commodity that can be demarcated, alienated, parceled, titled and owned and commercialized through application of Western legal systems that confer absolute ownership rights to land (Karanja, 1991). This contrasts with indigenous peoples' conceptions of their land where land is considered an embodiment of the Creator and therefore connected to spirit. Land is not just the physical space but is connected to the psyche and memory, extending to the universe to include the sky, seas, water, rivers and plants. It includes all the living and non-living universe as a place of knowing, of experiencing everyday living, closely linked to identity and self-hood (Dei, 2008). In the North American Native context, in the words of one Native American Indian speaking of the US government's colonization of Native American land,

> they knew it would kill us if they killed the land. That's what they tried, but someone was still praying and doing the ceremonies; that's why we're still here. (Colomeda, 1999)

To indigenous peoples, land, culture and spirit are interconnected and central to their ways of knowing and acting. The connection to the land is maintained and sustained through memory and articulated in stories. Land is held in a communal system that guarantees access to every member of the group. This conceptualization is well captured in the words of the aboriginal communities of Australia. According to one Aboriginal Elder, Big Bill Neidjie as quoted in the famous Australian Mabo case on Aboriginal land rights, Aboriginal people's conceptions of their land are not just as a physical entity but as a whole environment that sustains life and is sustained by people and culture (Mabo Case, 1992). This intricate relationship with the land and the universe is critical to indigenous worldview and healing.

## Land as a Site of Indigenous Healing

The unique relationship with the land for Indigenous people is critical in that Indigenous lands and languages provide the foundation for indigenous traditional healing, spirituality and knowledge systems with Indigenous healing seen as the vehicle through which a community's knowledge and spirituality are developed, revitalized and maintained (Robbins & Dewar, 2011). The centrality of land to healing, knowledge and spirituality is said to be dependent on the maintenance and renewal of the relationships with the land. For healing to take place, one must accept the teachings of how their illness ties to the laws of the universe and natural law, and must maintain strong relationships with the land as any break with the land is considered to be the most important cause of health problems (Robbins & Dewar, 2011). The Maori, for example, have a strong attachment to the land through mythology, traditions and stories that keep ties with the land alive and commemorate both history and local geology based on the five central elements of mind, body, land, family/genealogy and spirit (Mark & Lyons, 2010). The interconnectedness of these central elements is seen to be key to the process of restoring harmony at all levels of the earth and the universe (Dei, 2012; Wane, 2013).

(1) *Land as a Source of Medicine: Food as Medicine*

Plant-based medicines vary from region to region depending on each local community's healing practice and medicines and land; the universe, water, all living and non-living things or experiences are important sources of medicine and healing, connecting people with the greater flow of life (Colomeda, 1999). For First Nations, Inuit and Métis Peoples of Canada, land and territory are vital sources of plant-based medicines (Lavallée, 2007, p. 133). Likewise, Indigenous African healing practices and medicines also include plant-based medicines and herbs (Wane, 2013) while in traditional Thai healing, medicines as food are interrelated such that foodstuff is considered to be medicine and vice versa (Bamber, 1998; Pieroni & Price, 2006).

(2) *Land, Spirituality and Healing*

Indigenous worldview locates Indigenous People as having a deep spiritual and symbiotic relationship with the land. For example, Indigenous African spirituality hinges on the maintenance and renewal of relationships to the land, the environment, plants and animals, and all are crucial to the practice of traditional healing. Healing is said to occur when all elements of the human being, mind, body and spirit and wellness are in harmony with the natural laws of Creation and natural unwellness is, therefore, a consequence of being in violation of sacred social and natural law of Creation (Solomon & Wane, 2005). To create wellness, each person is expected to be responsible for his own wellness by attuning one to self, relations, environment and the universe (Portman & Garrett, 2006).

In some Indigenous communities, metaphors rooted in land establish the connection to spirituality and healing (Robbins & Dewar, 2011), with land being considered synonymous with life and as a life force. No distinction exists between the earth as life and as a source of life (Looking Horse, 2009). Alfred and Corntassel have contended that for Indigenous communities, land is life and connection with the terrain and geography of their indigenous heritage is crucial if they are to comprehend the teachings and values of the ancestors (Taiaiake & Corntassel, 2005). Connection with ancestors through spirit and spirit world provides the link between the living, the dead and the natural and supernatural worlds. In Africa, for example, ancestors communicate with the living through dreams and divinations in a cyclical relationship of stewardship (Mbiti, 1990).

### (3) *Land as a Physical Site of Healing*

For Indigenous peoples in Canada, healing practices incorporate rituals, ceremonies, vision quests, sweat lodges, smudging ceremonies, hot springs and ceremonies. These are considered sacred for communicating with ancestral spirits and as sites of healing ceremonies and rituals. Ceremonies allow for opportunities for giving thanks, performing rites of passage, connecting communities, commemorating important stages in life and events and marking important times of the year such as solstices. As well, burial sites are considered sacred as the resting places of ancestors and as sites for spiritually connecting with the ancestors. These ceremonies, healing practices and sacred places all connect to the land, and the practice of going back to the land is interpreted as spiritually connecting with these places (Portman & Garrett, 2006). In Indigenous worldview, the physicality of land and territories speaks to land, not as a commodity as conceptualized by Western science but as an entity that embodies connection to spirit and as a source of medicine and healing.

(4) *Reciprocity: Indigenous People and Land*

Reciprocity is a key aspect of the relational worldview of Indigenous people and requires honoring and respecting relationships with other forms of life and the universe. In Indigenous worldview, having a reciprocal relationship with the land includes land as encompassing all things living and non-living as well as the waters, air and the universe and the spirit world (Hart, 2010, p. 7). For example, the Tahltan tribe maintains a deep respect for the land as mother, providing food, shelter, knowledge and medicine. They believe that the people are keepers of the land just as they look to the land for sustenance, guidance and healing (Tahltan Central Council, 2018). Wane and Solomon have supported this argument by positing that for individuals, collective responsibility is needed to take care of oneself, each other, the earth and the universe to sustain life, and just as people get sustenance from the universe, including the land, they have a corresponding responsibility to protect the universe (Wane, 2013). This reciprocal relationship underpins the overwhelming sense of responsibility that indigenous people feel for protecting their lands and territories as the source of their sustenance, health and healing.

## Colonialism, Land and Indigenous Healing

While this chapter will not engage colonialism as a discursive subject, it is argued that colonialism and Eurocentrism have constituted the two main threats to Indigenous healing with Indigenous healing defined as not only including the absence of disease but also personal and societal recovery from violence, racism and oppression from colonialism (Robbins & Dewar, 2011). Colonialism has been defined as the act of gaining control over another people for the sake of what the colonial power has determined to be the 'common good' (Alfred & Corntassel, 2005). It is a narrative in which the settler's power is the fundamental reference and assumption point, inherently limiting indigenous freedom and imposing the colonizer's worldview on the colonized. It serves to disconnect people from their longstanding relationships with their homelands, cultures and communities and is best conceptualized as an irresistible outcome of a...process of forced dispossession... a disconnection from the land, culture and community (Corntassel, 2012).

Colonialism superiorized itself by creating and enforcing bifurcations, binaries and hierarchies of knowledges placing Western science at the top and subjugating other knowledges to give it colonial dominance over other knowledge forms. Through imperialism and Eurocentrism, colonial dominance was established to challenge the legitimacy of Indigenous/Aboriginal knowledges and the ability of Indigenous people to pass on their knowledges to subsequent generations (Faucault, 1972; Waldram, 2013). Eurocentrism has been defined as a Western ideology that ensures that the world is mediated only through the Western (European) worldview, and Indigenous worldviews are analyzed most often through a Eurocentric point of view (Anderson, 2010). Eurocentric thought claims to be universal, superior and steeped in synthesis, individualism, rationalism and scientism and is deeply rooted in the dyad of the knowing subject and the unknowing object, privileging Western science as the knowing subject and all other knowledges as inferior unknowing subjects. Eurocentric thought was initially spread through civilizing missions and has been spread more recently through modernization and globalization programs that view Western science as the only valid knowledge form and point of view to which all other knowledge systems should defer.

In the context of healing and medicine, colonial practices included the theft of indigenous lands and the denial and destruction/eradication of all physical symbols of Indigenous culture and healing practices as well as the denigration of indigenous healing ceremonies in an attempt to sever Indigenous people's relationship with the natural world (Corntassel, 2012). With the consequent loss of land and territory to colonization, Indigenous people lost access to healing plants, sacred sites, fishing, hunting, gathering and ceremonial healing sites. Robbins and Dewar have argued that the loss of land disrupted access to Indigenous knowledge sources including knowledges on healing practices and methodologies (Robbins & Dewar, 2011).

Colonization and Eurocentrism were premised on the denial of indigenous histories and identities in a well-orchestrated colonial process of dispossession. Archibald has argued that in the experience of being colonized, among other losses, the most far-reaching effect of colonialism to Indigenous people was the loss of land and their ancestral homelands and territories to the colonizers (Archibald, 2006). Dislocation and dispossession have continued to exist through continued loss of control over remaining lands and territories buttressed by the forces of commercialism, modernization and development projects and practices that cause injury to the land and disrupt access to indigenous medicine sites, healing practices and knowledge production sites.

Leanne Simpson has posited that in the loss of land, Indigenous people lost the ability to protect their knowledges from destruction and desecration by colonial practices (Simpson, 2004). Simpson has further argued that Indigenous knowledge comes from the land through the relationships indigenous people develop and foster with the essential forces of nature, and in the loss of land, they lost food, medicine and places to hunt, fish and gather (Simpson, 2004). As well, through colonialism, Indigenous people lost the ability to sustain themselves and suffered injury to their bodies, minds, spirits and memories (Corntassel, 2012). This marginalization and neo-colonialist Western policies have continued to contribute to the loss of indigenous peoples' relationship with the land, dislocation from their knowledge and healing sites and practices and sources of their medicines (Portman & Garrett, 2006).

## Centering Land as the Site of Indigenous Healing—A Decolonizing Project

So far, I have attempted to interrogate the concepts of indigenousness, conceptions of Indigenous healing and indigenous people's relationship with their lands. This analysis was crucial to underpinning the importance of land in indigenous healing and the inseparability of land and healing to argue that the loss of land meant loss of indigenous healing. In the section below, I will use a decolonizing framework to argue the centrality of land as the site of Indigenous healing and medicine. The argument I make in this chapter is that the continued colonial dispossession of indigenous people of their lands and territories is a neo-colonial project that deprives them of their medicines, healing and, therefore, health and, that decolonization is crucial to the reclamation of land to ensure sustainability of indigenous medicine and healing.

Centering land as the site of Indigenous medicine and healing is an inevitable decolonizing project that challenges the superiorization of Eurocentric knowledges and worldview (Dei, Hall, & Rosenthal, 2000). It allows for alternative and oppositional discourses to Western knowledges to offer indigenous pathways for reconnecting Indigenous nations with their traditional land, resources and heritage (Corntassel, 2012). Decolonization allows the resurgence of a harmonious relationship and balance with the universe based on the doctrine of relationality and is about reclaiming personal and community identity, language and knowledge (Robbins & Dewar, 2011). Decolonization calls for subversion of Eurocentric hegemonic worldview that subjugates other knowledges under Western science and demands acknowledgment of indigenous knowledges and healing practices as different knowledge systems equal to Western science. Oppositional to colonial ways of thinking and acting, it demands an Indigenous starting point and an articulation of decolonization as defined by Indigenous peoples themselves (Aman, Chandni, & Eric, 2012). Through decolonization, Indigenous healing is re-asserted as a legitimate healing system that predates Western medicine and is theorized as an alternative and equally effective system of healing. It also deconstructs and redefines healing by moving away from Western-based concepts of healing as treatment of disease to a more holistic indigenous form of healing that is intrinsically connected to the land and therefore underscores the centrality of land as a source and sites the knowledge of healing and medicine (Simpson, 2004).

As a decolonizing project, centering land as the site of indigenous healing positions land and healing as constitutive of each other, giving each other meaning and essence in a symbiotic and relational oneness that is complete and inseparable. Indigenous healing cannot exist without its source—the land, and the land separated from healing would not perform its role of sustaining and giving life its meaning and essence. Decolonization of healing aims at the restoration of land as the site of healing to its original owners. To this end, Indigenous healing cannot be embodied outside the land and its bearers without it losing meaning and context. Decolonization of healing involves a re-assertion and reclamation of the legitimacy of an indigenous healing system that stands on its own premise without needing Western scientific justifications or ratifications for its authenticity and existence to be validated.

The argument is offered here that it is disingenuous for colonizing forces to separate Indigenous healing from its land-based origin and to remove the bearers of indigenous healing knowledges from their lands and to still lament the loss of indigenous healing practices and knowledges. While the West has begun to recognize the crucial role of indigenous knowledges in the sustainability of global biodiversity (Daes, 1992), they fail to acknowledge the role of colonialism and neo-colonial forces in sustaining policies and practices that continue to dispossess indigenous people of their lands and sites of knowledge production. Alfred and Corntassel have posited that the true power of indigenous people lies in their relationship with the land, native languages and ceremonial life…that land is life and Indigenous people must connect with the terrain and geography of their indigenous heritage (Alfred & Corntassel, 2005). It is therefore imperative that any preservation of Indigenous healing must be premised on the preservation of the land as the source and site of healing. This requires the acknowledgement that interference with the sanctity of the land destroys the healing knowledge and teachings of the land, and that land and indigenous healing are interlinked and inseparable in a reciprocal relationship of custodianship and reciprocity.

## Futurity of Land as Site of Indigenous Healing

Decolonization calls for imaginaries of resurgent indigenous healing futurities that center land as the site of indigenous healing. It is a futurity that requires acknowledging that healing cannot take place only through Western biomedicine which has continued to fail the health of indigenous and other non-dominant communities (Wedel, 2009, p. 49). It is a futurity that sees indigenous healing as equal and complementary to Western biomedical treatment and rejects bifurcations, binaries and hierarchies of knowledges of healing and medicine. It acknowledges the historical origins of indigenous medicines as land-based and reclaims the land for its original owners. Futurity offers possibilities for decolonization of the self as critical to decolonization of healing, a process that requires renunciation of the seduction and privileging of Western biomedicine and enables epistemic equity of healing systems and knowledges and allows for indigenous people to reclaim and maintain discursive authority over their healing systems and knowledges. Already, this futurity is starting to become a reality in the resurgence of knowledges and traditions buttressed by rising indigenous resistance to colonialism and emerging international recognition of Indigenous knowledges as vital to protecting and sustaining the world's biodiversity and eco-systems (UN, 2007).

Imagined futurity will require sustainable stewardship of the land through re-engaging relationships of reciprocity with the land and consequently, its time-tested healing gifts—a process that of necessity requires indigenous lands returning to their rightful owners and custodians. Settler communities must interrogate, examine and challenge their own Eurocentric complicities that fail to engage the role of history in the colonial project and in the causes they now champion in neo-colonial destinations. As well, Indigenous people must jealously safeguard healing knowledges and develop strategies for wrestling indigenous healing systems from the negative consequences of cultural appropriation (Agrawal, 1995). Preservation of indigenous knowledges allows for the preservation of indigenous healing and medicine. Dei has postulated that the West does not have all the answers and indigenous people must trouble Eurocentric thought, hegemony and subjectivity to define their own terms of engagement (with the West) using the tools of resilience, creativity and resourcefulness (Dei, 2014).

## Conclusion

In this chapter, I have attempted to show the intrinsic relationship between the land and Indigenous healing and have argued that indigenous healing cannot be conceptualized separately from the land. It is critical then that discourses that seek to decolonize indigenous healing acknowledge the criticality of land to indigenous healing, medicine and well-being. Indeed, I would argue that any discourse that fails to acknowledge this crucial fact would not have a decolonizing objective. Land and relationship with the land are critical to Indigenous healing and the role of colonialism in disrupting those relationships is implicated in the loss of indigenous healing practices. Indigenous reconnections with the land must be prioritized for the continued sustainability of indigenous healing practices. The West must adapt to the humility of not knowing and listen to Indigenous voices on how indigenous healing can be reclaimed.

Just like the Indigene has never been lost (Dei, 2002), Indigenous healing was never destroyed by colonialism. It was only disrupted but land is crucial to its resurgence and growth. Decolonizing discourses must insist on epistemic equity of healing knowledges and any genuine dialogue on the future of indigenous healing must invoke land dispensations, the protection of land-based healing sites and a commitment to protect and preserve the land for indigenous healing to thrive. Land is truly the site of indigenous healing.

## References

Agrawal, A. (1995). Indigenous and scientific knowledge: Some critical comments. *Indigenous Knowledges and Development Monitor (IKDM), 3*(3), 3–6.

Alfred, T., & Corntassel, J. (2005). Being Indigenous: Resurgences against contemporary colonialism. *Politics of Identity, 9*, 597–614.

Aman, S., Chandni, D., & Eric, R. (2012). Towards the tangible unknown: Decolonization and the Indigenous future. *Decolonization: Indigeneity, Education and Society, 1*(1), 1–X111.

Anderson, J. (2010). *Issues paper—Indigenous/traditional knowledge and intellectual property*. Retrieved from http://web.law.duke.edu/cspd/itkpaper.

Archibald, L. (2006). *Indigenous experiences in the United States, New Zealand, Australia and Greenland*. Ottawa: Anishinabe Printing.

Bamber, S. (1998). Medicine, food, and poison in traditional Thai healing. *Osiris, 13*, 339–353.

Colomeda, L. A. (1999). *Keepers of the central fire: Issues in ecology for Indigenous people*. Sudbury, MA: Jones and Bartlett Publishers.

Corntassel, J. (2012). Re-envisioning resurgence: Indigenous pathways to decolonization and sustainable self-determination. *Decolonization: Indigeneity, Education and Society, 1*(1), 86–101.

Cumes, D. (2013, January/February). South African Indigenous healing: How it works. *Explore: Indigenous Medicine, 9*(1), 58–65.

Daes, E. I. (1992). *UN Conference on Environment and Development* (Paragraph 26.1 Agenda 21). Rio de Janeiro.

Dei, G., Hall, B. L., & Rosenthal, D. G. (2000). *Indigenous knowledge in global contexts: Multiple readings of our world*. Toronto: University of Toronto Press.

Dei, G. J. (2008). Indigenous knowledge studies and the next generation: Pedagogical possibilities for anti-colonial education. *The Australian Journal of Indigenous Education, 37*(Suppl.), 5–13.

Dei, G. J. S. (2002). African development: The relevance and implications of indigenousness. In G. J. S. Dei, B. L. Hall, & D. G. Rosenberg (Eds.), *Indigenous Knowledges in Global Contexts: Multiple Readings of our World* (pp. vii–x). Toronto: University of Toronto Press.

Dei, G. J. S. (2014). Personal reflections on anti-racism education for a global context. *Encounters on Education, 15*, 239–249.

Dei, G. S. (2012). Indigenous anti-colonial knowledge as 'heritage knowledge' for promoting Black/African education in diasporic contexts. *Decolonization: Indigeneity, Education & Society, 1*(1).

Ermine, W. (2009). Ethical standards for research involving traditional healing. *Conference: Our People, Our Health Conference, November 2009*. Ottawa: National Aboriginal Health Organization.

Faucault, M. (1972). *Archeology of knowledge and the discourse on language*. New York, NY: Pantheon Books.

Hart, M. A. (2010). Indigenous worldviews, knowledge, and research: The development of an Indigenous research paradigm. *Journal of Indigenous Voices in Social Work, 1*(1), 1–16.

Karanja, P. W. (1991). Women's land ownership rights in Kenya. *Realizing the Rights of Women in Development Processes: Women's Legal Entitlements to Agricultural Development and Financial Assistance, 10*, 109–135.

Lavallée, L. F. (2007). Physical activity and healing through the medicine wheel. *Pimatiwisin, 5*(1), 127–153.

Lavallee, L. F. (2010). Beyond recovery: Colonization, health and healing for Indigenous people in Canada. *International Journal of Mental Health and Addiction, 8*(2), 271–281.

Looking Horse, A. (2009). Indigenous philosophies and ceremonies as the basis for action. *Our People, Our Health.* Ottawa: National Aboriginal Health Organization.

Mabo Case, Mabo and Others v. Queensland No. 2. (High Court of Australia. June 3rd, 1992).

Mark, G. T., & Lyons, A. C. (2010). Maori healers' views on wellbeing: The important of mind, body, spirit, family and land. *Social Science and Medicine, 70,* 1756–1764.

Martin-Hill, D. (2003). Traditional medicine in contemporary contexts: Protecting and respecting Indigenous knowledge and medicine. *Our People, Our Health Conference.* Ottawa: National Aboriginal Health Organization.

Mbiti, J. (1990). *African religion and philosophy.* Garden City, NJ: Doubleday.

Pieroni, A., & Price, L. L. (2006). *Eating and healing: Traditional foods as medicine.* Binghamton, NY: Food Products Press.

Portman, T. A., & Garrett, M. T. (2006). Native American healing traditions. *International Journal of Disability, Development Education, 53*(4), 453–469.

Purcell, T. W. (1998). Indigenous knowledge and applied anthropology: Questions of definition and direction. *Human Organization, 57*(3), 258.

Randall, S. A., & Warner, E. K. (2013). *Climate change and Indigenous peoples: A search for legal remedies.* Orlando, FL: Edward Edgar Publishing.

Robbins, J. A., & Dewar, J. (2011). Traditional Indigenous approaches to healing and the modern welfare of traditional knowledge, spirituality and lands: A critical reflection on practices and policies taken from the Canadian Indigenous example. *The International Indigenous Policy Journal, 2*(4), 1–17.

Ryan, J. G. (2014). *The missing pill: The rise of energy medicine and conscious biospiritual transformation ... With an introduction to unity field healing.* Corcaigh Wilton, Ireland, UK: John G Ryan MPC.

Schiff, J. W., & Moore, K. (2006). The impact of the sweat lodge ceremony on dimensions of well-being. *American Indian and Alaska Native Mental Health Research: The Journal of the National Center, 13*(3), 48–69.

Simpson, L. (2004, Summer/Fall). Anti-colonial strategies for the recovery and maintenance of Indigenous knowledge. *The American Indian Quarterly, 28*(3&4), 373–383.

Solomon, A., & Wane, N. N. (2005). *Integrating traditional healing practices into counseling psychotherapy: Indigenous healers and healing in a modern world.* Thousand Oaks: Sage.

Tahltan Central Council. (2018, February 12). *Tahltan Band Council.* Retrieved from http://tahltan.ca/nation/people/.

Taiaiake, A., & Corntassel, J. (2005). *The politics of identity IX*. Oxford, UK: Blackwell Publishing.

UN General Assembly. (2007, October 2). *United nations declaration on the rights of indigenous Peoples: Resolution/adopted by the general assembly*. A/RES/61/295. Available at https://www.refworld.org/docid/471355a82.html. Accessed 10 September 2019.

Valiathan, M. (2003). *The legacy of Caraka*. Chennai, India: Longman Publishers.

Vaughan, M. (1994). Healing and curing: Issues in the social history and anthropology of medicine in Africa. *Social History of Medicine, 7*(2), 283–295.

Waldram, J. B. (2013). *Transformative and restorative processes: Revisiting the question of efficacy of Indigenous healing*. Saskatoon: Routledge.

Wane, N. (2013). African Indigenous healing practices. In N. Wane & E. Neeganagwedgin (Eds.), *A handbook on African traditional healing approaches & research practices* (pp. 7–29). Oakville: Nsemia Publishers.

Wedel, J. (2009). Bridging the gap between western and indigenous medicine in eastern Nicaragua. *Anthropological Notebooks, 15*, 49–64.

# PART II

# Body

CHAPTER 5

# Healing and Well-Being as Tools of Decolonization and Social Justice: Anti-Colonial Praxis of Indigenous Women in the Philippines

*Rose Ann Torres*

## Introduction

This chapter uncovers how Aeta women healers in the Philippines practice decolonization and social justice. Aeta Indigenous women have resisted oppression and colonization by nourishing individual and collective spirit as the core of human health and well-being. They have passed on their healing practices to younger generations after generation thus ensuring the survival of local knowledge in the face of colonization and exploitation. This chapter is based on my research conducted among Aeta women

Rose Ann Torres (✉)
Social Justice Education Department, Ontario Institute for Studies in Education, University of Toronto, Toronto, ON, Canada
e-mail: rose.torres@utoronto.ca



N. N. Wane et al. (eds.), *Decolonizing the Spirit in Education and Beyond*, Spirituality, Religion, and Education,
https://doi.org/10.1007/978-3-030-25320-2_5

healers in the Philippines in 2010 (Torres, 2012). Aeta is one of the Indigenous peoples in the Philippines, resisting colonization through their healing practices.

Their knowledge of healing was passed to them by their ancestors through the word of mouth. Healing for Aeta women healers is about focusing on overall well-being of an individual which is spiritual, mental, physical, and psychological. To them, if one of their aspects of themselves is not functioning, then it will result in "*sakit*" or sickness. Their focus is to ensure that their children are knowledgeable about their worldviews, cultures, and traditions. This chapter is aimed at providing historical evidence of the healing power of Aeta women healers in the Philippines and how they use their healing practices and the well-being as a form of resistance against imperialism. I will also discuss healing and well-being as a form of decolonization and social justice. I employed talking circles as a methodology which Aeta women healers have been employing for their teachings to transmit their culture and healing practices. Talking circle is one of the Indigenous decolonizing research methodologies (Kovach, 2009; Restoule, 2004; Smith, 1999). The methodology gives the participants a chance to share their knowledge and to question the researcher (Kovach, 2009; Torres, 2012). Through this methodology, colonial research process is questioned and troubled to center narratives from the margins. It transforms the politics between the researcher and the participants in such a way that they are co-producers of knowledge. It is also a methodology that gives equal power to the participants and the researcher (Kovach, 2009; Torres & Nyaga, 2016).

Aeta women healers know that society is changing and that they need to start having written materials that relate to their culture and healing practices, as both a means of reaching out to the people outside of their community and a means of sustaining their knowledge. They know that non-Aeta people need to build relationships with them in order to change their perceptions of the Aeta people and that of other Indigenous peoples in the world. I employ the following questions to guide me through this chapter: How can the spirit be healed? What is healing of the spirit? Why is the healing of the spirit important for the body? Can the spirit be corrupted?

My questions enabled me to hold a conversation with the healers who indicated to me that, first and foremost, the spirit is central to our well-being. If the spirit is week, then the mind and the body are weak. If the spirit is weak, certain rituals are held to bring back balance and harmony. For the outsider, the ritual has a semblance of ordinary prayers; however, these are special ways of communicating with the Creator and the ancestors. The healers engage in conversation with the "spirito" or spirit by chanting and calling ancestral spirits to join them in the healing practice. Once the spirit is healed, the healers focus on the mind and the body of the person to achieve holistic healing. In relation to the corruption of the spirit, the healers explained that a spirit cannot be corrupted but can be possessed. In order to make sense of the conversation that I held with the healers, I will provide narratives from them. My intention is not to engage in an analysis of these narratives, but to leave it to the reader to have a moment to reflect on the words of the healers. That is through this ritual, the spirit's well-being is restored. In addition to healing practices, I will provide historical evidence of how Aeta women healers employed their healing practices as a form of resistance against imperialism. I situate this work on anti-colonial theory.

## *Anti-colonial Framework*

Anti-colonial framework speaks to Aeta women forms of resistance to colonization. Anti-colonial work recognizes the body of knowledge that is embedded in the history, experiences, and cultures of the subjugated and brings their experiential reality to the forefront. It violently dismantles the colonial mind-set in the lives of the colonized and reminds the oppressed to look back and admire what they have lost both culturally and spiritually in their communities. The axiomatic claim of the paradigm is that lost culture is worth reclaiming as is the restoration of the lost pride of the endemic population. To many colonized people, their language was taken away through the education system. This robbed them of their cultural ways of knowing. The Aeta women, who participated in this study, lamented the fact that the young people had lost their local language. Wa Thiongo (1986) explains the importance of local language. By acknowledging the local dialect, Wa Thiongo (1986) sees this as a standpoint through which full emancipation of the colonized can be realized. He believes that culture is embedded in the language that we use and so, to define ourselves, full emancipation has to start from where we missed the step. To him, language is an imperative tool in decolonization. The Aeta women healers concede that language is a prerequisite for the preservation of their culture and traditions. Through their language, they know that they are able to put into context the love that their ancestors gave them. They speak Agta and Ilokano and they use these languages to educate their children about the importance of adhering to Aeta morals and values.

Anti-colonial theory teaches us how to "resist oppression, assimilation and annihilation by encouraging us to use alternative knowledge, oral histories, literatures, and cultural products as a counterpart to hegemonic forms of knowledges" (Dei & Asgharzadeh, 2005, p. 65). This is what the Aeta women did. They held on to their spiritual healing practices. We need to be aware of the full spectrum of oppressive techniques because the colonialists, "through their methods of writing and teaching, as well as through production, validation, and dissemination of knowledge, [compel] the colonized subjects to view themselves, their cultures, their language, their ancestors, their histories and their identities negatively" (ibid.). Anti-colonial theory "encourages the colonized bodies and communities to define themselves and to articulate their condition through their own voice" (ibid., p. 66). Anti-colonial theory places Indigenous knowledge that would have been excluded from the academy at the center of academic discourse. However, placing Indigenous knowledge at the core of discourse does not mean excluding other forms of knowledge.

Anti-colonial theory captures the importance of Indigenous knowledge in the academy as well as the anti-colonial struggle against imperialism, racism, sexism, impoverishment, homophobia, and other forms of colonial domination. Anti-colonial theory can speak to the issues faced by Aeta women healers because it focuses on agencies and resistance that Indigenous peoples practice and because it recognizes marginalized groups as subjects of their own histories, knowledge, and experience (Dei, 2002; Fanon, 1963; Foucault, 1980; Memmi, 1965). It is because of the focus on the wide variety of pertinent themes, such as the contribution of women, dismantling of dominating influences, use of language in the battle against colonialism, agency, and resistance or race, highlighted by the anti-colonial theory, that this study selected to this framework as a means of bringing forth the significance of the role of the Aeta healers.

Finally, anti-colonial theory captures the essence of why we need to acknowledge the Aeta cosmology and practice and why we need to dismantle the notion that knowing by means of Western knowledge is the only valid way of knowing. Anti-colonial theory celebrates the different forms of resistance of the colonized (Wane, 2009). It brings the histories of knowledge production, "epistemology of the colonized, anchored in the Indigenous sense of collective and common colonial consciousness" (Dei,

2002) to the spotlight. It also recognizes the complicities and responsibilities of every colonized individual, hence its appropriateness for this paper.

### *Complexities of Spiritual Healing*

Spiritual healing, I came to make sense of, is a complex phenomenon. This is revealed by Aludig words:

> I can tell when somebody is being possessed by a "dakes nga spirito" or bad spirit through their eyes, actions, and behavior. One day, I was in the farm. I was tilling the land when somebody started shouting. The person was not drunk or drugged. I looked at him on the eyes and it was so sharped and red. And so..., I started talking to the spirit. I asked, I know you are not Juan (the name of the person who was possessed), who are you? The spirit said something that I did not understand. I believe, the spirit had demands, but, I said "you do not belong to this world, and right now I want you to go back to where you belong, and do not disturb Juan again". Then, I prayed and suddenly, Juan fell on the ground. I waited for few minutes, then I talked to Juan and he responded in a respectful way. I knew then, that the spirit of Juan is healed. That is why we must nourish our own spirit through love and care of one another. The nourishment of our spirit is like the way we take care of our mind and our body. We must ensure that we do good things, we eat good food. We need to know how to share, and we must help one another. These things cannot be done by an individual alone, it must be done by the whole community.

The above captured what many healers understanding of being possessed. Conversation with a spirit that is inhabiting a human being is easily identifiable by looking at their eyes. What is amazing is the healers know the names of the bad spirits that are creating chaos for the person they have taken over their mind, body, and spirit. During the healing process, relationship building is important. In this relationship building, the healer and the patient must trust and respect one another. If the patient does not trust and respect the healer and vice versa, the process becomes complicated. This relationship building can be attained through open communication between the healer and the patient as well as the spirit.

Aludig narrative above reveals that it is not just removing of the bad spirit, but the importance of self care, through nourishment of the body and mind, through food and love, respectively. The question to ask is, can all the dispossession of the spirit have emanated from colonization? Of course, I am alluding to the fact that we did have dispossession of the spirit before colonization. What we do know is that when the colonizer came to the Philippines hundreds of years ago, they knew that the first thing they needed was to disturb the spirit of a person. Some who were not spiritually prepared to resist colonization were dislocated and completely alienated from the spirit of our ancestors.

The practice and assumptions are neither the value system nor the methodological standard practices of Western trained healers; instead, they bear remarkably similar insights to those of many other Indigenous cultures. The American South West Navaho have the concept of Koyaanisqats or "life out of balance." The concept speaks about the violation of nature and imbalance leading to "illness" or absence of wellness. These are ideas now embraced by many, arguing for an ecological and environmental approach to health and life. Aeta women healers systemically argue that it is deleterious for the body because it creates imbalances in the system that result in headaches and body pains, among other ailments. Their healing practice therefore is to counter the work of colonization and, more recently, the work of global capitalism, whose aims are to generate profits. These women probably have not read Amy Chua's "World on Fire" (despite the fact that she is Chinese-Filipino/American) yet their life and cultural experiences material reality and ontological insights lead them to similar conclusions about the pejorative effects of exporting "global democracy" and its resulting racism, environmental degradation, and acrogenic consequences. Aeta women healers also know that while colonizers from Britain or Spain may no longer be present in the Philippines, their presence on ontological curricular models, informal learning and "taken for granted truths," and cultural prejudice continues to be felt (2003).

Aeta healers have maintained the healing practices that their ancestors employed as a way of resisting these oppressive forces. They work in the possibility of hope, a hope that gives them the strength to carry on their culture and tradition. They know that their identity has been damaged; they have been essentialized on the basis of their gender, race, and class and have been ridiculed on the basis of their culture, and Sterling (2002) documents that her grandmothers possess the knowledge we need in order to live a successful life. They have the experience and knowledge about how to heal and how to maintain the well-being of their community. They are the cultural professors. They know what it takes to be healthy. Their healing practices go beyond making the physical body strong, instead adopting a holistic focus on ensuring that the social, emotional, and spiritual well-being of a person is also taken care of. They can communicate with the terrestrial world as well as the celestial world. They believe that everything is related and interconnected. We cannot live without the presence of the "other." They believe, like many African tribes, and Indigenous groups in both North and South America and across the globe, that it is a circle of interrelationship in which a break can be the cause of the loss of social, cultural, and political, as well as economic and personal well-being. To Aeta women healers, their environment should be respected if they are to live in harmony.

According to Nyaga and Torres (2015, p. 753) that:

> The Aeta women healers' "credentials", which are to be represented, are based on their spirituality and the extensive experiential study of how this plays out in nature, medicine, and healing practices. Their spirituality is the source of their strength and power in the struggle against colonization. Their spirituality is an instrument for sustaining both their identity and agency. Their spirituality is one of their sources of healing. It gives them the confidence to heal and to perform their responsibilities as members of their community. They acknowledge their awareness of Christianity and attend to its truths rather than summarily dismissing it. In fact, they respect the teachings and recognize that it shares common truths with their own beliefs; we are, after all, human—all with the same strengths and flaws. Nonetheless, they would like to maintain the spirituality that they learned from their ancestors and sustain it despite having different struggles, oppressions, and dismissals. They would like to be identified by their spirituality because this would explain who they are and what morals and values they have in life. If the non-Aeta people appreciate Aeta spirituality, then the Aeta women healers believe that the stereotypes about the Aeta will cease.

The above quotes give us a glimpse of the source of healing powers of the Aeta women healers. While foregrounding the historical legacy of Aeta women's healing power in the Philippines, this passage above endeavors to campaign for the maintenance and sustenance of the knowledge of these women. For the Aeta women, their identity is marked by their healing practices. They are proud to carry that responsibility for the well-being of their community. Their spiritual healing practices are their form of teaching. According to Nyaga and Torres (2015) that:

> The history of Philippine medicine historically required the use of herbs and followed the belief that sickness was brought on by the spirits. Historians thus concluded that the earliest practice of medicine was in line with the indigenous healer practices (De La Cruz 1984). Nevertheless, when Spaniards established their colony in the nineteenth century in the Philippines, they brought with them physicians from Spain. Indeed, the creation of public health and Western medicine "were integral parts of the ideology of empire" (King 2002: 765). This "ideology of colonial healing" is one of the justifications given by colonizers for their invasion on the pretext that they were bringing the best quality of life for indigenous peoples. The idea that the Spaniards were out to save the newly found heathens from their uncivilized way of living was implanted in the minds of the indigenous peoples. (p. 753)

Indigenous medicine has provided balance for the Aeta community for hundreds of years. However, when the colonizers arrived in the Philippines, they did recognize the herbs or the rituals that this community employed. The colonizers came to save the Aeta community, even when their justification for saving the society was fraudulent. Let me turn to a deeper analysis of the narratives of the Aeta women spiritual healers.

## Discussion on the Narratives of Aeta Women Healers Using the Anti-colonial Framework

How can healing and well-being be used as tools for decolonization and social justice? What is decolonization? What is social justice? For Aeta women healers, decolonization is about recognizing the impact of colonization in the lives of the people. It is also about knowing how to reclaim the practices, traditions, ways of knowing, and among others that have been affected by colonization. For example, one of the impacts of colonization in the Philippines is division and hatred among the populace. There is a division between the Indigenous peoples and one of them the Aeta people and the colonized Filipinos. There has been an ongoing problem of grabbing the land of the Aeta people, or abuse when they go to town. Aeta women healers know the root cause of all these problems. They decided to focus on their healing practices to reclaim and restore the peace and unity of the Philippines. They know that it takes a while to do the work, like Aludig mentions:

> To heal is not a one-time process. In fact, it can take a long time. But, I do not focus on the time. But, I focus on the purpose of the healing. And that

> is to attain well-being of the people that will result to peace and unity that have taken away from us (colonizer). For example, our neighbor who have been suffering of sickness for a long time came to me and asked me why he has been sick for such a long time. I begun my healing with her through a conversation about her life histories, then moving on to her life styles and so on. I decided to do a healing that compose of rituals, offerings and taking herbs for her strength. It is still an on-*going process. But, I have faith she will get well.*

Through this, they believe that social justice can be attained. Amay states what social justice entails:

> We can say that there is social justice if we enjoy the same rights as human being. It is an absence of abuse, brutality, discrimination against, and violation of human rights.

In just this material and intellectual understanding, the Aeta women healers form part of the vanguard of organic intellectuals who have been utilizing their healing knowledge to reclaim their political, social, cultural, and spiritual power outside of their community. Aludig explains:

> My healing is for all… I heal Aeta people or other people that do not belong to our community or group. I believe that being healthy is not only for the benefit of an individual but for the nation. I always think that if we are all healthy than we can always fight against injustices in our small places that we belong to. And what I mean by well-being is about being healthy spiritually, emotionally, psychologically, and physically. That is why my healing is for all.

They actively participate in reclaiming their indigeneity in a practical sense. These "intellectuals" fully understand that societies house machinations and encoded rules as well as patterns of governance, and they are ready to make changes that suit the well-being of the whole society. Rima states:

> My knowledge of healing was passed to me freely. I believe that I was given this talent and skills of healing not for my own benefit. Healing for me is for all those people who need it and believe it. What I mean "believe" is acknowledging the power of healing because without believing it, then, it is impossible for somebody to get healed. Healing is for all because we belong to one community and to one nation. If we are all healthy than we will be able to help each other economically, politically, socially, and spiritually. But, if one of us is not well than it can affect all of us. One of the common disease

> that I usually hear from people is "high blood pressure". I heard that people who have this kind of problem takes a lot of medication. I cannot judge the efficacy of this medication, but, a person who came to me with this health problem, I asked him to take an herb that can normalize his blood. I also ask him to pay attention to the food that he takes and his relationships to others.

They are experienced and knowledgeable in their endogenous and external cultural practices, laws, and norms and are ready to overcome oppression as engaged activists (Rima, Aeta healer).

In addition, Jose Rizal and Andres Bonifacio, among others, were the leaders of revolutionary movements in the Philippines. Jose Rizal wrote novels, such as *Noli Me Tangere* and *El Filibusterismo,* to expose the grievous act of the Spaniards against the Filipinos, while Andres Bonifacio led his troops to the mountains to end the injustices of the colonizers. Aludig, states:

> There have so many on-going injustices in this nation. Like for example, killing one another, raping women and children, mining, using dynamite in fishing, and so many others. When you try to talk to people and beg them to stop what they're doing, they even abuse you. So, to me my way of helping my community is to include them in my prayers and in my offerings. Because, that our creator will intervene. And so when a person comes and asks me to heal her/him, it is a joy for me. Because I know that this is a beginning of healing the whole community as well. I begin my healing through heart conversation. We talk about the Philippines before the coming of colonizer (dayuhan). Then, we talk about the problem of our community. Then I begin the process of healing.

Though they all came from different vantage points when analyzing the colonial nature, we can see that they had unity in their goal: to resist and to explain the work of colonization while simultaneously reclaiming decolonization. Fear was not sufficient to trump action since without such proactive steps; cultural genocide and domination would result. It was cultural survival that maintained the claim to human self-determination which was itself the prize. Amay explains:

> I know in my heart that when a person is healthy or "nasalun-at" than the whole community is also healthy. And when we are all healthy than we can stop acknowledging the power of colonization in us. I believe that all of us are better off without outsiders in our community. My healing is all from

> nature and believing that our creator will help us in order to achieve a healthy community.

According to Young (2001), "...many histories, rebellions, political campaigns, cultural identification and theoretical formulations that evolved during the twentieth century as part of the anti-colonial struggle that together, at great human cost, freed the world from colonial domination in a remarkably short period of time" (pp. 427–428). However, these could not have happened without the help of women. Women had a role to play, supplying men with both food and Indigenous medication made from their herbs. Talna also explains:

> Healing for all, means achieving and practicing social justice. There are many injustices in this country. In our community alone, outsiders have taken away some parts of our ancestral land. Some of us are being beaten up, rape, or harassed. We are not given the rights to vote and our opinion are being considered by the government. We are considered as being illiterate people therefore we do not know anything, and so on. Everything that I told you in this circle are not many, but, it serves as an example of injustices in our society. I chose to be a healer to attain social justice. That in my healing I heal the mind, the body, and the spirit. I have this strong belief that if we are healed holistically we refrain from committing injustices in our community. For example, in our community one way of preventing social injustices is to practice sharing and reciprocity. If others need so food and you have some, share to do those who do not have. We usually practice these kinds of values in our community.

Fanon (1963) expresses his recognition of and confidence in the capacity of women in overthrowing colonization: "the women could not be conceived of as a replacement product, but as an element capable of adequately meeting the new tasks" (p. 48).

In addition to these proponents of anti-colonial thought, this paper includes here the Indigenous peoples in the world, including the Aeta women healers who have been resisting tyrannical pedagogies and reclaiming their space. Maya notes:

> Philippines is so divided. Aeta people versus the Filipino people became enemy because of psychological impact of colonization. We are at war at each other. Therefore, we need to be healed to have peace in this nation. We

> need to examine our values-how do we see each other? Why do we need to discriminate others?

Human collective success always works at many levels as we have tried to do. It is important to acknowledge the important epics and paradigmatic models written about anti-colonialism while neither devaluing nor forgetting the work of ground-level intellectuals who were and are the front-line personnel and ground-level organic intellectuals of anti-colonial struggle and thought. Since the inception of colonization, Indigenous peoples—with the Aeta women healers as both a text book example and role models—have been skirmishing against oppression and challenging false cultural characterizations.

A holistic and full account of the anti-colonial struggle involves laying out the schematic and diagrammatic parts of the struggle. Hence, it is essential to describe anti-colonial thought while simultaneously acknowledging that the original people who exemplify resistance work against colonization are the Indigenous peoples, including the Aeta. Amay expresses her opinion:

> I am hopeful for our nation despite our differences I believe we can attain justice. For me, I heal everybody, Aeta, non-Aeta, men, women, children, adults. Because I believe that if I show kindness and love and compassion through healing this will resonate to others. That is why, when I was called by a family of a police, I went not just to heal him, but, to show, that it is fine to be kind and loving to those people who do not belong to the same community.

This is not to romanticize the Indigenous peoples but rather to fill in unspoken segments of the empirical basis of human life from all humanity and to therefore start acknowledging those who are frequently excluded or (misrepresented) for both political and economic convenience (from the colonial perspective of) knowledge production of theory and "fact." We must exert due diligence in our own method and rigor in our investigations of critical work or we may end up re-colonizing and misrepresenting the actual richness of cultural belonging to the Indigenous peoples in our theories and "thick descriptions" (Geertz, 1973). We have to highlight the dynamics, intelligence, and uniqueness of their ways of life and how they have mastered the struggles resulting from being eclipsed by reductionist representation, and in these representations, we must be sympathetic yet critical as we watch the unfolding strategies of how Indigenous people like the Aeta are standing firmly for their cultures and traditions and not succumbing to domination and marginalization. Talna explains what well-being as a form of social justice is:

> The root cause of injustices in our nation is complex and cannot be solved by medicine. It is systemic, in fact it's already ingrained in our psych that it is "okay" to commit injustice especially when you don't feel good about other people. This kind of behavior is "sick" in nature. That is why I heal everybody, anybody because well-being for all is necessary to counter injustices. When a person is well, he/she has the capacity to determine right or wrong, then, he/she's wellness is a result of justice in our community.

This paper further notes that anti-colonial analysis does not sufficiently highlight the contributions of both non-Indigenous women and Indigenous women against colonization (Spivak, 1995) and "often reproduce patriarchal, hierarchical models as the ideals for sovereignty" (Kuokkanen, 2007, p. 8). This paper seeks to partially address this oversight and is the central reason for the inclusion of the Aeta women healers with the tactical and intellectual hopes of chronicling and recording their voices as part of the growing chorus rising as anti-colonial proponents. Again, this paper addresses the gap created by the absence of the Aeta from the literature. Anti-colonial theory is nevertheless relevant in theorizing how the Aeta women healers have been rupturing the work of colonization in their community through their healing practices, and how the agency of Indigenous peoples has been celebrated since it gives us an analytical template that fits many who endured the Euro-colonial paradigm.

According to Amay,

> If we do not act now, when? I believe personally that healing and the well-being can counter the work of colonization. When we heal, we also discuss what we need to do as community. We discuss strategies, issues, and different forms of healing. We also identify who needs healing in our community. I also teach my children and the children of others to heal so that I am no longer strong, then somebody can continue the work. And as we continue to heal, to support, and to love one another, the work of "dayuhan" (colonizer) will cease.

Amay expresses the urgency of decolonization because she knows that every time we sit back and think that colonization is over, then, this is the time that we let colonization continue to colonize us. That is why for Amay and all the healers, healing is a continual process to achieve decolonization. And as long as colonization is ongoing, then healing is also ongoing.

## Conclusion

This paper concludes that Aeta women healer's knowledge of healing and well-being is a tool and the optimal strategy for decolonization of their community. Their success, persistence, and generosity offers a model of knowledge production that the academic community would do well to learn from. In the course of many honest exchanges and the simple, but powerful, act of listening, the Aeta healers in the circle taught me that I should always be ready to reference the ultimate library of knowledge: what our Mother Nature is willing to give to us. These are lessons in limits and possibilities, and truths such as that we are made from nature and neither the controller nor arbiter of the possible. These ecological, biological, physical, and emotional truths are such that Western science and ecology are only now rediscovering. When I met them, this set of caring women taught me how to pay attention to their way of life and practices. The study methodology—talking circle—is a safe place for them (and as I discovered to my delight, also for me). It symbolizes interconnection, love, respect, and openness to one another. The women taught me not to impose upon their lives, but, rather, to respect and be willing to make changes.

Finally, I offer empirical findings and a conclusion about the women with whom we discussed decolonization as a process that has to be dealt with. Despite the continued challenges from outside their community that they must endure, the women's determination not to give up only increases. They make a concerted effort to use their healing practice as a tool for change in their community, as they interact with both their own people and the non-Aeta people. They may not have received a Eurocentric education, but they apprehend what is happening externally. Nonetheless, however, through their healing practices, they believe that their race will continue to exist. They are human, highly intelligent, and understand life and nature, including the dynamics of power assimilation, knowledge production, and the healing power of caring.

The strength of this chapter is in highlighting and documenting the knowledge of the Aeta with respect to healing physical, emotional, social, and spiritual well-being as a tool for decolonization. My ethnographic records from the circle thematically document and emphasize the distinct identity of the Aeta in general and of their women healers in particular. My thematic elements focus on their different forms of agency and resilience and strive to comprehend the empirical and conceptual schemata. This schemata is conceptually rich and complex since it describes the interplay of society, nature, and human adaptation. This chapter documents that the Aeta women are not docile, primitive or backwards. Alternatively, they are healers, community custodians and sages. My chapter chronicles the cultural richness of the Aeta women healers.

## References


Chua, A. (2003). *World on fire: How exporting free market democracy breeds ethnic hatred and global instability*. New York, NY: Doubleday.

Dei, G. J. S. (2002). *Spiritual knowing and transformative learning* (NALL Working Paper No. 59). For full text http://www.oise.utoronto.ca.myaccess.library.utoronto.ca/depts/sese/csew/nall/res/59GeorgeDei.pdf.

Dei, G. J. S., & Asgharzadeh, A. (2005). The power of social theory: The anti-colonial discursive framework. *Journal of Educational Thought, 35*(3), 297–323.

Fanon, F. (1963). *The wretched of the earth*. London, England: Penguin Books.

Foucault, M. (1980). *Power/knowledge: Selected interviews and other writings, 1972–1977*. New York, NY: Pantheon.

Geertz, C. (1973). Thick description: Toward an interpretive theory of culture. In C. Geertz, *The interpretation of cultures: Selected essays* (pp. 3–30). New York, NY: Basic Books.

Habermas, J. (1996). Modernity an un-finished project. In P. Maurizio & B. Seyla (Eds.), *Critical essays on the philosophical discourse of modernity* (pp. 97–123). Cambridge: MIT Press.

Kovach, M. (2009). *Indigenous methodologies: Characteristics, conversations, and contexts*. Toronto, ON, Canada: University of Toronto Press.

Kuokkanen, R. (2007). Myths and realities of Sami women: A postcolonial feminist analysis for the decolonization and transformation of Sami society. In J. Green (Ed.), *Making space for Indigenous feminism* (pp. 72–92). Halifax, NS: Fernwood Publishing.

Lopez, I. J. (1995). The social construction of race. In R. Delgado (Ed.), *Critical race theory: The cutting edge* (pp. 163–177). Philadelphia, PA: Temple University Press.

Memmi, A. (1965). *The colonizer and the colonized*. Boston, MA: Beacon Press.

Nyaga, D., & Torres, R. (2015). The politics of cultural representation. *Sociology Study Journal, 5*(9), 744–758. https://doi.org/10.17265/2159-5526/2015.09.

Omi, M., & Winant, H. (1993). *Racial formation in the United States from the 1960s and to the 1990s* (2nd ed.). New York, NY: Routledge.

Restoule, J. (2004). *Male aboriginal identity formation in urban areas: A focus on process and context* (Doctoral dissertation). Toronto, ON, Canada: Ontario Institute for Studies in Education of the University of Toronto.

Smith, L. (1999). *Decolonizing methodologies: Research and Indigenous peoples.* London, UK: Zed Books.

Spivak, G. C. (1995). Can the subaltern speak? In B. Ashcroft, G. Griffiths, & H. Tiffin (Eds.), *The post-colonial studies reader* (pp. 28–37). New York, NY: Routledge.

Sterling, S. (2002). Yetko and Sophie: Nlakapamux cultural professors. *Canadian Journal of Native Education, 26*(1), 4–10.

Thiongo, N. W. (1986). *Decolonizing the mind: The politics of language in African literature.* Portsmouth, NH: Heinemann.

Torres, R. (2012). *Aeta Indigenous women healers in the Philippines: Lessons and implications* (Dissertation). Toronto: University of the Philippines.

Torres, R. A., & Nyaga, D. (2016). Discussion of power through the eyes of the margins: Praxis of post-colonial Aeta Indigenous women healers in the Philippines. *International Journal of Asia-Pacific Studies, 12*(2), 31–56.

Wane, N. (2009). Indigenous education and cultural resistance: A decolonizing project. *Curriculum Inquiry, 39*(1), 159–178.

Young, R. (2001). *Post-colonialism: A historical introduction.* Oxford, UK: Blackwell Publishers.

CHAPTER 6

# Decolonizing Western Medicine and Systems of Care: Implications for Education

*Jacqueline Benn-John*

## Introduction

Canada's colonial history has generated many attempts at assimilating Indigenous people into Western institutions and systems. These efforts include rhetoric and practices that both subjugate Indigenous knowledge, cultural traditions, languages, and spiritual practices as well as those that attempt to re-appropriate these into Western institutions and systems (Dei, 2012; Hill, 2008; Wane, 2014). Recognizing traditional medicine and healing practices as legitimate and fruitful healing tools is limited as Canadian institutions of health—shaped by hegemonic notions of White superiority and capitalistic motivations within a globalized context—define the parameters of health, knowledge, and legitimate expertise. Drawing on anti-colonial and anti-racist theories, this chapter interrogates these hegemonic neo-colonial values and methods that privilege Western biomedical systems of care. This work then offers recommendations for decolonizing

J. Benn-John (✉)
Department of Social Justice Education, Ontario Institute for Studies in Education, University of Toronto, Toronto, ON, Canada
e-mail: jacqueline.benn.john@mail.utoronto.ca



N. N. Wane et al. (eds.), *Decolonizing the Spirit in Education and Beyond*, Spirituality, Religion, and Education,
https://doi.org/10.1007/978-3-030-25320-2_6

Western medicine and systems of care, thereby increasing options of care for all. In particular, this chapter advocates for widespread use and support for traditional medicine and healing methods.

The Canadian healthcare system clearly differentiates between Western medicine, often just referred to as *medicine*, and traditional or Indigenous medicine, which is referred to as *alternative medicine*. Singer and Fisher (2007) refer to the former as *orthodox* medicine, which is based on scientific knowledge and constructed as superior to other models of health care past and present. However, it is less clear what falls within the boundaries of "alternative" or "traditional" medicine.

A review of academic literature reveals many definitions for alternative medicine: However, notably, most often "alternative" and "traditional" refer to *who* administers the medicine or practice, and the *practices* it includes. For example, Amzat and Abdullahi (2008) define "traditional medicine" as "a term used to describe Chinese medicine and various forms of indigenous medicine like the African traditional medicine" (p. 154). Therapies may include "herbs, animal parts, minerals as well as non-medicine like acupuncture, manual therapies and spiritual therapies which may involve incantations to appease the spirits" (p. 155). More broadly, the World Health Organization has defined traditional medicine as

> the sum total of the knowledge, skills, and practices based on the theories, beliefs, and experiences indigenous to different cultures, whether explicable or not, used in the maintenance of health as well as in the prevention, diagnosis, improvement or treatment of physical and mental illness. [It incorporates] plants, animals, and or mineral based medicines, spiritual therapies, manual techniques and exercise applied singularly or in combination to maintain well-being as well as to treat, diagnose or prevent illness. (2002, p. 155; 2013, p. 16)

Key in both World Health's and Amzat and Abdullahi's definitions of traditional medicine is the identities (i.e., social locations, including racialization) of the practitioners—that is, Asian, African, and Indigenous. In addition, both identify practices that diverge from the hegemonic pharmaceutical, technological, and biomedicine traditions of Western medicine.

Aligning with these points, in "Indigenous Healing Practices among Rural Elderly African Americans," Harley (2006) refers to Indigenous healing or traditional medicine as

> the practices and knowledge that existed before the advent of modern conventional medicine that were used to promote, maintain, and restore health and well-being. Indigenous knowledge represents the accumulated experience, wisdom, and know-how unique to a given culture, society, and/or community. (p. 433)

Clearly, the alternatives to Western medicine are diverse and can include practices that are community-based and experiential. In this chapter, I use the term *traditional medicine/healing* to refer to pre-colonial and current health practices employed by some Indigenous groups to prevent disease and maintain or improve health (including practices that help people to cope with unexplainable conditions). In this paper, *Indigenous* refers to belonging to a place and the original inhabitants are from that place (Hill, 2008).

An Indigenous understanding of health and healing strives for harmony and balance among humans and the universe. In this model, one component of health and healing does not precede or supersede the others. Indigenous understandings of health and healing recognize and respect the interdependent relationship between humans and the universe in which they live (Dei, 2012; Wane, 2001). Similarly, Baskin (2011) argues that since all creation is interconnected, everyone is both dependent and connected with others in the environment. Drawing on the works of Wane (2001) and Dei (2012), this chapter reflects the above components in *traditional medicine/healing* models and practices. In addition, Indigenous knowledge in *traditional medicine/healing* includes the management of how the community deals with health and sickness.

In this chapter, I consider the Canadian healthcare system within the framework of anti-colonial and anti-racism discourses. In Dei and Kempf, George Dei identifies that contemporary race inequities are rooted in a global history of colonization (Dei, 2000). An anti-colonial perspective is useful in challenging racial inequities wrought by colonialism, emphasizing decolonization and "affirming Indigenous knowledge and culture" (Pon, Gosine, & Phillips, 2011). *Anti-colonialism* is defined as "the political struggle and active resistance of colonized peoples against the ideology and practice of colonialism. It emphasizes decolonization and affirms Indigenous knowledge and culture, while establishing Indigenous control over Indigenous national territories" (Pon et al., 2011, p. 400). *Anti-racism* is "an action-oriented, educational and political strategy for institutional and systemic change that addresses the issues of racism and the interlocking systems of social oppression (sexism, classism, heterosexism and ableism)" (Dei & Calliste, 2000, p. 11).

Applying anti-colonialism and anti-racism frameworks to hegemonic beliefs about biomedicine and traditional medicine can help us to understand how colonialism and racism continue to structure Canadian medicine and systems of care today. These frameworks can also point to possibilities for active cultural and community-based resistance practices in response, such as increasing awareness and legitimacy of alternative health care and healing pathways (Gahayr, 2011). These frameworks also challenge the institutional powers and structures established by colonialism, instead offering a divergent privileging of the cultural knowledge and expertise of marginalized "Others." Anti-colonialism and anti-racism frameworks offer strategies for interrupting the production of social inequalities within Western medicine (such as the geographical inaccessibility and costliness of biomedicine, and a lack of traditional medicine healthcare options) and its systems. In these ways, this chapter aims to both disrupt colonial constructs of medicine and suggest decolonizing alternatives.

## My Epistemological Standpoint

I am a Black African woman who was born in Trinidad. I immigrated to Canada from Trinidad as a one-year-old. My early understanding of a healthy body was informed by the cultural knowledge in my mother's teachings on the role of West Indian foods and herbal concoctions in maintaining health or in treating common conditions (colds and menstrual cramps, for example). My mother had learned about traditional healing and herbal medicine from her mother when she was a girl. Even today, the message from our culture and family members is consistent: A healthy body can only be achieved by eating healthy food. Immigrating to Canada, however, complicated my family's access to the herbs and plants that grew in abundance in backyards in Trinidad. This shift impacted my understanding of the usefulness of these resources. As I became acculturated to Canadian society, I embraced hegemonic Western ideals and began to view my cultural traditions as inferior. In particular, I rejected traditional healing methods. My reference points for defining valuable and non-valuable methods of healthcare were largely those of colonial health, medicine, and religion. Rather than consuming my mother's bitter concoctions, I opted for fast-acting extra-strength painkillers.

Until recently, my narrow definition of health and healing, whether of the mind, body, or spirit, reflected Western hegemonic notions of health and healing. As part of my decolonizing journey, I grew to challenge these notions. Instead, I have developed an understanding of Indigenous health and developed a deeper appreciation for my own cultural knowledge. This journey has been heavily influenced by the works of scholars such as Amzat and Abdullah (2008), Tsey (1997), Akomolafe (2010), Pederson and Baruffati (1985), Jagtenberg and Evans (2003), Harley (2006), Tupper (2009), and Tilburt and Kaptchuk (2008), and their insights are reflected in this chapter. In particular, they have helped me to recognize a pre-colonial perspective on health and healing, which I adopt in this chapter. Some of the implications of this perspective are that I've stopped denouncing my cultural knowledge, and I recognize and appreciate the work of traditional healers. I believe and have experienced the medicinal powers of food, and I now support the efforts of Indigenous societies around the world who resist the marginalization of their healing practices.

This chapter is itself an act of resistance to the colonization of Indigenous healing. My hope is that the decolonization of Western systems of care will allow Indigenous healing to become a viable option for anyone wishing to access it.

## Alternative or Indigenous Medicine?

Language has a role in creating categories of social *inclusion* and *exclusion*. This is relevant to the construction of both healthcare systems, our understandings of well-being and our understandings of "legitimate" care options. For example, the term "alternative" health care implies a system of health care that is second or inferior to "mainstream" healthcare practices. When applied to healing and medicine, the adjectives "alternative" "traditional" or "Indigenous" perpetuate a dominant discourse—and, in this, an accompanying discourse of difference.

The language of our post-colonization society describes non-Western health care as health care created by and for racialized bodies: It is implicitly situated as by and for the Aboriginal, South Asian, Asian, and African. This "Othering" of the medical and health practices of Indigenous societies, which are also usually located in a fixed period of time (before modernity, for example), delegitimizes and disregards the efficacy of healing practices employed by colonized societies today. Differentiating traditional healing with labels of exclusion (i.e., "alternative medicine") also helps to constitute Western medical systems: By default, Western models are legitimate, scientific, evidence-based, and universally relevant (Pederson & Baruffati, 1985, p. 5). Western medicine is grounded in biomedical understandings of the body, health, and wellness. In *Biomedicalization: Technoscience, health and illness in the US,* biomedicalization is broadly described as practices that "emphasize *transformations* of medical phenomena and of bodies, largely through...technoscientific interventions" (Adele, Mamo, Fosket, Fishman, & Shim, 2010). Biomedicalization, the authors note, is organized around a number of interactive processes, including "the technoscientization of biomedical practices where interventions for treatment and enhancement are progressively more reliant on sciences and technologies, [and] are conceived in those very terms" (ibid.). By and large, this model and interventions stand in contrast to other practices and treatments described as "alternative" or "traditional."

Language can also concretely impact *who* is included or excluded in a sector or profession: for example, which populations, which histories, and which knowledges retain value, social repute, or visibility. For example, populations that are included in the definition "Indigenous" are closely tied to Western-defined racial hierarchies and cultural hegemonies, in which persons and communities of white-skin privilege are situated highest on social hierarchies. With this in mind, Harley (2006) argues that African Americans meet the definition of Indigenous because they have "witnessed, been excluded from, and have survived modernity and imperialism" (p. 434); currently experience exclusion and discrimination from full citizenship and during colonialism; "remain culturally distinct with many of their native belief systems still alive" (ibid.); and "survive outside their traditional lands because they were forcibly removed from them and their connections" (ibid.). The exclusion of African Americans from the definition of *Indigenous* reproduces and reinscribes colonial notions of inferiority and exclusion on the bodies of Africans. While Indigenous knowledge is considered inferior to Western knowledges, African knowledge is not even included in the category *Indigenous.* Like many other Indigenous healing practices, the African and Caribbean tradition of obeah—a spiritual and healing practice—is not recognized in Western medicine. It has been dismissed as superstition and holds negative connotations aligning with myths of racial degeneracy and backwardness.

Yet despite its illegitimacy within Western frameworks, traditional medicine is shared around the world. For example, around the world, traditional medicine has been shared within communities through demonstration and practice as well as orally through speech, instruction, song, and story. This mode of knowledge transmission has transcended time and geographical boundaries, as Indigenous people migrated to Western nations. Dyck (2006) illustrates how cultural knowledge of health and illness is transmitted through immigrant women's storytelling. For example, South Asian migrant women living in British Columbia, Canada, transmitted knowledge about *desi* medicine (a concoction of *sarnaa, samf, kalkhand* and *malka* to ease *kavi*, or constipation) to their children and husbands. These women also transmitted knowledge of desi medicine to each other orally and acquired new Indigenous knowledge from immigrant co-workers with different healing traditions. Dyck's (2006) study underscores not only women's acceptance of Indigenous knowledge, but the critical role of oral transmission in India, as knowledge is passed on from mothers and grandmothers. Similarly, in her research on Embu rural women, Wane (2001) cites the work of Dei (2000) and Grenier (1998), highlighting the practice of imparting Indigenous cultural values, belief systems, and worldviews to younger generations through community elders.

Dei (2012) asserts that "knowledge is embedded within particular contexts and resists appeals to master narratives, transcendent experiences, or a universal 'human nature'" (p. 105). The above examples of South Asians in British Columbia and women in Embu reveal this resistance in practice: The practice and transmission of traditional medicine continue, despite the ongoing presence of a colonial and Western healthcare hegemony.

## (De)Legitimizing Indigenous Knowledge and Healing

In spite of this—and in spite of the accessibility, convenience, and accuracy with which Indigenous knowledge is transmitted—dominant discourse continues to delegitimize Indigenous knowledge and oral transmission as primitive and backward. In fact, delegitimizing Indigenous knowledge is a strategy employed by the colonizer to control knowledge, including its transmission (Wane, 2014). Indigenous values of collectivity, oral tradition, spirituality, cultural ties to the local, and ecology do not fit neatly into neocolonialism's globalizing homogenous tendencies (Tupper, 2009). Following this, much Indigenous medicine has also been systematically marginalized: Jagtenberg and Evans (2003), for example, note that "the historical lineage of herbal medicine is *outside the square* as far as Western mainstream has been concerned—since at least the scientific revolution and arguably the advent of a Christian Europe" (p. 321). In this context, Indigenous medicine and healing practices have been further delegitimized by their cultural roots in shamanism and nature worship.

One consequence of this is that the colonized person also becomes the recipient of the colonizer's brand of knowledge and medicine. This remains true even as there is a growing interest in and use of traditional herbal medicine among White Westerners. For example, in "The impact of co-option on herbalism: A bifurcation in epistemology and practice," Singer and Fisher (2007) identify a new trend in the West to modernize herbal knowledge and align this knowledge with principles of biomedicine and biomedical dominance. This not only reifies Western biomedical traditions and model, but also results in further marginalization of the "Other" and their healthcare practices (ibid.) by selectively "legitimizing" some Indigenous knowledge and healing. In this way, Canadian medical and health-care industries can exploit Indigenous knowledge and healing practices for profit, without challenging the racial and cultural hierarchies that belie them.

## Decolonizing Western Medicine and Systems of Care

The North American health industry is a billion dollar industry, and this sector is increasingly profiting from the commodification and appropriation of Indigenous medicine, research, treatment, and advice. Singer and Fisher's (2007) work on herbal medicines identifies this; Tilburt and Kaptchuk (2008) report that worldwide, nearly $60 billion (US) is spent on herbal medicine products each year. In 2005, $33 million (US) was spent on herbal medicines by the National Center for Complementary and Alternative Medicine at the National Institutes of Health (p. 595), and in 2004, the National Cancer Institute "committed nearly US 89 million" to researching traditional therapies (p. 595). This drive to mainstream and profit from Indigenous medicine has led to the category within the dominant heath care system of "complimentary alternative medicine." This term has been "endorsed by the biomedical elite in order to assert control over non-orthodox practices through grouping together a vast range of practices under one umbrella" (Baer quoted in Singer & Fisher, 2007, p. 20).

The appropriation and co-option of Indigenous culture and healing take many forms. In some contexts, it mirrors early contact between Indigenous societies and colonizers. One such example is what Singer and Fisher (2007) refer to as "mainstreaming" of Indigenous practices. Rather than accepting, recognizing, and co-existing alongside different Indigenous knowledges, practitioners in the North American healthcare industry react to the clear success of Indigenous practices by co-opting the "Other's" knowledge resources for profit (Singer & Fisher, 2007). Just as Columbus and those who followed him extracted profit from colonized Indigenous societies, the healthcare industry responds to the resources of the Indigenous community not by building a beneficial and collaborative bridge between the two, but by selectively appropriating discrete components of Indigenous systems. For example, a medical doctor may take "a short course in the use of herbs for which there is 'evidence' of safety and efficacy" (p. 20). The doctor is then able to prescribe "herbal tablets to treat specific diseases, such as St. John's Wort for depression" (p. 20). Singer and Fisher describe a West-identified doctor, who, in wanting to be "seen as 'holistic' might engage an herbalist to consult for within their medical practice without necessarily engaging in a collaborative referral system" (p. 20). These are all examples of mainstreaming—and co-opting—Indigenous practices into the Western health system.

Mainstreaming and commodification may also occur in a more direct manner. For example, Australians spend twice as much on non-orthodox medicine than on orthodox medicine. In response to this rising market, healthcare providers and institutions have commodified Indigenous healing methods by packaging and marketing goods to sell in grocery stores not only to settlers, but also to Indigenous people living there. In Canada, major grocery stores typically have aisles offering "ethnic" foods and "organic" or "wellness" products. "Indigenous" roots, herbs, mixtures, and plants are marketed as authentic, despite the fact that mass production and profit motives not only affect the quality of the product, but remove the product from the context in which it has been used to heal.

All of these processes are occurring in the context of International capitalism, which creates national and trans-national inequalities that greatly impact Indigenous medicine and its practitioners. Peasant farmers cannot compete in the global marketplace, against corporations that rape the land for its natural resources (herbs and plants, for example). Another effect of globalization, regulatory legislation under the banner of improved safety and efficacy for consumers (Jagtenberg & Evans, 2003), has had a profound effect on small, low-tech manufacturers of traditional herbal products who cannot easily meet regulatory conditions. According to Jagtenberg and Evans, over the last 15 years many small herbal manufacturers have been taken over or simply could not compete with "larger herbal companies and pharmaceutical companies" (p. 323). These realities illustrate the imposition of Western medicine's reliance on standardization, universalism, and globalization onto Indigenous systems of health and healing. In an increasingly standardized and globalized market, Indigenous societies' dependence on cultural knowledge, local communities, and local ecology is neither acknowledged nor accommodated.

Despite the continuing devaluation of Indigenous medicine, its use is increasing. Traditional healing methods have had notable clinical success in treating major illnesses such as HIV/AIDS, infertility, and mental illness (Flint, 2015). I believe that the way forward is for Western medicine to use its energies and power to *decolonize itself*, rather than continuing its efforts to consume the "Other." Imagine the possibility of multiple healing systems operating in tandem, with a plurality of healthcare systems in which people could choose the care and methods best suited to their circumstances. More importantly, people could choose *not* to access methods and practices that are incongruent with their beliefs, values, or presenting needs. Decolonizing Western medicine can offer practical and accessible strategies for improved health that, if practiced consistently, will yield improved health and well-being for all. Here, I detail a number of concrete strategies for decolonizing Western (and, by extension, Indigenous) medicine.

Western medicine can start a decolonization process by learning how traditional knowledge on medicinal and health practices is reproduced or transmitted from one generation to another—including the social contexts within which these practices occur. This is a foundational step to demystify the "Other," bring legitimacy to their knowledges, and help neo-colonialists to recognize that the constructed gap between Western medicine and Indigenous healing is not as wide as they have made it to be. I also recommend an intentional change in terminology that eliminates language of hierarchy and exclusion. Western professionals and institutions must acknowledge that there are many ways of knowing, including methods that are not amenable to scientific or other empiric tests. The "Other" must be accepted in all of their diversity—binary assumptions about the relative qualifications and knowledge of "Indigenous" healers vs. Western-trained doctors should no longer be the dominant discourse in discussion of diverse healing and systems of care. While regulation ought to be imposed, regulations ought to be applied in a way that encourages equity and access for small farmers and local healers.

In the context of terminal illnesses, the Western heathcare and pharmaceutical industries should make life-saving medications available to those who need them, not those who can afford them, and should ensure a steady supply of effective medications (full strength, for example) to developing countries and to low-income and racialized communities.

Western medicine can also decolonize itself by reconsidering the ways in which it delivers mental health systems and services. For example, the delivery of culturally diverse healthcare practices would reduce the effect of "Othering" racialized individuals and increase access to and success of services. In addition, referrals to Indigenous healers and partnerships with Indigenous healing associations and shamans will help to ensure that those in need of mental health support can receive a full spectrum of care for their needs.

The strategies presented above are by no means exhaustive. However, I put them forward in an attempt to demonstrate how the decolonization of Western medicine can begin to challenge the institutional powers and structures established by and maintained through colonialism. The strategies discussed in this chapter that are involved in the continuation of traditional medicine are evolving. In fact, this is the reason traditional medicine and worldviews continue to transcend geographical borders, time, and space—therefore, traditional medicine is a key factor in decolonizing Western medicine.

## Conclusion

This chapter has advocated for the widespread use and support for traditional medicine. It did not advocate for the integration of traditional medicine and healing practices into Western systems of care, due to the belief that this perpetuates hegemonic neo-colonial values and methods by subsuming traditional medicine and healing into a supporting branch of Western health care. We know that one size does not fit all, and history has demonstrated the danger of a "single story" (Adichie, quoted in

Akomolafe, 2010). Indeed, there is no "single story" about health, healthcare, or healing. I argue that we need a variety of healthcare options, including Indigenous systems, that can respond to the unique needs of individuals. This approach recognizes the diversity of the populace and leaves space for the emergence of new healing methods. It is therefore imperative that the dominance of the single model of Western medicine be interrupted. Through the decolonization of Western medicine, the transmission, practice, and promotion of diverse cultural knowledges and healing methods will thrive.

## References

Adele, C., Mamo, L., Fosket, J., Fishman, J., & Shim, J. (2010). *Biomedicalization: Technoscience, health and illness in the US*. Durham, NC: Duke University Press.

Akomolafe, A. C. (2010). Decolonizing the notion of mental illness and healing in Nigeria, West Africa. *Critical Psychology in Changing World*, 726–740. Retrieved from https://thediscourseunit.files.wordpress.com/2016/05/nigeria-726-740.pdf.

Amzat, J., & Abdullahi, A. A. (2008). Roles of traditional healers in the fight against HIV/AIDS. *World Health, 2*, 153–159.

Baskin, C. (2011). *Strong helpers' teachings: The value of Indigenous knowledges in the helping professions*. Toronto, ON: Canadian Scholars' Press.

Dei, G. J. S. (2000). Rethinking the role of Indigenous knowledges in the academy. *International Journal of Inclusive Education, 4*(2), 111–132.

Dei, G. J. S. (2012). Indigenous anti-colonial knowledge as 'heritage knowledge' for promoting Black/African education in diasporic contexts. *Decolonization: Indigeneity, Education & Society, 1*(1), 102–119.

Dei, G. J. S., & Calliste, A. (2000). Mapping the terrain: Power knowledge and anti-racism education. In G. J. S. Dei & A. Calliste (Eds.), *Power, knowledge and anti-racism education* (pp. 11–22). Halifax, NS: Fernwood.

Dyck, I. (2006). Travelling tales and migratory meanings: South Asian migrant women talk of place, health and healing. *Social and Cultural Geography, 7*(1), 1–18.

Flint, A. (2015). Traditional healing, biomedicine and the treatment of HIV/AIDS: Contrasting South African and native American experiences. *International Journal of Environmental Research and Public Health, 12*(4), 4321–4339. https://doi.org/10.3390/ijerph120404321.

Gahayr, S. (2011). *Invisibility, disappearance and reclamation: A sociological investigation into the locations(s) of Aboriginal and African women in Canada* (Master's thesis). Retrieved from Ontario Institute for Studies in Education, University of Toronto Online database.

Grenier, L. (1998). *Working with Indigenous knowledge: A guide for researchers.* Ottawa: International Development Research Centre.

Harley, D. A. (2006). Indigenous healing practices among rural elderly African Americans. *International Journal of Disability, Development and Education, 53*(4), 433–452.

Hill, (Gus) Louis Paul. (2008). *Understanding Indigenous Canadian traditional health and healing* (Theses and Dissertations [Comprehensive], 1050). https://scholars.wlu.ca/etd/1050.

Jagtenberg, T., & Evans, S. (2003). Global herbal medicine: A critique. *The Journal of Alternative and Complementary Medicine, 9*(2), 321–329.

Pederson, D., & Baruffati, V. (1985). Health and traditional medicine cultures in Latin America and the Caribbean. *Social Science Medicine, 21*(10), 5–12.

Pon, G., Gosine, K., & Phillips, D. (2011). Immediate response: Addressing anti-native and anti-black racism in child welfare. *International Journal of Child, Youth and Family Studies, 3,* 385–409.

Singer, J., & Fisher, K. (2007). The impact of co-option on herbalism: A bifurcation in epistemology and practice. *Health Sociology Review, 16*(1), 18–26.

Tilburt, J. C., & Kaptchuk, T. J. (2008). Herbal medicine research and global health: An ethical analysis. *Bulletin of the World Health Organization, 86*(8), 594–599.

Tsey, K. (1997). Traditional medicine in contemporary Ghana: A public policy analysis. *Social Science Medicine, 45*(7), 1065–1074.

Tupper, K. W. (2009). Ayahuasca healing beyond the Amazon: The globalization of a traditional Indigenous entheogenic practice. *Global Networks, 9*(1), 117–136.

Wane, N. (2001). Narratives of Embu rural women: Gender roles and Indigenous knowledges. *Gender Technology and Development, 5*(3), 383–408. https://doi.org/10.1177/097185240100500303.

Wane, N. N. (2014). *Indigenous African knowledge production.* Toronto: University of Toronto Press.

World Health Organization. (2002). *Traditional medicine strategy 2002–2005.* Retrieved from https://www.who.int/.

World Health Organization. (2013). *Traditional medicine strategy 2014–2023.* Retrieved from https://www.who.int/.

CHAPTER 7

# BLOOD-ANGER: The Spirituality of Anti-Colonial Blood-Anger for Self-Defense

*Stanley Doyle-Wood*

My focus in this chapter on what I call blood-anger started to take shape in another piece of work as a methodological starting point in my attempt to write about the power of resistance and the subsequent death of Kajieme Powell. Kajieme was a young 25-year-old Black/African-American man who was murdered by two St. Louis police officers on August 19, 2014, just ten days after the St. Louis police murdered Michael Brown a Black/African American child/teenager in Ferguson, Missouri. My intention was to write about the racialization of murder. I put my fingers on the computer keys. I type in a few words and then I stop. I break down. I want to talk about Kajieme but I can't move. I can't speak. My body won't let me. I try repeatedly. Each time I stretch my arms out and move my fingers to the keyboard

S. Doyle-Wood (✉)
New College/Transitional Year Program, University of Toronto, Toronto, ON, Canada
e-mail: stan.doyle.wood@utoronto.ca



N. N. Wane et al. (eds.), *Decolonizing the Spirit in Education and Beyond*, Spirituality, Religion, and Education,
https://doi.org/10.1007/978-3-030-25320-2_7

to write. I start to type out a few words and every time I do so I draw on the fragments of Kajieme's story that I have read and taken in with my whole body. Each time I break off. I can't seem to do it. The pain is excruciating. I see Kajieme's face in a photograph in a newspaper story (Bates, 2014). He is sitting on a bench with a smile on his face that exudes love of/for life. In that moment of camera click, state terror seems to be paused, suspended, refused. It's like Emmett [Till] posing for a picture in his living room, his arm resting on a television with that beautiful smile on his face. My body's emotion/heart/blood wants to hold that moment, to freeze it, to stop him going into that store to be accused by that White woman, to stop the pain that we as a Black collective feel as we imagine his fear and terror at the hands of White supremacy as they took him from his bed in the night and we wish and wish that he hadn't felt any terror and any pain but we know he must have and we keep wishing that it hadn't happened and we keep wishing we could wish it away. And all of this clashes with my body's memory of Kajieme's photo which clashes against the images of his life and being. My body has stored multiple stories, images and fragments of stories that news media outlets have disseminated about Kajieme. It has stored the contradictions and filtered the depersonalizing from the personalized/the dehumanizing from the re-humanized, the re-membered from the dis-membered. It has stored his family's remembrance of him coming from New York, of his plans and dreams, of how he would love his grandma's cooking and the care and love of his family all around him, and how he would say, "[o]h granny this is so good" (Bates, 2014) just like my own son as a child when he would sit in front of the TV with a big smile on his face, his favorite food on a plate on his lap and say contentedly, "ahh, this is the life". My body has a speaking blood-memory then that speaks of my children and my family and our histories and those we know and those we have known and for whom the collective is *we*. I go to the bathroom to compose myself. I go to the bathroom to look at myself in the mirror. I'm crying. I look at myself partly to reassure myself and partly to compose myself, to *manage* my emotions so that I can go back and write. I say to myself, pull yourself together. You need to do this. In the bathroom I am wiping my tears away. I am doing this because those knowledges/those epistemologies that my body is drawing on to speak tell me that in order to speak, in order to fulfill the task I have set myself, I must separate my mind from my body. I must create an emotional distance between the subject matter that I am writing about and the subject matter that is also the matter of my body. I must not only split/bifurcate myself, I must reject my body completely as a place of language, knowledge, blood-memory, blood-anger and blood enunciation. Through this process of negation I must tie up my body-tongue that historical racial scheme that Fanon (1952) speaks to as a "definitive structuring" of the self shaped through a historical violent encounter with a colonizing "spatial and temporal world" (p. 91). This "structuring" is (for the historically racialized and colonized body) "woven" as Fanon says, out of a thousand White supremacist and colonial "details, anecdotes and stories" (p. 91). It is a "body scheme" (p. 91) manifested in bone, muscle, tissue, blood, corpuscles, synapses and spirit by the blood-memory of thousands of overt and covert dis-intacting assaults, injuries, woundings, negations, disconnections and dis-locations accumulated now in my body not only through my experiences and navigations of an oppressive world since birth but through the experiences and blood-memories of my ancestors who reside in me and who make up my DNA. In my back and forth from the keyboard to the washroom to wipe my tears, to compose myself, to manage my emotions, and then back to the keyboard only to freeze-up-in-my-body-splitting movement, I am negating the embodiment of the historical racial schema in me and so cannot speak outside of colonial constraints without neurosis and pain. Through this process I am negating the relationship between the racialized body [my body] and the world. I am negating, repressing and amputating my body's blood-memory and in doing so I am negating the body-language (that of blood-anger) that my body uses to translate its blood-memory, that it uses to organize its defense against dis-intactness and injustice and to analyze and contest the fucked-upness of the world I have been born into. In the absence of this blood embodied connection I am paralyzed by trauma. It is only when I make the decision to refuse this negation in my writing that my body begins to untie itself and I begin to speak. Blood-anger and its anti-colonial promise are my methodology. My writing from this point on will be a whole-bodied blood-anger process.

## Blood-Anger/Blood-Memory

Blood-anger is the boned-in, muscled-in, tissued-in, corpuscled and blood-celled organic body-tongue of the historically oppressed. It is the body's organizing mechanism of/for self-defense against colonialism's historical and ongoing murderous enforcements of alienation, disembodiment, dis-intactness and disconnectedness. It is an organic embodied organizing mechanism that defends the body in an embodied intensely focused fight-back/strike-back way that says, physically, psychologically, physiologically and emotionally, fuck-you to anything and anyone that threatens what blood-anger reads as an assault against the intactness of its individual and collective body. Blood-anger does not simply emerge from nothing. It is an anger grounded in the historically oppressed body's blood-memory of oppression, resistance and struggle.

The Indigenous writer Thomas King (2003) talks about how the truth about stories can be broken down to one thing, which is, that's all we (as human beings) are, stories. I read this to mean that there is an understanding and acknowledgment [recognition] that our bodies, the physicality, the physiology, the emotionality, the psychology and the soul/spirituality of our bodies as holistic beings/as historically oppressed peoples are constitutive of the collective experiences, memories, wounds, lesions, struggles and resistances gathered by our peoples in their struggles with oppression and in their journeys and practices of survival, resistance and being in their/our world. In this moment of a re-membering of myself as a member of the historically oppressed I hold true to myself and that of my own ancestors who reside in me that stories of survival, of resistance, of joy and of trauma do not just live in our bodies, they *are* our bodies. They are inextricably entangled in the sinews, in the blood, the bone, the synapses, the nerve reactions as a spiritual collective memory that is in and of itself embodiment. Blood-anger as the body-tongue of blood-memory is therefore grounded in a blood epistemology. Within the conceptual frameworks of Indigenous knowledges, cosmologies, ontologies and epistemologies, blood-memory is a "living memory" (Holmes, 2000, p. 42). It contains and speaks to an "ancestry of experience that shapes dreams, desires, intentions [and] purposeful activity" (p. 46). In this way, blood-memory opposes and transcends Eurocentric colonial notions of time, space and mind/body-splitting. At the same-time blood-memory as a physical, physiological and spiritual force that is place, present and presence in its embodiment assures us that our bodies are constitutive of the collected/collective cultural memory of our peoples and their relationships to one another, to land, to consciousness, to the spirit world and to the cosmos. In this sense, our stories are more than narratives, they are the blood-memory of our bodies and blood-anger is the body-tongue of that blood-memory.

Blood-anger is not simply an emotional reactive force, fired up in one minute only to subside and to lose its hold in the next. As the boned-in body-tongue of the historically oppressed it is always existentially present, presence and place because it emerges from the body's blood-memory of oppression, struggle and resistance. If we are to engage in an embodied process of untying our tongues, a process where our body-tongues untie themselves away from the constraints of those colonial epistemologies that our blood-angers too often times use to both translate our blood-memories and organize their self-defense, if we are to nurture our bodies toward a lived spiritualized holistic connectedness with all of our relations, one that is grounded in the practice of an anti-colonial blood-anger that is central to resistance, freedom and opposing auto-destruction and the colonial structure as a whole, then a critical, love-of-self-centered consciousness of how blood-anger informs our individual and collectively racialized, gendered, sexualized, dis/abled and classed positioned lives and relations and how it defends our individual and collective bodies in ways that may or may not be detrimental to our survival and liberation as historically oppressed peoples is an urgent necessity.

There are few examples of not only the nature of present, presence and place of blood-anger as the body-tongue of blood-memory for self-defense but also its auto-destructive impact and anti-colonial possibilities than in Toni Morrison's novel *The Bluest Eye* (1994). The work is central to bell hooks' analysis of rage in *Killing Rage* (1995), and while there are multiple sites of difference that structure the blood-anger and blood-memory of the oppressed in the novel, I want to foreground race and gender to speak to blood-anger and blood-memory's relationship to identity and embodiment. According to hooks the novel's "narrator says of the dehumanized colonized little black girl Pecola that there would be *hope* (my italics) for her if only she could express her rage, telling readers 'anger is better, there is a presence in anger'. Perhaps then it is that 'presence,' the assertion of subjectivity colonizers do not want to see, that surfaces when the colonized express rage" (p. 12). Pecola's body yearns for love, to be loved. It yearns for intactness in a colonial order that disconnects and dis-intacts. But hooks does not provide the full story. The narrator is speaking of a moment when Pecola, after being racially disregarded, degraded and dehumanized by a White storeowner Mr. Yacobowski, notices a bunch of dandelion flowers on the ground, flowers that (like herself) are disregarded by everyone as ugly, as weeds. The narrator tells us that for a brief moment a "dart of affection leaps out from Pecola to them, but they do not look at her and do not send love back. She thinks then, yes 'they *are* ugly. They *are* weeds'. Preoccupied with that revelation, she trips on the sidewalk crack. Anger stirs and wakes in her: it opens its mouth, and like a hot-mouthed puppy, laps up the dredges of her shame. Anger is better. There is a sense of being in anger. It has reality a presence. An awareness of worth. It is a lovely surging" (p. 50). The narrator is an African-American girl-child named Claudia. Claudia does not use the term "hope". She does not pathologize Pecola. What Claudia tells the reader is that Pecola's anger does not hold. As Claudia says, Pecola's "thoughts fall back to Mr Yacobowski's [racist] eyes and his phlegmy voice". "[T]he puppy is too easily surfeited. Its thirst too quickly quenched, it [anger] sleeps" (p. 50). Claudia's reading of anger in this moment is not one that conceives of anger as blood-anger. Like hooks, anger is conflated with rage, a force that erupts quickly and is soon gone.

Blood-anger as the body-tongue of blood-memory, however, is always present. On a constant basis, it organizes itself to defend Pecola and Claudia's bodies against the disconnectedness and dis-intactness that is the effect of White supremacy and the systematic imposition/enforcement of anti-Black racism. For Pecola, blood-anger organizes the self-defense of her body in a yearning for Whiteness that is crystalized in a desire for blue eyes. While Claudia's blood-anger navigates a similar terrain, there is a brief anti-colonial departure. It is anti-colonial because for a moment blood-anger's self-defense is in the offense at the colonial structure. Claudia's defensive in the offensive fuck-you-the-system blood-anger destroys White "baby dolls" and dreams of bringing pain to White children. Claudia tells us that, "the dismembering of dolls [though] was not the true horror. The truly horrifying thing was the transference of the same impulses to little white girls. The indifference with which I could have axed them was shaken only by my desire to do so. To discover what eluded me; the secret of the magic they waved on others. When people look at them and say, 'Awwwww', but not for me? The eye slide of black women as they approached them on the street, and the possessive gentleness of their touch as they handled them. If I pinched them, their eyes—unlike the crazed glint of the doll's eyes—would fold in pain, and their cry would not be the sound of an icebox door, but a fascinating cry of pain" (p. 23).

She goes onto say, "[w]hen I learned how repulsive this disinterested violence was, that it was repulsive because it was disinterested, my shame floundered about for refuge. The best hiding place was love. Thus, the conversion from pristine sadism to fabricated hatred, to fraudulent love. It was a small step to Shirley Temple [the colonial structure's representation of White-child beauty, innocence, and perfection]. I learned much later to worship her, just as I learnt to delight in cleanliness, knowing, even as I learned, that the change was adjustment without improvement" (p. 23).

So, anger for Claudia does not seem to hold. But although anti-colonial blood-anger doesn't hold blood-anger certainly does. Blood-anger in its defense of the body from oppression through the seeking out of a place-of-refuge [by any means necessary and wherever even if it's in Whiteness and self-hate] holds. It's not the revolutionary fuck-you anger at the system that June Jordan mourns the loss of sure (Parmer, 1991), but we got to love, embrace and become conscious of the embodiment of the former [or what some folks might call "destructive" anger] before we can get to understand this latter. The question is why does Claudia's anti-colonial-fuck-you-the-colonial-system blood-anger not hold? I would argue that it is because her body-tongue has no epistemological defense. Claudia's flicker of anti-colonial anger is disconnected from her body and is drowned out and rendered conceptually invisible by colonial definitions of what anger is in the first place (i.e., a negative reactive emotion that must be silenced/controlled). This occurs even as Claudia's blood-anger organizes itself to defend her disconnectedness through a rejection of Blackness and a fleeing toward Whiteness, cleanliness and Shirley Temple as the place of refuge. And though Claudia understands anger as not holding in its fuck-you the system form, because of the epistemic violence she and her collective have been subjected to, she has no epistemological means of understanding anger outside of these disembodied individualized, damning colonial paradigms and constructions. Her conception of anger is one delinked and utterly evacuated from a conception of blood-anger as the self-defensive body-tongue of blood-memory and so it cannot be heard. How can blood-anger be nurtured away from an avoidance and rejection of the self as a method of self-defense and more toward an anti-colonial position that defends the body as an individual and as a collective through contesting and opposing the colonial structure (external and internal to our bodies) if we cannot see, hear, listen or talk with our body-tongues in the first place or if we fail to recognize blood-anger's self-defensive embodiment as present, as presence and as place always?

There is a self-defense-of-the-body constancy to blood-anger as the body-tongue of blood-memory that is present, presence and place in Morrison's *Bluest Eye* (1994). It is a constancy that's narrated by Claudia even as it remains unnamed. Everywhere blood-anger as the body-tongue speaks but is not heard. Blood-anger as the body-tongue for self-defense is present in the bodies of the boys who taunt and verbally attack Pecola's Blackness. These are Black boys, whose blood-anger organizes the blood-memory of "their exquisitely learned self-hatred, their elaborately designed hopelessness and sucked it all up into a fiery cone of scorn that had burned for ages in the hollows of their minds [and their bodies] and then cooled- and spilled [it] over [their] lips of outrage, consuming whatever was in its path. They danced a macabre ballet around [Pecola], whom, for their own sake, they were prepared to sacrifice to the flaming pit" (p. 65). Blood-anger as the body-tongue of blood-memory, as the body's organic auto-protective/self-defense mechanism in these seeking-a-place-of-refuge contexts, is not only a process by which the body of the oppressed defends itself against the threat and encroachment of dis-intactness and depersonalization by attacking its own collective self through the amputation of itself from that very collective, it is also the body's mechanism for displacing (as a method of/for self-defense and self-protection) that which it refuses to acknowledge, the colonial order.

Blood-anger's "war of position" (Gramsci, 1971) in this moment lies in a refusal to acknowledge that colonial order while refusing to acknowledge any political place in that order. In other words, blood-anger organizes an individualized displacement/avoidance/and at times violent rejection of its politically "damned" collective self as a strategy of/for physical, psychological and emotional self-defense and self-preservation in the face of threat, fear and danger. As Fanon (1968) writes, it is through intercommunal conflicts or "vendettas" that the oppressed try to persuade themselves "that colonialism does not exist, that everything is going on as before, that history continues" (p. 54). There is then no "mindless" anger of the colonized. There is no "mindlessness" to blood-anger as blood-memory as far as the colonized and oppressed are concerned. Even if these young African-American boys had physically brutalized and obliterated Pecola (and certainly they are complicit in doing so at the whole-body-spirit level), this would not/does not constitute "mindless anger" (hooks, 1995, p. 19). Blood-anger as blood-memory in this instance/in these situations/under these colonial conditions/is the colonized body's "death reflex when faced with danger" (Fanon, 1968, p. 54). In these contexts, the danger/threat/fear is that of dis-intactness of dis-connectedness, of disembodiedness. It is a death reflex that subconsciously (via the penetrations of colonialism) disembodies/dismembers, amputates and avoids its political self. In its defense of its self (individually not collectively), blood-anger has not moved toward its anti-colonial possibility. It seeks a place of refuge in the negation of its whole racialized, gendered, sexualized, abled, classed embodied self. But in embodied relational terms, blood-anger as the body-tongue of blood-memory is *present*; blood-anger as the body-tongue of blood-memory is *presence*; blood-anger as the body tongue of blood-memory is *place*. And as members of the historically oppressed (individually and collectively), we see/feel/hear/know/refuse/negate blood-anger as the body-tongue of blood-memory on these terms/in these real, material existential contexts. We can see/hear/feel/know/refuse/negate blood-anger as the body tongue of blood-memory as present, presence and place in the *Bluest Eye* (Morrison, 1994) character Geraldine, the "sugar brown Mobile" woman. Once again blood-anger's self-defense/its presence, its place of refuge, lies in the place that is a *not* Black place and space. It is a relentless, rejecting, policing blood-anger. Self-defense is a rejection, suppression and hate of her body and of all things emotional, of all things passionate, of all things "funk" and "funkiness" (p. 83), of all the things that Geraldine's blood-anger as the body-tongue of blood-memory associates with Blackness.

The place of refuge lies in an embodied worrying and attacking fuck-you movement away from Blackness and toward all things closest to White. It lies in bodily cleanliness, in behavior, in movement, in *not* funk. Geraldine's blood-anger works to read, police, root-out, scream at and do violence to, the body sounds, smells and fluids of a funkiness imagined as Blackness's presence. Blood-anger's self-defense organizes its protection of Geraldine's body through a studying and worrying of funkiness' appearance "wherever it erupts" in/on her body, in/on her body's extension, her child Junior (who yearns to utter the word "fuck" like the Black children who play outside) and in/on her collective, the "sugar brown mobile girls". It is "this funk", that blood-anger "wipe[s]" away "where it crusts" (p. 83). Blood-anger "dissolves" it. "[W]where it drips, flowers, or clings", blood anger "find[s] and fight[s] it until it dies" (p. 83). Blood-anger "fight[s] this battle all the way to the grave" (p. 83) in a self-defensive war for intactness against dis-intactness and disconnectedness. In this war—of position organized around a flight from [and an assault on] Blackness in itself/in its body, it polices, harries and fights "[t]he laugh that is a little too loud, the enunciation a little too round; the gesture a little too generous" (p. 83). In its place of refuge as *not* Black as *not* funk, blood-anger's reading/alertness/policing/worrying works for the sugar brown girls as a collective blood-anger drawn from/driven by a collective blood-memory of White supremacist grounded/driven fractionalizing violence, terror and rape. And as blood-anger as the body-tongue of blood-memory organizes the bodies of the sugar brown girls in a worrying mode of/for self-defense, it holds "their behind[s] in for fear of a sway too free" (p. 83). It worries their bodies "when they wear lipstick [so that] they never cover the entire mouth for fear of lips to thick" (p. 83). Blood-anger as the body-tongue of blood-memory worries and attacks its own individual and collective body constantly, relentlessly, unremittingly, especially the "edges of their hair" (p. 83). It brings an accumulative, creeping, choking/strangulating death to the entire collective.

Blood-anger too is present, presence and place in Pecola's mother Mrs. Breedlove. Once again it defends by seeking refuge in all things White, in the love of/for the White child of the White family and the White home she cares for. It finds refuge in the "smells of their linen", in "their silk draperies", "[t]he child's pink nightie, the stacks of white pillow slips", in the bathing of the White child, in a "porcelain tub with silver taps", in running hot water, "clear water", in the drying of the White child with "fluffy white towels", in the brushing of the White child's "yellow hair", in "enjoying [the] roll and slip of it between her fingers" (p. 127).

The refuge of avoidance of Blackness is the place of rejection, hate and contempt. Blood-anger's attack is its defense. And so there is contempt and rejection for Pecola's mother's own household's "zinc tubs, buckets, stove heated water [and] stiff greyish towels washed in a kitchen sink" (p. 127). There is contempt for "the dusty backyard and the tangled black puffs of rough wool [hair] to comb in a [White] world more delicate more lovely clean, neat" (p. 128). Relationally, and by extension and association, Mrs. Breedlove's blood-anger as the bodies organizing method of self-defense mobilizes contempt, neglect, rejection, avoidance and punishment of/for Pecola and all Black children in her sphere. But the blood-memory of Pecola's mother's body-tongue is a racialized and gendered memory of anti-Black violence and oppression. It is a blood-memory of bruises collected "from moving about the earth -harvesting, cleaning, hoisting, pitching, stooping, kneeling, picking always with young ones underfoot" (p. 138). It is a memory of "laughter lost in youth that had been more touch than sound", of an "edging into life from the back door" as a grown-up, into a racialized, violated Black woman of "becoming" where "[e]verybody in the world was in a position to give [her] orders", where "White women said 'do this', White children said, 'give me that'. White men said, 'come here'. Black men said, 'Lay down'" (p. 138). It is a blood-memory of running the houses of White people, a blood-memory of White people beating Black men, and of cleaning up the blood of Black men then going home to "receive abuse from the victim" (p. 138). Self-defense in these self-preservatory, self-protective, unconscious, individualized, body-splitting and politically decontextualized, brutalized, dis-intacted and disconnected colonial contexts finds blood-anger as the body-tongue of blood-memory organizing and directing the body toward a place of refuge and safety manifested in an avoidance of coloniality, in an avoidance/rejection of its own multiplicative embodied difference, its memory and collective self.

How then do we nurture and shift blood-anger away from an avoidance and rejection of the collective self as a method of/for an individualized self-defense and toward an anti-colonial blood-anger-war-of-position that defends the body collective through a fuck-you opposition and contestation of the colonial structure in its entirety? What does anti-colonial blood-anger look like/feel like? How do we get there? How is it practiced? What are its elements? How is it sustained/lived/held on to?

## Untying the Body-Tongue/Anti-colonial Blood-Anger

There is a spirituality to anti-colonial blood-anger that is contingent on the untying of the body-tongue of the oppressed. Untying is the embodied movement away from silencing practices. It is about the speaking of our embodied truths (Riggs, 2006). It is the fuck-you refusal in the face and teeth of colonial power's parasitic coercions and categorizations to amputate the complexity, depth and wholeness of our embodiment as oppressed peoples and more widely as human beings. Untying is the extrication of our bodies away from those body-splitting colonial epistemologies and ways of knowing that our blood-anger as the body-tongue has relied upon to understand, translate, interpret and respond to our blood-memories. As an ongoing process untying is central to the praxis of anti-colonial blood-anger for self-defense. To nurture and practice anti-colonial blood-anger for self-defense is to engage constantly in the process and struggle of untying our body-tongues. There is nothing fixed here. There is nothing arrived at. Marilyn Dumont (2014) notes that in *Buffalo on*, one of the short stories in Leanne Simpson's *Islands of Decolonial Love, Stories and Songs* (2013), the narrator in the story says, "right off the bat, let's just admit we're both from places that have been fucked up through no fault of our own in a thousand different ways for seven generations and that takes a toll on how we treat each other, it just does". As Mrs. Breedlove, Pecola,

Claudia and the entire Black collective in Morrison's novel can bring testimony and witness to, yeah, it takes a toll on how our bodies treat and speak back to themselves as individuals and as members of the collective. Untying is grounded in these contexts. It is a reflexive struggle that comes with setbacks and gains. It is not clean. It is a messy, snotty, shitty, bloody love of self that embodies a fuck-you the colonial structure freedom. It requires/demands first and foremost a commitment to engage in the practice of active re-membering. Denise Nadeau and Alannah Young (2006) talk about re-membering as an embodied process. Re-membering on the part of the body is the re-membering that "all things are connected" (p. 94). It is a re-membering of ourselves as members of our collectives and as members of all of our relations. Re-membering constitutes a re-connection of that "broken connection between us and the rest". As Nadeau and Young say, it "involves recovering historical and collective memories of culture and spirituality.... These are body-memories of spirit-of-grace, connection and vitality. The word re-*membering* [my italics] plays on the image of reordering the members (as in bodily members), creating a counter [embodied] memory or refraining in the body of goodness, spirit, and interconnection. It involves both affirming sacred moments in one's past and acknowledging the sacredness of the self in the present. It includes reconnecting with spiritual and cultural traditions that have meaning for one's life now and re-membering the body's connection with the Earth" (p. 94). Active re-membering as relational to untying and therefore anti-colonial blood-anger for self-defense are all of this and more. It is a constant, reflexive, ongoing and embodied action. Active re-membering is an epistemological position that is lived/alive. It is tactile. It burns. It breathes. It screams. It spits fire. It whispers. Active re-membering requires that our blood-anger as the body-tongue of our blood-memory talks with and back to our bodies. It requires that our blood-anger engages in conversation with our blood-memories which at this point have become radically politicized and de-victimized. This talking, this conversation, this dialogue (with-and-by blood-anger to-and-from blood-memory and the whole of the self) are a whole-bodied listening, hearing, feeling, re-connecting, re-membering, anti-colonial blood-anger talk. It is the talk that our blood-angers make when they begin to organize our whole bodies to say fuck-you to the colonial structure and its body-splitting, disconnecting and dis-intacting murderous agenda.

The process of untying our body-tongues through active re-membering as relational to self-recovery and as a critical component of anti-colonial blood-anger for self-defense necessitates in its radical politicization that our body-tongues begin to recognize, hear, listen, talk-to-and-talk-with our blood-memories of longing and yearning for a tactility of connectedness to all of our relations that have been lost and remain lost to the bodies of the oppressed from one generation to the next because of the colonial fuckeries of 1492 and its genocidal impact and aftermath. Active remembering knows that these connections have not so much been lost to us as much as stolen/erased/amputated from our consciousness even though all of our relations exist in our bodies and even though all of our relations *are* our bodies. It is those colonial epistemologies that have been imposed on/in us that deny us the ability to recognize them or, if we do so fleetingly, then force us to reject and dismiss them. Our bodies in their colonized split-up tied-up state yearn/long-for that which is already present, for that which continues to speak and for that which is silenced and left unheard. In the blood-memory of my body, my family and my immediate collective lie the plantation systems of Barbados in the mid-1800s, the struggles and practices of death, survival and resistance as the property of the enslavers called Worrell who brand their name on us but cannot fully brand it into us. There is too, the blood and anguish, torture, terror, fuck-you rebellion and relations of love formed under holocaust conditions sweated and congealed into the soil and earth as the earth in turn is congealed into our bodies. There are the struggle, pain, terror and murderousness of the middle-passage and the congealment of water and land (D. Chin, personal communication, April 21, 2017). Our blood-memories sing the struggles, survivals and blood stories of our peoples the Kalinago. They sing our ancestors' resistance in St. Vincent and all across the Caribbean to the murderousness of Columbus and his conquistadorists. Blood-memories such as these influence our body-tongues to organize the self-defense of our peoples against dis-intactness through the creation of our own ways of knowing, our own epistemologies and our own ways of doing that continue in the present even though we may not be conscious of it.

Like the way we have for generations taken the nable-strings (those little stumps of the umbilical cord) of our newborns and placed them in our little tins, covering them in talcum powder to protect them and keep them safe. And like how when we take them out we see how they have turned to stones that are now polished like gems, like onyx. And when we touch them we know (in a fuck-you opposition to colonialism's cosmologies) that we touch our ancestors, our mothers, fathers, grandmothers, grandfathers, sisters, brothers, nephews, nieces, cousins. We know in this tactility of connectedness that they came into the world and that they live beyond the world. We know that they existed/lived even though we have never seen them, and we know they still live, and we know that they are the earth and all are we. And from this we know (and it is confirmed to/by/with and through our body-tongues) that we are a collective, and that everything is connected, everything talks/speaks/hear/listens/breathes/has knowledge/has wisdom/has memory. It is these blood-memories of yearning and longing for connectedness that drove the body-tongues of my family to regularly climb high up into the mountains of the Northern Range of Trinidad to touch the Kalinago rock. That huge rock standing alone in the middle of a forest of thick bamboo. No other rock or stone around, not even a pebble. And its like that rock in the creation stories of the Kalinago, the one that saves our peoples from a massive flood by telling them to climb up onto it but warns everyone to be careful because the floods will come again and if they are to be saved they must listen only to the rock's voice who will warn them when the floods are about to start, but they don't listen, they forget to listen. They have forgotten how to listen. They forget to hear. They have forgotten how to hear. They forget to talk to the rock. They have forgotten how to talk to the rock. They have become disconnected from the rock and the land. The floods return and they die (Legends of the Caribs, 2009). The Kalinago rock felt/feels like that same rock. Etched into it are figures, peoples, living beings, just like in the story of Tamosi, the creator who starts life again by carving all living things on the side of a rock which then come back to life. I remember/re-member how we payed homage to the sacredness of those traces/voices of our communities and their presence from a thousand years ago that spoke back to us in the present.

We slid our fingers into the etched-out lines and traced the same embodied movements of those who made the carvings and when we did this our body-tongue's yearning/longing to be re-connected with an existence beyond 1492, beyond all of those colonial ways of thinking that have told us who we are, what we are, where we come from, how we come to be, how we should think about space and time and our relations with each other and with land and with everything around us seemed to be realized. Our body-tongues and our blood-memories had/have always told us that we are more than what we have been forced to accept, that we are sacred, that we have a collective "soul as vast as the world…as deep as the deepest of rivers.... [that we have]....the power to expand to infinity" (Fanon,

1952, p. 119). In that moment of spiritual tactility we hear, we know, we believe. In that moment our body-tongues in their re-membering for self-defense are becoming untied and anti-colonial. But when we leave the rock, when we come down from the mountain, the same disconnectedness we have tried to escape from returns. All around us our blood-anger as the body-tongue of blood-memory in its collective sense organizes its self-defense against dis-intactness and disconnectedness in avoidance, amputation, self-hate or a slave-master like domination over those it considers inferior and/or property. In all of this colonizing fucked-upness that *dis*-members, causes mental unwellness and turns everything to shit this is the place of refuge that our blood-anger has been forced to put us. I see a body lying on the street. People look on in shock and pain. The body is draped in a covering. I see two small scuffed-up tennis-shoed feet showing from beneath the covering. I hear later that night that a man murdered a woman.

All around us and inside us our collective blood-anger as the body-tongue of our blood-memory is tied-up and tied-down with body-splitting, individualizing, dis-membering colonial epistemologies of gender, sexuality, race, color, disability and class. All around us and inside us our blood-angers are directing a fuck-you strike-back back toward ourselves. All around us our blood-angers are relying on these same colonial epistemologies and ways of knowing to diagnose what is the cause of our wounds (Gaztambide-Fernandez, 2014), how we should understand and relate to our wounds, how we should know and understand our bodies, what it means to be a collective, what it means to be a community, how to move, how to defend ourselves, what self-defense means, how to bring balance and equilibrium, how to relate to each other, our relationship to land, how to survive, how to live in the past in the present and for the future, and how we should liberate ourselves. Each time our blood-angers defend our bodies in relation to all this in their dis-membered, disconnected state by killing/murdering the collective and the very multiplicativeness that is the core of we-self. Under these body-splitting, dis-membering dis-intacting epistemically violent conditions our blood-angers have no epistemological frameworks that will allow them to make that revolutionary connection and distinction between the colonial structural violence that starves us, exploits us, demoralizes us, executes us, punishes us, murders, hurts and terrorizes us and the self-destruction that it causes and brings into being when the oppressed are forced to live in fear and do battle against themselves in the struggle and scramble for survival (Fanon, 1968).

Active re-membering as the core element of anti-colonial blood-anger is the defense, the antidote and the opposition. As an epistemological fuck-you-war-of-position it works to untie our bodies. It is conscientisized to the splitting that our bodies have been subjected to and it makes the move as an embodied practice of self-defense to oppose and restore that splitting. Self-defense in these contexts is a defense then of all of the relations that constitutes the body of the historically oppressed. Its self-defense lies in a re-membering and restoration of the multiplicativeness of our bodies, of the connections between our bodies and the land and a re-membering and restoration of the presence of that same land that resides in our bodies. Fundamentally, active re-membering works to restore the connectedness between blood-memory and blood-anger as the body-tongue of blood-memory. This shift/this embodied movement for self-defense of the collective whole is anti-colonial blood-anger in action. In its shift toward its anti-colonial promise blood-anger takes up an embodied listening/hearing/talking back war-of-positionality with itself, and against the oppressor within, one that is imbued with revolutionary love of self, one that educates and coaxes back our blood-angers away from those moments when they want to take us back to that refuge of avoidance and rejection of the collective self in defense of a colonial individualized self, or when there is a slippage toward a colonial translation of our blood-memories that convinces us that we are helpless, powerless victims of oppression bereft of agency. Active re-membering's restoration of our blood-anger-blood-memory relations, its reclamation and politicization of our blood-memories, its consciousness of what it means to be a collective and what it means to defend and re-member that collective and all its relations, is the epistemological grounding that allows blood-anger's self-defense of the body to make the shift toward a radical anti-colonial offensive against the colonial structure that is external and internal to our bodies.

## Conclusion

There can be no decolonization without anticolonization. Active re-membering is the process whereby the oppressed find their anti-colonial center. This is what makes for the spirituality that is anti-colonial blood-anger. It demands that blood-anger speaks to and with blood-memory as a prerequisite for my interactions with all of my relations and as a methodological prerequisite for writing this chapter. This is self-recovery. Self-recovery in agency. Self-recovery in writing. Self-recovery in and through a fuck-you-the-structure self-defense of the collective[s].

## References


Bates, D. (2014, November 23). Exclusive: 'They filled him with bullets then hoped it would go away'. Devastated family of black man, 25, shot dead in St. Louis days after Michael Brown lash out at police for dragging heels with investigation. *Daily Mail*. Retrieved from https://www.dailymail.co.uk/news/article-2845846/Devastated-family-black-man-25-shot-dead-St-Louis-days-Michael-Brown-lash-police-dragging-heels-investigation.html.

Dumont, M. (2014). Pain and reassertion: Leanne Simpson's islands of decolonial love. *Arc Poetry Magazine*. Retrieved from http://arcpoetry.ca/2014/08/28/pain-and-reassertion-leanne-simpsons-islands-of-decolonial-love/.

Fanon, F. (1952). *Black skin white masks*. New York: Grove Press.

Fanon, F. (1968). *The wretched of the earth*. New York: Grove Press.

Gaztambide-Fernandez, R. (2014). Decolonial options and artistic/aesthetic entanglements: An interview with Walter Mignolo. *Decolonization, Indigeneity, Education & Society, 3*(1), 196–212.

Gramsci, A. (1971). *Selections from the prison notebook of Antonio Gramsci*. New York: International Publishers.

Holmes, L. (2000). Heart knowledge, blood memory, and the voice of land: Implications of research among Hawaiian elders. In G. Dei, B. L. Hall, & D. G. Rosenberg (Eds.), *Indigenous knowledges in global contexts multiple readings of our world* (pp. 37–53). Toronto: University of Toronto Press.

hooks, b. (1995). *Killing rage: Ending racism*. New York: H. Holt.

King, T. (2003). *The truth about stories: A native narrative*. Ottawa, ON, Canada: Canadian Broadcasting Corp.

Legends of the Caribs. (2009). Retrieved from http://www.oocities.org/thetropics/shores/9253/legends3.html.

Morrison, T. (1994). *The bluest eye*. New York: Plume Book.

Nadeau, D., & Young, A. (2006). Educating bodies for self-determination: A decolonizing strategy. *Canadian Journal for Native Education, 29*(1), 87–148.

Parmer, P. (1991). *A place of rage*. London: Hauer Rawlence Productions, Channel Four Television.

Riggs, M. T. (2006). *Tongues untied*. Berkeley, CA: Signifyin' Works.

CHAPTER 8

# In my Mother's Kitchen: Spirituality and Decolonization

*Janelle Brady*

Only my grandmother understood
Only my grandmother understood how connected I felt once again
Only my grandmother understood what being in that kitchen meant
Only my grandmother understood that I was stepping into a spiritual realm
Finding connection to what was lost on this earth, in this life, by being in the kitchen and reaching out to the person I love again
Only my grandmother understood

Washing chicken and vegetables
My hands hold the memory which was passed down from my ancestors
My connection to these memories came from my mother, my aunts and my grandmothers

J. Brady (✉)
Department of Social Justice Education, Ontario Institute for Studies in Education, University of Toronto, Toronto, ON, Canada
e-mail: janelle.baptiste.brady@mail.utoronto.ca



N. N. Wane et al. (eds.), *Decolonizing the Spirit in Education and Beyond*, Spirituality, Religion, and Education,
https://doi.org/10.1007/978-3-030-25320-2_8

I washed away tried to reclaim and understand her pain
I washed away with rejuvenation, understanding the sacredness of her gift to me, life
I washed away again and again

I peeled and felt connected to my mother's struggle
Her struggle in the face of anti-Black racism
Her struggle in the face of patriarchy
Her struggle in the face of white supremacy
Her struggle in raising me
Her struggle in a world expecting her to be a strong, Black woman and what that meant
I peeled away knowing this was not a single story

I peeled and unraveled years of intergenerational trauma
Trauma passed down to Black mothers
I peeled away and chopped, understanding, but not fully
Knowing, but not with mastery,
Instead with a humility of accepting what I do not know
I remembered her words to me in the kitchen to "Move yuh hand fast" and how we would laugh
We would laugh because it was comical, but true, no time to delay, and as she would say, you need to "cut n go tru"
Our race and gendered realities do not allow for us to sit back and wait
We cannot wait for privileges and systems of warmth and welcome
Built on Others, othering, and people lives devalued, expendable and lost at all cost
To uphold a system that claims to built by those who fought or earned their place
I peeled away

I prepared and tasted
I remembered that we need to foster resistance through sisterhood, motherhood, friendships and our ancestors
I remembered her trying
I remembered she said "Everyday that we are living, we are dying"
She resisted in every aspect she could and challenged me to resist and live a life that she would
I prepared and tasted

My hands never held such strength
I do not owe this to my own-doing or merit
I understand, that I do not understand everything, but I understand this comes from years and generations of preparation
Preparation which I do and do not understand
I understand the life-long process and how she'd say, we're all "a work in progress"
I understand that we must learn to unlearn, continue to resist and insist
Together by building solidarities we did not know exist

She was my messenger, my mentor and friend
She continues to guide me to the end
Holding her strength in my hands
I wash away, peel away, prepare and taste
Most importantly I serve
Reclaiming a realm I cannot understand
She guides me and puts strength in my hands
But on this journey to reclaim that which is now lost, only my grandmother understood the tears behind that sauce

CHAPTER 9

# Reclaiming Cultural Identity Through Decolonization of Food Habits

*Suleyman M. Demi*

## Introduction

Critical scholars of Indigeneity in North America and globally have argued that decolonization is not arrival at some political destination, but an ongoing and historical process of unlearning deeply internalized perceptions fostered through colonization and domination (Dei, 2002; Thiophene, 1995; Wane, 2006). This chapter, therefore, is a starting point to unlearn

This chapter is part of major research leading to MA thesis title "African Indigenous Food Crops: Their Role in Combating Chronic Diseases in Ghana". Submitted to the Department of Social Justice Education and School of Environment of the University of Toronto, Toronto, Canada.

S. M. Demi (✉)
Department of Social Justice Education of the Ontario Institute for Studies in Education and School of the Environment, University of Toronto, Toronto, ON, Canada
e-mail: suleyman.demi@mail.utoronto.ca



N. N. Wane et al. (eds.), *Decolonizing the Spirit in Education and Beyond*, Spirituality, Religion, and Education,
https://doi.org/10.1007/978-3-030-25320-2_9

some of the Eurocentric theories that I have imbibed in pursuit of my academic career and conversely, re-learn some Indigenous ways of knowing as legitimate forms of knowledge that value personal experience. Before my studies at the Ontario Institute for Studies in Education (OISE), my research interest was focused mainly on how to modernize agriculture to make food available to people in need and also to reduce poverty, particularly in developing countries. My understanding of food at the time was quite narrow as I considered only food items sold on the world market. However, my engagement with a critical scholarship at OISE resuscitated my consciousness to begin to look at issues more holistically. I start by describing my personal experience in food-related issues and how it has shaped my understanding and interest in food. The chapter critically examines misconceptions about African food systems by Western food scholars and highlights link between food and culture and the effects of colonization on food systems of the colonized countries and the consequences on environment.

I argue that one of the colonial legacies visible among Indigenous communities is the destruction of the cultures of the people. The erosion of Indigenous cultures through colonization was a deliberate attempt to delink Indigenous people[1] or racial bodies from their identity. Thus, the erosion of culture leached upon the Indigenous people globally has culminated in the loss of identity and self-esteem among some communities of Indigenous people. However, food cultures have not only been influenced by colonization but also capitalism. Since the introduction of commercial agriculture, new technologies were introduced to address what the Western capitalists considered the bottleneck of farming. Hence, technologies including artificial irrigation were introduced to reduce reliance on natural rainfall and allow farmers to produce food all year round. Secondly, modified species of crops and animals were introduced to shorten the maturity period of most crops and animals to allow farmers to produce food to meet immediate market demand. Thirdly, the introduction of storage facilities on and off-farm to prolong the shelf life of most farm products. The absence of these conditions hitherto made farming unattractive for business-oriented individuals and corporations. As some would describe agriculture as the most significant breakthrough in human history (Crosby, 2003), others considered agriculture as "the worst mistake in the history of human race" (Diamond, 1987, p. 95).

Nevertheless, the improvement in agricultural infrastructure made farming profitable and enabled Western capitalists to capitalize on food as a business empire and allow market forces (demand and supply) to dictate world food prices to the disadvantage of the poor. Also, it enabled Western countries, especially the United States and the United Kingdom, to dominate the world food market and also turn the developing countries into dumping grounds for their subsidized, excess and lower-quality foods. Susan George argues "this is what food has become: A source of profit; a tool of economic and political control; a means of ensuring effective dominance over the world at large and especially over the 'wretched of the earth'" (cited in Raschke & Cheema, 2007, p. 663).

However, in traditional communities, food is not only about nutrition but intertwined with culture because the culture of a specific group of people defines their food system and food system of a group of people constitutes their culture. Hence, reclaiming past Indigenous food cultures, therefore, constitutes a significant act of decolonization. As argued by Fanon, colonialism attacks the present, the past and the future; hence, we cannot fully decolonize without reclaiming the past. He wrote:

> ...colonialism is not content merely to impose its laws on the colonized country's present and future. Colonialism is not satisfied with snaring the people in its net or of draining the colonized brain of any form or substance. With a kind of perverted logic, it turns its attention to the past of the colonized people and distorts it, disfigures it, and destroys it. (Fanon, 1963, p. 149)

Re-invigorating Indigenous food cultures, therefore, constitutes a way by which colonized people can re-assert their agency and reclaim their past glory due to the relevance of food in humans' life. Food is the basic need of all living organisms that must be satisfied to provide the impetus to meet other needs. Food gathering, preparation, preservation and consumption started long ago since humans realized feeding themselves from the wild was unsustainable as people begin to live in clusters. Historical accounts have shown that long experimentation with what was in humans' immediate surroundings, as well as intuition and revelations from God, gods and ancestors, determined what could be regarded as food (Logan, 2012). Food has, therefore, been ingrained in cultures of most Africans and other Indigenous communities across the globe.

Scholars have long argued that food is a crucial component of African culture (Blair, 1966; Dei, 1989, 1991) and consequently, connected to local spirituality. Blair established the link between food and the culture of African people: "food habits are a basic part of every African culture. They have developed over a long period in response to the number of primary factors. The foods eaten are determined by environment, cultural contact and migration, barter, and trade" (Blair, 1966, p. 53). The process of acquiring food in Africa takes place in a manner that ensures the continued existence of peace, harmony and sanctity in nature. Sustainability of the environment constitutes a critical issue considered in food production and consumption practices. This is linked to the Africans' belief and spirituality that humans are connected to the earth; hence, their existence depends on respect accord to the earth. Such belief also admonishes local people to make peace with plants, animals (both domesticated and wild), stones and so on (Wangoola, 2000). The soil was assumed to be a deposit account from which the account holders (people) drew only part of the accrued interest without ever touching the principal (Wangoola, 2000). Hence, apart from nutritional value, food helps to shape individuals' lives, personal dispositions and spiritual connection. The next section, therefore, presents my self-reflection on food-related issues.

## Self-Reflection

Growing up in Ghana, I was sent to live with my grandmother. As one of her favorite grandchildren, it became my responsibility to assist in food preparation in our home and I was introduced to a variety of African Indigenous Leafy Vegetables (AILVs) which were not sold on the local market. I also learned that sometimes, foods were prepared to meet the physiological needs of people. Hence, if someone fell ill, she or he was not supposed to eat certain foods, particularly those with higher fat content. Again, the food for expectant mothers or women who had just delivered a baby were differently made to meet their physiological needs such as the production of breast milk for the newborn baby and also for faster healing of wounds sustained during childbirth. There were specific AILVs and spices such as grain of paradise (*Aframomum melegueta*), Negro pepper (*Xylopia aethiopica*) and calabash nutmeg (*Monodora myristica*) for these purposes.

Typical examples were the occasions when my aunties would come to our home to give birth instead of the hospital in the cities. My grandmother would prepare special food using a mixture of local leaves (e.g., "nuunum" by the Akan) for the new mother. Again, on occasions where my grandmother had complications in delivering a baby, she gives the woman in labor some local herbs to eat and within a few minutes, the baby would be delivered without any further complications. My grandmother used these herbs to deliver several babies without any incident or complication.

I grew up with the understanding that food is eaten to satisfy hunger or heal people from sickness. But my experience in the Eurocentric boarding school structured by the British was different. There were strict rules and regulations regarding dinner time and eating manners, and students were prohibited from carrying food outside the dining hall. The food we were exposed to was the ones sanctioned by the board of directors of the school as a balanced diet and Indigenous African grains such peal millets, sorghum and AILVs were considered of less value and hence, were absent in our menu. The decisions as to what we ate were entirely in the hands of the school authorities with little to no input from students. Eating with the hands was considered archaic—hence, the need for authorities to orientate us by taking us through lessons to mimic the Western style of eating. How to hold and where to place a fork, knife and spoon on a dining table and how to sit at the dining among other things were the pre-occupation of our matron and kitchen staff who themselves had become "a commodity of western ideology" (Wane, 2008, p. 187). Those who were inclined to their Indigenous upbringing and had difficulties in catching up quickly with the Westernization were laughed at and labeled village folks. Our communal way of eating was broken and individualism encouraged. Each student had his/her unique cup, plate, spoon, fork, etc., for which they were not transferable.

At the end of my boarding school experience, my eating habits and food preferences completely changed. My desire for Western foods over traditional foods increased. To compliment my newfound diets, I began listening to country music, blues and foreign gospels. Local foods and music became outdated to me and I began questioning the traditional way of life. I had no desire to eat in a group as we used to do before going to secondary school. I started asking for my separate bowl of food, which was frowned on by my grandparents, aunties, uncles and siblings as it implied a sign of division, breaking the bond that existed in the family. Soon I gained my "freedom" when I entered university. Now I decide what to eat, where to eat and how to eat it. I later became so engraved to more refined Western foods. I only became aware of the dangers of my eating habit when I fell sick and I was advised by a physician to avoid taking certain foods that I considered healthy and modern. Then I began to appreciate what my grandmother used to prepare for us.

I vividly remember my grandmother used to prepare a meal consisting of leaves called "Zoogala gandi" (in the Hausa language) and mixed with "gari" (a food from cassava) and oil. After boiling the leaves, my grandmother would sieve the mixture to separate the leaves from the liquid. As children, we sipped the remaining liquid, an action that received no reprimands from my grandmother because she knew its medicinal value. According to her, she inherited it from her great-grandparents. About ten years later, after I had graduated from the university and was teaching in the city, I heard of a wonder plant called "moringa" which according to scientists cures several diseases. The leaves are dried, grinded and the powdered form sold to schools, corporate organizations, as well as individuals in Ghana to incorporate in their food. Our school purchased the seedlings of moringa to plant on our school compound. To my utmost surprise, the wonder plant is no other plant than "Zoogala gandi" that we were exposed to several years earlier. This encouraged me to value our food cultures bequeathed to us by our ancestors.

The connection between people and food was demonstrated in one of the courses I took—"Cultural Knowledges, Representation and Colonial Education"—offered at the Ontario Institute for Studies in Education of the University of Toronto in the fall of 2013. As part of a presentation, my group decided to do an exhibition to conceptualize our topic "Museumization and showing of cultures." A colleague brought species of pepper commonly found in Latin America, the Caribbean and most parts of Africa. At the end of our presentation, we asked the class to comment or ask questions regarding our presentation. Surprisingly, among the entire exhibits, the one that caught the attention of students who originated from the Caribbean and Africa was the pepper. Most of the "after the presentation" discussions centered on the pepper. Many students showed how the pepper had re-connected them to their ancestral home and brought back some memories which demonstrated the relevance of food to our culture, identity and spirituality. The next section critiques some views expressed by Western food scholars on African food system.

## Critical Examination of Misconceptions About African Food Systems by Western Food Scholars

A Ghanaian Akan proverb states, "if somebody who does like you want to mimic your dancing style, she or he twists the wait in an awkward position to discredit your dancing moves." This proverb suggests that stories or facts can be twisted to suit a specific narrative. Consequently, one story can be told differently by different actors depending on who is saying it and the motivation behind the narrative. It, therefore, implies that we cannot vouch for the authenticity of every statement purported to have come from scholars/academicians as the absolute truth without subjecting those statements to scrutiny. The second adage, which is common among Ghanaians, is translated as "until the lions begin to tell their own stories, the tales of hunting will always glorify the hunters." Drawing from these proverbs, it follows that stories of racialized groups told by dominant are often couched in a way to portray a state of hopelessness or helplessness to warrant colonial intervention. Prah (1997) argues that minority groups need to resist the insulting notion that others know them better than they know themselves. Critical scholars have criticized the attempts by Western scholars to devalue the knowledge systems and worldview views of Indigenous/minority groups as "epistemic racism" (Escobar, 2004; Maldonado-Tores, 2004).

For instance, some Western food scholars argued Africa lacked suitable food crops for human sustenance. However, this chapter limits its critiques on views expressed by two Western food scholars. Diamond (1997) argues that Africa was not blessed with the most promising domesticable food plants and animals in global terms; as a result, few crops and animal species were exported from the continent. Crosby (2003) corroborated Diamond's (1997) assertion that Africa lacked suitable crops:

> [t]he importance of American foods in Africa is more obvious than in any other continent of the Old World, for in no other continent, except the Americas themselves, is so great a proportion of the population dependent on American foods. ***Very few of man's cultivated plants originated in Africa***...and so Africa has had to import its chief food plants from Asia and America...As for the influence of these crops before 1850, *we might hypothesize that the increased food production enabled the slave trade to go on as long as it did without pumping the black well of Africa dry.* (Crosby, 2003, pp. 185, 188)

Crosby quote raises several questions that need to be unpacked. However, it is important to note that McNeil who wrote a foreword for Crosby in the same book was the first to discover factual inaccuracies in Crosby's assertion. McNeil highlighted Crosby's silence on African contribution to the world food system partly because of inadequate information on African food system. McNeil notes:

> Though they came in chains part of their fauna and flora came with them including African rice, okra, yams, black-eyed peas, millets, sorghum, sesame and the pathogens that cause yellow fever and malaria. Coffee came from Africa though not in slave ships. (McNeil, 2003, as cited in Crosby, 2003, p. xiii)

This quote from McNeil highlights the fact that even in shackles, the enslaved Africans relied on their Indigenous food contrary to Crosby's (2003) accounts. Preserving their foods as enslaved Africans did in Americas demonstrates Indigenous people of Africa resisted the colonizing power while maintaining a significant source of sustenance under colonization. As enslaved Africans practiced their Indigenous food cultures (e.g., soul food) in captivity in the Americas, it re-established their spiritual link to continental Africa.

Crosby's argument that "Very few of man's cultivated plants originated in Africa" requires further interrogation. Does Crosby (2013) suggest Africans contributed little to European cuisine? Or Africa contributed meagerly to the world food systems? In both cases, the statement is debatable because how did Crosby account for many Indigenous foods consumed by Africans which are not sold on the world market? For instance, in traditional communities, what constitutes a food to a particular group of people can be object of worship for some, or taboo to others or pet to many (Demi, 2014).[2] The Western hegemony in the categorization of plants and animals as food in global terms was challenged by Sahlins (1976) who argues "the exploitation of American environment, the mode of relation to the landscape, depends upon the models of a meal that includes a central meat element with periphery support of carbohydrate and vegetables" (p. 176). Sahlins (1976) further argues that the humans would have witnessed an entirely different structure of agricultural production and articulation to the world market if for instance Western countries particularly "Americans" ate dogs and horses, both of which are edible in some parts of the world. Food production, therefore, is governed by the cultural construction of consumption along with symbolic taboos and valuation (Dietler, 2007). Hence, focusing on food consumption offers a vital premise to understand the social and cultural relevance of food and its role in colonialism (Dietler, 2007).

Again, Crosby's argument by inference seeks to suggest that the new crops introduced into Africa stimulated rapid population growth to replace population loses during slavery; hence, slavery did not significantly affect the African population. Ironically, Walter Rodney in his book *How Europe Underdeveloped Africa* showed that population growth in Africa was stagnant between the period of 1600 and 1900, the period in which most of the foreign crops were introduced into Africa compared to growth rates in other continents (Rodney, 1982).

Rodney's (1982) argument was corroborated by recent studies by Carney & Rosomoff (2010) and Inikori (1994) who corroborated Rodney's argument by showing how slave trade drastically reduced the population of Africa and deprived some communities of exuberant farm laborers. Therefore, the slave trade partly necessitated the adoption of early maturing crops like maize compared to millet and sorghum or less labor-intensive crops like cassava compared to yam (Logan, 2012). It is also worth emphasizing that Indigenous African farmers select not only high yielding crops but also crops that can withstand environmental shocks (Logan, 2012). Hence, there is an in-built mechanism in African Indigenous farming systems to ensure farm diversification and mixed cropping[3] which contrasts the monocropping.[4] The mixed cropping guards against total crop failure during natural disasters such as drought, flood or bush fire because different crops respond differently to these disasters.

Contrary to the views expressed by Crosby (2003) and Diamond (1997), recent empirical studies have demonstrated with ample evidence that Africa has contributed immensely to world food systems. Kiambi, Atta-Krah, Schmelzer and Omion (2003) found that out of 150 plant-based foods used by humans, 115 (76.7%) originated from Africa. Additionally, the world's major regions of crop diversity include the Ethiopian highlands, the Sahelian transitional zone, the delta of Niger River and the humid forest zones of West and Central Africa (Kiambi et al., 2003). The term "endemism," which refers to the proportion of species not found anywhere else in the world, is also high in Africa (Kiambi et al., 2003). It is estimated that tropical Africa is endemic to 45% of crop species (Sayer, Harcourt, & Collins, 1992). Researchers working at Plant Resource of Tropical Africa (PROTA) have isolated 275 plant species as vegetables and 528 species which are used as food, medicine or ornamental purposes (Grubben & Denton, 2004; PROTA, 2005). Their study reveals 75% of the vegetables are Indigenous to Africa, 16% are traditional and only 8% were considered exotic to Africa (PROTA, 2005). According to Smith and Eyzaguirre (2007), Indigenous food crops of Africa are those that have their natural habitat in sub-Saharan Africa and traditional food crops are those that were introduced over centuries ago, and due to their prolonged use, they have become part of subcontinent food culture.

It is evident from the above discussion that Africa has promising food crops. However, recent food security challenges in Africa can be traced to several factors, including policies of the World Trade Organization (WTO), which has turned Africa into a market for Western food products. Until recently, Africa was a net exporter of food (Bello, 2008). Some have also argued that the persistent food insecurity reported in some parts of Africa was the result of abandoning African Indigenous food crops (AIFCs) that were suited to the African climate (Culwick & Culwick, 1941; Raschke & Cheema, 2007; Sambo, 2014; Smith, 2013). Another phenomenon that contributed to the underutilization of AIFCs is the globalization of the world food systems by Western economies resulting in many governments-based research institutions paying little or no attention to African Indigenous crop species and their potential for local crop improvement (Adebooye, Ogbe, & Bamidele, 2003; Adebooye & Opabode, 2005).

Furthermore, most research institutions are funded by foreign donors who set the priorities for research based on what they consider relevant. In such cases, Indigenous crops that have little international appeal or do not promote global trade have less incentive to research. It is important to emphasize that most food crops dominating on the world food market presently have been modified through breeding or genetic manipulation for higher yield. McCann (2001) described how maize, for instance, was transformed through genetic and breeding to become the leading cereal on the world market: "modern genetic alchemy has transformed maize's personality from an obligingly adaptive vegetable crop into a hegemonic leviathan that dominates regional diets and international grain markets" (2001, p. 250). This quote suggests that it is possible to transform African cereals such as sorghum, millet and rice to the level of maize and other cereals especially when sorghum and millet contain higher nutrients (e.g., protein and vitamins) than most of the leading cereals on the world market. However, Indigenous communities have a broader understanding of food beyond a means of nourishment. Food production, preparation and consumption are linked to culture, identity and spirituality of the people. Hence, farmers may resist any attempt to genetically modify their food crops by either rejecting hybrid seeds or breed their own seeds to adapt to their soil condition as a way of keeping these knowledges sacred from colonization (Hellin, Bellon, & Hearne, 2014; Mark, 2017). Hence, maintaining the originality of Indigenous seeds or food crops is considered as an act of resistance among Indigenous people. The next section discusses the role of colonization on food systems and environmental sustainability.

## Colonization, Indigenous Food Culture and Environmental Sustainability

Prior to the colonial era, production and consumption of foods were always done with key considerations governed by norms, values and taboos that evolved from customs, traditions and cultures among Indigenous communities. These traditional rules and regulations were instituted to ensure the sustainability of the environment, mother earth and all that live within her. The social structures of Indigenous people changed drastically with the onslaught of colonization. The food dynamics within the world particularly in Africa, Americas and other colonized places came to a drastic change with the arrival of the Europeans. European agriculture "manipulated the environment to meet the needs of the settlers for food, shelter and other resources" (M'bayo, 2003, p. 191). Mutwa (1999) argues that since imperial forces of Europe began expanding their empires through the colonization of sub-Saharan Africa, ancient Indigenous knowledge including a wealth of knowledge about food habits, local pharmacology and health and longevity has progressively been eroded. The attrition of traditional knowledge of food and health was also reported in North America and Australia (Bodirsky & Johnson, 2008; Rowley et al., 2000). Colonization, therefore, altered the fauna and flora of most colonized areas in the world. As M'bayo succinctly put it:

> Domesticated animals from Europe arrived, thrived, and multiplied into enormous herds. Their eating habits, trampling hooves, and droppings and the seeds of weeds they brought left a deep impact on the environments that became their new homes. In the end, colonialism changed and reshaped the world because most continents lost many natural plants and animals due to the human introduction of overpowering species. And in many instances,

> colonized regions were adversely affected by the introduction of animals, diseases, and plants from another environment, which dominated the existing Indigenous flora and fauna. (M'bayo, 2003, p. 191)

The alteration of the ecology brought economic gains to the colonizers and untold hardship to local indigenes. Ironically, Indigenous communities who maintain their responsible roles to nature suffer the most severe consequences of environmental colonialism (Beinart, 2000). McCann (2001) argues "maize and cassava together were the nutritional wedge of a human assault on the forest landscape, intended to convert the forest's biomass and energy into useable carbohydrate" (p. 258). The exploitation of forest resources initiated by the colonizers persists long after political independence in most developing countries because the structures that ensure outflow of resource from colonies to Europe remain intact. This is witnessed in most parts of Africa where forest reserves are being eroded annually and several wildlife species face imminent extinction as reported in some studies (Attuquayefio & Fobil, 2005; Wiafe, 2013). Slocum and Saldanha (2013) revealed the fallacies in the description of the landscape of most colonized countries to pave the way for resource appropriation. They argue, "Cultivation is strongly coded masculine labour; landscapes are called wild or virgin, awaiting the white man to penetrate, survey, and subdue them. A field, like a woman, becomes barren" (p. 6). The notion that soils in developing countries, for example Africa, were poor but their forest reserves were considered wild and therefore good enough for exploitation was described by Slocum and Saldanha (2013) as "productivism," and it was criticized for its sexist implications (Trauger, 2004) as well as its Whiteness (Anderson, 2003).

According to Bodirsky and Johnson (2008), contrary to the Western Christian gospel that God bestowed on humans dominium over the rest of creation and instructed them to subdue and rule over the earth, the Creator spirit of Indigenous people gave no such right to humans. To the Indigenous people, humans are the most vulnerable and weakest link in the vast chain of nature (Wangoola, 2000). The world was not for them to conquer but to live in peace, harmony and respect (Wangoola, 2000). According to many Indigenous stories, "the Creator instead instructs the plants and animals to have pity on their younger siblings, the humans, and to teach them how to live successfully with the rest of creation" (Bodirsky & Johnson, 2008, p. 2). To demonstrate the interconnection between humans, the earth, the plants and the animals, an old Kenyan woman showed how they reciprocate the benevolence of the nature through some farming practices:

> Carry some seeds with you. If you get to the farm before me, scatter the seeds before you start your harvest. When you do that you are giving back to the land. Give thanks to the Creator for providing for us, then you can start your harvest. If you do not give back, next year I will have no food and you will be far away to feel the effects of failing to observe one of our basic principles of life. (Wane, 2002, p. 90)

The above quote rooted in the spirituality of Indigenous people demonstrates how Indigenous farmers humanize the earth and show gratitude. By throwing part of the previous harvest onto the ground implies feeding the ants, termite, insect, birds and all other animals, and those that enter the soil either germinate or turn into manure to feed the plants. This kind gesture ensures that the cycle of sustainability and reciprocity is intact. This type of knowledge is lacking in conventional agriculture where the desire to make profit overrides any other considerations. The Indigenous measures of managing critical resources are always downplayed in the scientific world and often characterized as unscientific, accidental or conservation was not the prior objective. As Orr (2004) argues, it is elusive to think that we can manage the earth using appropriate scientific technologies. According to Orr (2004), it is more beneficial to control human desires, our economy and political expediencies. The current environmental challenges facing the world defy the universalist approach—hence, the need to combine Western science and Indigenous knowledges to solve environmental problems. The need to incorporate Indigenous Knowledge into policies is, therefore, needed now more than ever.

## Conclusions

This chapter explored a wide range of issues regarding food habits and culture. The chapter critically examined misconceptions about African food systems by Western food scholars and provided fact and figures to support the critiques. Contrary to popular views held by some Western food scholars that Africa lacked suitable food crops and animal species, the chapter demonstrated with ample findings from empirical studies that suggest Africa is the hub of over half of the world's food diversity. However, the marginalization of African Indigenous food crops due to the globalization of the world food systems has contributed to the underutilization of most Indigenous crops of Africa. The marginalization and underutilization of AIFCs are partly responsible for rising food insecurity in Africa. To address this problem, it requires the re-invigoration of Indigenous food culture as form of resistance and connecting to local spirituality. Going back to Indigenous foods could help solve numerous environmental issues associated with industrial agriculture.

## Notes

1. The phrase "Indigenous people" is used in this paper as an international category.
2. For example, cattle are food for most people but an object of worship among Hindus in Indian; dogs and cats are popular pets in Europe and the Americas but food for some tribes in Africa and some part of the world; and crocodiles (alligators) are delicacy for some tribes in Africa but they are totems for some tribes (e.g., my tribe)—hence a taboo to eat their meat or cross the water which was used to wash crocodile meat and thrown on the floor.
3. Growing of different types of crops on the same piece of land.
4. Growing a single crop on a piece of land which is the focus of Western agronomic practices.

## References

Adebooye, O. C., Ogbe, F. M., & Bamidele, J. F. (2003). Ethnobotany of Indigenous leaf vegetables of Southwest Nigeria. *Delpinoa, 45,* 295–299.

Adebooye, O. C., & Opabode, J. T. (2005). Status of conservation of the Indigenous leafy vegetables and fruits of Africa. *Africa Journal of Biotechnology, 3,* 700–705.

Anderson, K. (2003). White natures: Sydney's royal agricultural show in post humanist perspective. *Transactions Institute of British Geographers NS, 28*(4), 422–441.

Attuquayefio, D. K., & Fobil, J. N. (2005). An overview of biodiversity conservation in Ghana: Challenges and prospects. *West African Journal of Applied Ecology., 7*(1), 1–18.

Beinart, W. (2000). African history and environmental history. *Africa Affairs, 99,* 269–302.

Bello, W. (2008). How to manufacture a global food crisis. *Development, 51*(4), 450–455.

Blair, T. L. V. (1966). Continuity and change in African food habits. *Journal of the Institute of Food Technologies, 20*(6), 53–58.

Bodirsky, M., & Johnson, J. (2008). Decolonizing diet: Healing by reclaiming traditional Indigenous foodways. *The Journal of Canadian Food Cultures,*

*1*(1), 1–10. Retrieved May 12, 2013, From http://wwwerudit.Org/Revue/Cuisine/2008/V1019373ar,Html.

Carney, J., & Rosomoff, R. N. (2010). *In the shadow of slavery: Africa's botanical legacy in the Atlantic world*. Berkeley: University of California Press.

Crosby, A. W. (2003). *The Columbian exchange: Biological and cultural consequences of 1492* (30th Anniversary Edition). Westport, CT: Praeger Publishers.

Culwick, A., & Culwick, G. (1941). Nutrition and native agriculture in East Africa. *East African Medical Journal, 6,* 146–153.

Dei, G. J. S. (1989). Hunting and gathering in Ghanaian rain forest community. *Ecology of Food and Nutrition, 22,* 225–245.

Dei, G. J. S. (1991). Dietary habits of a Ghanaian farming community. *Ecology of Food and Nutrition, 25*(1), 29–49.

Dei, G. J. S. (2002). *Rethinking the role of Indigenous knowledges in the academy* (NALL Working Paper #58).

Demi, S. M. (2014). *African Indigenous food crops: Their roles in combating chronic diseases in Ghana* (Master's thesis). University of Toronto, Department of Social Justice Education and School of the Environment, Toronto, ON, Canada. Retrieved from https://tspace.library.utoronto.ca/bitstream/1807/68528/1/Demi_Suleyman_M_201411_MA_thesis.pdf.

Diamond, J. (1987). *The worst mistake in the history of the human race*. Discovering Magazine. Retrieved from http://www.sigervanbrabant.be/docs/Diamond.PDF.

Diamond, J. (1997). *Guns, germs and steel: A short history of everybody for the last 13,000 years*. London, UK: Vintage.

Dietler, M. (2007). Culinary encounters: Food, identity, and colonialism. In C. T. Katheryn (Ed.), *The archaeology of food and identity* (Center for Archaeology Investigations, Occasional Paper No. 34). Southern Illinois University.

Escobar, A. (2004). Beyond the third world: Imperial globality, global coloniality and anti-globalization social movement. *Third World Quarterly, 25*(1), 207–232.

Fanon, F. (1963). *The wretched of the earth*. New York, NY: Grove Press.

Grubben, G. J. H., & Denton, O. A. (Eds.). (2004). *Plant resources of tropical Africa 2: Vegetables*. Wageningen, The Netherlands: PROTA Foundation.

Hellin, J., Bellon, M, R., & Hearne, S. J. (2014). Maize landraces and adaptation to climate change in Mexico. *Journal of Crop Improvement, 28*(4), 484–501. https://doi.org/10.1080/15427528.2014.921800.

Inikori, J. E. (1994). Ideology versus the tyranny of paradigm: Historians and the impact of the Atlantic slave trade on African societies. *African Economic History, 22,* 37–58.

Kiambi, D., Atta-Krah, K., Schmelzer, G. H., & Omion, E. A. (2003). Plant genetic resources in the global and Africa settings. In *Plant resources of tropical Africa. Proceeding of the first PROTA International Workshop* (pp. 33–52), 23–25 September 2002. Nairobi, Kenya: PROTA Foundation.

Logan, A. L. (2012). *A history of food without history: Food, trade, and environment in West-Central Ghana in the Second Millennium AD* (Ph.D. thesis). University of Michigan, United States. Retrieved from https://deepblue.lib.umich.edu/handle/2027.42/96047.

Maldonado-Tores, N. (2004). The topology of being and the geopolitics of knowledge; modernity, empire coloniality. *City, 8*(1), 229–234.

Mark, G. S. (2017). *What ancient corn framers can teach us about engineering crops for climate change?* Retrieved from https://massivesci.com/articles/ancient-corntortillas-farming-genetic-engineering.

M'bayo, T. E. (2003). *Environment, colonialism: An international social, cultural, and political encyclopedia* (pp. 190–191). Santa Barbara, CA: ABC-CLIO.

McCann, J. (2001). Maize and grace: History, corn, and Africa's new landscapes, 1500–19991. *Comparative Studies in Society and History, 43*(2), 246–272.

Mutwa, V. (1999). *Indaba, my children.* Johannesburg, South Africa: Grove Publisher.

Orr, D. (2004). Introduction: What is education for? In *Earth and mind* (Tenth Anniversary Edition). Washington: Island Press.

Prah, K. (1997). Accusing the victims—Review of in my father's house by Kwame Anthony Appiah. *Codesria Bulletin, I,* 14–22.

PROTA. (2005). Comparative data on 275 vegetables. In C. H. Bosch, D. J. Boras, & J. S. Siemonsma (Eds.), *Vegetables of tropical Africa: Conclusions and recommendations based on PROTA 2: "vegetables".* Wageningen, The Netherlands: PROTA Foundation.

Raschke, V., & Cheema, B. (2007). Colonisation, the new world order, and the eradication of traditional food habits in East Africa: Historical perspective on the nutrition transition. *Public Health Nutrition, 11*(7), 662–674.

Rodney, W. (1982). *How Europe underdeveloped Africa.* Washington, DC: Howard University.

Rowley, K. G., Gault, A., Mcdermott, R., Knight, S., Mcleay, T., & O'Dea, K. (2000). Reduced prevalence of impaired glucose tolerance and no change in prevalence of diabetes despite increasing GMI among Aboriginal people from a group of remote homeland communities. *Diabetes Care, 23,* 898–905.

Sahlins, M. (1976). *Culture and practical reason.* Chicago: University of Chicago Press.

Sambo, B. E. (2014). Endangered, neglected, Indigenous resilient crops: A potential against climate change impact for sustainable crop productivity and food security. *Journal of Agriculture and Veterinary Science, 7*(2), 34–41.

Sayer, J. A., Harcourt, C. S., & Collins, M. M. (1992). *The conservation atlas of tropical forests.* New York, NY: Sim & Scuster.

Smith, I. F. (2013). Sustained and integrated promotion of local, traditional food systems for nutrition security. In J. Franzo, D. Hunter, T. Borelli, & F. Mattei (Eds.), *Diversifying food and diets: Using agricultural biodiversity to improve nutrition and health* (pp. 122–139). Abingdon: Routledge/CTA/Biodiversity International.

Smith, I. F., & Eyzaguirre, P. (2007). African leafy vegetables: Their roles in the world health organization's global fruits and vegetables initiative. *African Journal of Food Agriculture Nutrition and Development, 7*(3), 1–17.

Slocum, R., & Saldanha, A. (2013). *Geographies of race and food: Fields, bodies, markets.* London; New York, NY: Routledge.

Thiophene, H. (1995). Post-colonial literature and counter-discourse. In B. Ashcroft, G. Griffiths, & H. Thiophene (Eds.), *The post-colonial studies reader* (pp. 95–98). New York: Routledge.

Trauger, A. (2004). Because they can do the work: Women farmers and sustainable agriculture. *Gender, Place and Culture, 11*(2), 289–307.

Wane, N. N. (2002). African women and spirituality: Connections between thought and education. In E. V. O'Sullivan, A. Morrell, & M. O'Connor (Eds.), *Expanding the boundaries of transformative learning: Essays on theory and praxis* (pp. 135–150). New York: Palgrave.

Wane, N. N. (2006). Is decolonization is possible? In G. J. S. Dei & A. Kempt, (Eds.), *Anti-colonialism and education: The politics of resistance* (pp. 1–24). Rotterdam: Sense Publishers.

Wane, N. N. (2008). Mapping the field of Indigenous knowledge in anti-colonial discourse: A transformative journey in education. *Race, Ethnicity and Education, 11*(2), 183–197.

Wangoola, P. (2000). Mpambo, the African multiversity: A philosophy to rekindle the African spirit. In G. J. S. Dei, B. Hall, & D. Golden-Rosenberg (Eds.), *Indigenous knowledges in global contexts: multiple readings of our world.* Toronto: University of Toronto Press.

Wiafe, E. D. (2013). Status of the critical endangered Roloway Monkey (Cercopethicus Diana Roloway) in dadieso forest reserve, Ghana. *African Primates, 8*, 9–16.

PART III

# Mind

CHAPTER 10

# A Journal on Ubuntu Spirituality

*Devi Mucina*

I would like to start this Ubuntu greeting by expressing my deep gratitude and respect to the Lekwungen-speaking people, on whose traditional territory the university that I work for stands. My family and I also live and play on the territories of the Songhees, Esquimalt and WSÁNEĆ peoples. I acknowledge your historical relationship with these lands, which continues today and into the future. I also want to acknowledge that I am here through the colonial settler project and therefore implicate myself in the colonial project, which endeavors to dispossess you of your lands. As we dialogue, I am awakening to our colonial reality. My act of relationally seeing you is leading me to decolonizing scholarship and actions. Hence, my first action as an Indigenous Ubuntu (being) is to request that you allow me to raise my hands so I may acknowledge you as Ubuntu. As Ubuntu when we meet, we extend to each other an Indigenous Spiritual Ubuntu greeting. I would like to offer this Ubuntu greeting to you and to my people of African descent, scattered across the globe, "Sanibonani," meaning

D. Mucina (✉)
Director of Indigenous Governance, Faculty of Human and Social Development, University of Victoria, Victoria, BC, Canada
e-mail: dpdee@uvic.ca



N. N. Wane et al. (eds.), *Decolonizing the Spirit in Education and Beyond*, Spirituality, Religion, and Education,
https://doi.org/10.1007/978-3-030-25320-2_10

"We see you" but also implying that at a deep spiritual level, I am never alone as my ancestors are always with me and in me. Subsequently, we see you. The response to this is "Yebo Sanibonani," meaning "Yes we see you too." Again, the implication is that you, the reader, and your ancestors agree collectively about your observation of us. So, to our ancestors, to our elders, to our parents, to our sisters and brothers, to those yet unborn and to all of creation, "Sanibonani." But, let me also request that we exercise caution, because we know that the act of speaking can also be used to deny, refuse and ignore our relatedness. So, as I give voice to our relatedness, I also acknowledge the relationships that we have also erased and silenced. May the ancestors be with us as we try to renew and re-establish familial bonds. May the sacred cycle of breath connect us as one, Ubuntu.

## My Context and Location

Brothers and sisters of Turtle Island my remembering is occurring through our relational bonds. To me, you are Ubuntu, which is to say I cannot distinguish where you end and I begin, yet I do not say this as a way of imposing my voice, I say this as a way of making space. In the same manner that you have made space for me to speak. I hope you will find resonance in some of the things I say, while seeing our differences as communicating the uniqueness of our contextual knowledge. May we continue to learn from each other. May we continue to inspire each other to enact everyday acts of decolonizing Indigenous resurgence. May we enact decolonial love in spite of how colonialism has positioned us against each other. I also want to apologize for any transgressions that I make, as what I say is grounded in Ubuntu spirituality, with some remembering influence from our dialogues.

I was born in Zimbabwe, in the rural lands of Makoni on the colonially created reserve of Chendmuya to Joyce Nyamunda. This makes me thankful to my Shona relatives on my Amai's (mother) side. Without them, we would have no life. I am because they are. This is the genealogical blood memory that connects me to my maternal family. Yet our Ubuntu Indigenous traditions dictate that when I am in the Shona territory of Zimbabwe, I am a welcomed familial visitor as my rightful place is with my paternal family according to our Ubuntu traditions. Through my Baba's (father) lineage, I am Maseko Ngoni and Chewa from Lizulu, which is on the colonial border of Malawi and Mozambique; again, we see how colonialism fragmented our Indigenous nations, because as many of you know, colonial boundaries speak to a colonial context, which renders us silent in our own territories. The silence that colonial reality and context create in our territories is well captured in *Moving the Centre* by Ngugi Wa Thiong'o (2008). My Baba is Peter Dee Mucina and my totem is Khomba (bush baby). Even before I understood my location among my paternal Maseko Ngoni and Chewa family, my names, which are Devi David Peter Dee Mucina Khomba, to the knowing Maseko communities, communicated my blood ties but as I heard when I went home to LiZulu, it is my actions, which have led to the whole community claiming me. My highest sense of responsibility and accountability is to my families and communities in Southern Africa, which raised me. The colonially created reserve of Chendmuya could not sustain the needs of my family, so my father had to leave his family in the early 70s and go to the city of Harare to find a job as a cheap laborer but his sporadic jobs did not pay him enough to support his growing family. Many years later, my mother reported to me that she did unspeakable things to try and keep us alive, but as hard as she tried she saw her babies die one by one from malnutrition and poverty. Colonially fragmented from each other, Amai and Baba struggled against the colonially imposed poverty, while being isolated from each other. It was inevitable that the colonial created White supremacy governance structure would make them evaluate each other against its colonial expectations of capitalistic accumulation. Not surprisingly they found each other wanting within the colonial capitalistic structure of White supremacy. Again, my Amai reports that it was around this period my Baba started having psychotic mental health breakdowns. Although my Amai feared for my well-being, she ultimately understood that I would die from malnutrition and poverty, which had already claimed my younger brother and sister. Under such duress, my Amai and her family demanded that my Baba come and take me away, this was around 1977–1978.

This is how I became the child that was raised by many Indigenous communities on their territories or on other Indigenous peoples' territories. I was other-fathered by the other Indigenous African men; who let Baba and I stay with them illegally in the servants' quarters. I was other-fathered by the older Indigenous boy who slept in the phone booth with me, because I was scared of being beaten by my own biological Baba. Mark Mathabane (1986), in the preface of his autobiography entitled *Kaffir Boy,* has this to say about his Baba: "They turned my father - by repeatedly arresting him and denying him the right to earn a living in a way that gave him dignity - into such a bitter man that, as he fiercely but in vain resisted the emasculation, he hurt those he loved the most" (Mathabane, 1986, p. X).

Yet, there were others who stepped in, and I am truly thankful for being other-fathered and other-mothered by the Indigenous support staff, like Bambo Colin, Bambo Raymond, Bambo Filamord and Amai va Cuda, at the orphanage, St. Joseph's house for boys. Especially around 1982–1991, these other-parents and community parents loved and cared for me when I wanted no association with them because they were Indigenous Africans and I wanted nothing to do with my Indigenous heritage or spirituality. You see I had been seduced even at this early age by the power of White supremacy as embodied by Whiteness, capitalism and patriarchy. Here I would like to acknowledge how I referenced and borrowed from Njoki Wane's work titled Reflections on the mutuality of mothering: Women, children and othermothering (2000), to develop the term other-fathering in reference to men nurturing beyond biology. It is through such deep physical and spiritual nurturing that I have come back home to be accountable and responsible to the Ubuntu governance structures. All that is Ubuntu is me and I am all that is Ubuntu. Are the ancestors not in me as I was once in them? Do you see how Ubuntu spirituality connects the past, the present and the future into one, Ubuntu?

Another important spiritual ancestor for me is Gogo (Grandmother) Amanat Mucina and it is my sense that our ancestral and familial bonds are deeper than was communicated to me. Baba addressed her as mother. Without asking Baba, I changed my surname from Dee (my grandfather's name) to the praise name that Baba used to honor me, Mucina (Gogo Amanat's name). I will admit that in the beginning, this change was hard for folks from my paternal family but after having their questions answered about the name change these family members are now comfortably addressing me using either Khomba or Mucina. This also shows that names are not static and can be changed. Whether we welcome it or not, change is coming. At times change seems to be taking us away from our traditions when in fact it is taking us toward our traditions and when we are comfortable in traditions, change comes. Still, honest honorable individuals can transcend a tainted family name through the collective will of the community to immortalize such individuals. For example, Baba has never let me forget that the name Khomba connects me to the spirits of my paternal family. When I meditate to and with my ancestors, I direct my engagement to the great spirits of my Seano (totem) of Khomba[1] (bush baby).

As I locate myself in southern Africa among the Ubuntu, while living here on Turtle Island, I am cognizant that I am a visitor and an unwelcome settler on Indigenous territories. Colonial governance structures and other settlers welcomed me to these Indigenous territories. I also acknowledge our ancestors that were brought here forcibly, those that lost their lives in the middle passage and our relatives that continue to leave their territories due to war and political prosecution. I raise my hands to you in recognitions of the tensions you experience about being here, but I particularly want to acknowledge that as I speak about Ubuntu spirituality, I am cognizant that I am privileging a particular Indigenous spirituality while being in the spiritual context of Turtle Island and its Indigenous peoples. The friendships and familial bonds I have developed with Indigenous peoples on these territories are saving me from colonial amnesia and trickery. I know home physically and spiritually because you have welcomed me into your colonial struggle. Our engagements about Indigenous resurgence shape my everyday actions. Through our relational bonds, I am learning to walk, play, live and work more responsibly. May we continued to turn toward each other with each passing day.

## The World Sense That Gives Rise to Ubuntu Spirituality

The fragment memories and experiences that I know to be Ubuntu have also been nurtured through relational bonds with other Indigenous folks in Canada. I left Southern Africa at the age of 21 (relationally and intellectually, I left Africa a lot sooner) and have lived in Canada for 24 years. Within this context, I have nurtured my Ubuntu scholarship through centering my childhood memories of Ubuntu teachings, researching texts as a way of addressing the gaps in my memories and as a way of gaining new knowledge, which I cross reference by having open dialogues with other Indigenous scholars who center their personal, political and spiritual realities of relational connectivity, which for me is Ubuntuism. Doing this helps me communicate how we as Indigenous peoples matter to each other in the world, while also communicating our convergent and divergent stories as relationally connected. Yet here is the particular knowledge that I know about Ubuntu.

Ubuntu is a Black philosophical and ethical system of thought, from which definitions of humanness, togetherness and social politics of difference arise. I engage Ubuntu philosophy in a more fulsome way in an article published by *The Journal of Pan African Studies* under the title of "Ubuntu orality as a living philosophy," Mucina (2013). Spirit in the Ubuntu worldview is the energy flux in all things. It is the energy that creates the building blocks of all elements, because it is the energy (life force) that we recognize in all things (relation). Spirit is also the energy, which connects all matter to the living energy source of Unkulunkulu (The Great Deviser or The Great Spirit). For me spirituality is the principles and values that allow me to connect to the life force that created all of creation. It is valuing that I am connected to all living forces. It is understanding that everything that I do has an impact on this universe, that we share with other beings. It is understanding that I am part of the web of life. It is knowing that I am the representation of the creative forces that made all of life possible on our planet, Blackness. Yet, I want to be clear that the assertions I make about Blackness are political strategies not meant to discredit other beings or undermining the significant relational connections we have to other beings. I am just asserting what it means to be a spiritual Black Ubuntu, while leaving room for others to assert their own definitions. For me this energy of Blackness is the eternal creative energy of all living material and all of life. Blackness is the eternal energy flow that is the building block of everything. Everything flows back into Blackness and Blackness is unending. Unkulunkulu is this eternal black energy of which I am. My quest to understand Unkulunkulu is my quest to understand my higher self (energy flowing, into, among and emerging out of energy). Spirituality is the active paths that I take to attain and understand this higher self, which is the eternal life energy, Unkulunkulu.

There is much more to Ubuntu philosophy than this. Yet, I am only trying to engage Ubuntu relational worldsense to show our spiritual Indigenous education. It is important that I convey to you my other understanding of Ubuntu and how it relates to you, and why it should matter to you. Ubuntuism can also be viewed as a complex worldsense (beyond privileging the single sense of site as the central sense in knowledge acquisition) that holds in tension the contradictions of trying to highlight our uniqueness as human beings among other human beings. In *The Invention of Women: Making an African Sense of Western Gender Discourses* (1997), the Nigerian theorist, Oyèrónkẹ́ Oyěwùmí, finds the Eurocentric term of worldview unacceptable when speaking about Indigenous African knowledge production because it privileges only one sense of knowing when Indigenous cultures center multiple ways of sensing and knowing the world. To address this shortcoming she has termed the multiple Indigenous ways of knowing the world as worldsense. So, to engage the politics and tensions of the human condition in a diverse world the Indigenous worldsense of Ubuntu centers relational reciprocal engagement in the web of life. I believe this teaching is central to most Indigenous teachings if not all, and its teaching is important to future generations. I hope I have made it clear how I use Ubuntuism as the Indigenous paradigm for understanding and exploring individual actions that add to the collective actions of decolonizing Indigenous spiritual resurgence.

## Orature as Methodology for Spiritual Work

Orature, the encoding into Indigenous memory sacred knowledges through storytelling, is a specific Indigenous Ubuntu methodology that I use to engage my spiritual self, while exercising critical reflections on our social political context so that I am responsible and accountable to the impacts of my actions in our socially changing relationships. All the oratures that I hold convey that we do things in relation to others, meaning all of creation, inclusive of inanimate and animate beings because the materialization of myself occurs in my diverse relations. I am never alone, even in my own body. Like I have said, earlier on, "Was I not in the ancestors as they are now within me?" Yet, in order to survive in the colonial context, Malidoma Patrice Somé (1994), in *Of Water and the Spirit*, reminds us that due to capitalistic colonialism, neo colonialism and the marking of our bodies as erasable commodities, some of us have had to forget the power of our Ubuntu spirituality and the oratures that connected us to these knowledges as a way to survive while, on the other hand, some of us have had to remember our Ubuntu ways in order to survive. To those Black people who have remembered our African ways, I hope the stories that I will share encourage you to keep educating us, the segments of our Black communities that have forgotten our Blackness as a means of survival. To those Black people who have had to forget, suppress and hide their Blackness in order to survive, I hope our intellectual engagement is carving a path for you to spiritually start finding the fragments of our Indigenous Ubuntu knowledges. As diverse as Black scholarship is, it certainly makes one salient point, we are still strong, and we still remember who we are, even if it is only in fragments. If we share our fragmented stories, we get a fuller and richer picture of our Black knowledges, which helps us understand who we are. The Ubuntu has always used the art of orature to extol the power of experience as a teaching tool. I can use no other research tool as this land mass called Africa, for it is the first story and Ben Okri assures us:

> Africa breathes stories. In Africa everything is a story, everything is a repository of stories. Spiders, the wind, a leaf, a tree, the moon, silence, a glance,

> a mysterious old man, an owl at midnight, a sign, a white stone on a branch, a single yellow bird of omen, an inexplicable death, an unprompted laughter, an egg by the river, are all impregnated with stories. In Africa things are stories, they store stories, and they yield stories at the right moment of dreaming, when we are open to the secret side of objects and moods. (2002, p. 115)

Here I quote Ben Okri's narration of stories in an effort to explicate that stories enable the encoding of my embodied forms of knowing and learning, as expressed by Stuart Hall (1997). To me, an Ubuntu, orature is a functional and viable (re)-search approach that one ignores at one's own peril. History reminds us that orature is done with the purpose of maintaining cultural continuity while, at other times, oratures allow for cultural directional change. An orature can allow a culture to regenerate itself because the only constant in our lives is change. Put simply, our oratures are our efforts to create shared interpretation structures about experience so that change has shared meaning. This means for me that spirituality is a process of discovery and relational reunion, which cannot be scripted and must unfold through Sankofa, which is a going back to reclaim that which is good and useful from our past, so that we may proceed into the future with reference about some of our personal, familiar, communal, cultural and creational (all beings) political responsibilities. All this occurs in our Ubuntu African worldsense and when we understand it from our own perspective then we are ready to share and learn from other diverse worldsense that exists in our diverse world. Knowing other worldsense before our own only creates fragmentation within us, because foreign structures are made from the context of their own people and therefore only center their own imagined reality at our expense (Thiong'o, 2008). I would like to conclude this section by stating that even our collective Ubuntu spirituality is an orature about our personal relation to the universal energy, which connects us to everything, Ubuntu. As we are social beings, we try to share these unique experiences through symbols, texts, cultural rituals, which can all be captured as Oratures. Stories are our way of trying to matter to each other, of trying to find common meaning from our unique experiences as this confirms our interrelatedness. Spirituality allows us to understand our common relatedness without undermining our individuality and uniqueness because we all come to know each other through stories.

## Can the Spirit Be Colonized?

The answer to this question is no, but let me put this answer in context. Among the Ngoni and Chewa, adulthood is not measured through the milestones of years lived; this is not to say that years of living do not equate to knowledge gained. The point is that a person acquires adulthood through developing their spiritual self in relation to community and all of creation. To understand such realities and spiritual truths requires great strength of character and maturity. This is why in the past the community unanimously decided on who was ready to perform the spiritual ritual of coming of age. Although there was an integral part of communal engagement and participation, the spiritual ritual of coming of age was primarily an inner journey of acquiring self-knowledge, wisdom and medicine to understand one's connection and relation to the universe, as part of it and being of it. Such knowledge was and is essential for our spiritual survival and physical well-being. However, colonialism every single day tries to undermine this way of being through its imposition of foreign worldsense, spirituality and governance. Here I mean spirit to mean relational connection to each other and to all beings because as Ubuntu, we come from the energy flux, which is in us, around us and in everything (Mutwa, 1969). Spirits can also be more than just people because there is the spirit of animals, plants, sacred places and sacred waters, which can speak to us and advise us. Owen Burnham, in *African Wisdom,* reports that the African world:

> ...is a world in which wisdom and knowledge are the keys to survival in the multi-dimensional spiritual universe where we are never far from the past, present and the future as represented by the ancestral spirits that are all around us. (2000, p. 12)

Yet, I would like to tell you the truth as I know based on our oratures, which have cascaded into my memories and experiences. As I prepare to tell you these oratures, I am suddenly aware that colonialism and its insidious diversionary trickery have failed to colonize my spiritual self because to tell you these oratures I must journey into the depths of my inner spiritual self, which paradoxically leads me to the universal energy flux. From this inner spiritual self, I find our medicines, which heal my body and my mind by connecting me to my universal self, the energy flux of Blackness. I am aware that I am using Blackness as a political strategy in this context, but how else can I breathe power, energy and life into the sleeping energy flux of Blackness, which has been lulled into sleep by colonial racism. I must waken the spirit of Black people. To share an orature is to reach out, to reach out is to express a sense of connection, a sense of connection is to believe in oneness. I share because of our spiritual oneness and hope my story sharing demonstrates that we can still get to our inner selves and acquire the medicines that we need to be spiritually and physically whole. I tell you all this, because I want you to remember that the spirit cannot be colonized. Our bodies can be fooled, our minds can be fooled but the spirit is beyond the philosophy of the physical world. Spirit is the energy in all things. Spirit is a relational connection beyond the political power maneuvering of social relations. Spirit is relational connection in the chaos of political maneuvering, and because it cannot be colonized, it creates hope by showing us the possibilities of re-establishing relational connections. I would like to share two dream oratures that demonstrate that the spirit cannot be colonized.

Reading the work of Leela Fernandes (2003) *Transforming Feminist Practice: Non-violence, Social Justice and the Possibility of Spiritualized Feminism* made me remember a dream that I had some time back. In the dream I was back in the orphanage, where I lived from 1982 until I "left care" in 1991. In this dream, I had gone back in time, yet I was still in my adult body. It seems my spirit was sending me back to confront the abusive traumas that I experienced at the hands of the Anglican priest, who ran the orphanage. Father Little was a priest who firmly believed that if you spared the rod then you spoiled the child. Yet, when investigations began into his actions, due to sexual abuse accusations, it seems he was not willing to face the same level of hushed disciplinary measures that he so generously merited out and instead chose to commit suicide. Dressed in his church service clothes, and I am sure he carefully chose the right colors to communicate the appropriate message as priests do with specific robes. I wonder what he was saying in death that he could not say in life. There is a lot to talk about here, but in this case, I am here to address the dream. Being an Englishman, Father Little was a stickler for good English table manners. Slouching on the table or having your elbows on the table could earn you a strapping from blackjack. Blackjack was half a meter of black rubber floorboard trimming. Depending on your misdemeanor, blackjack could be administered on your hand or ass. When you showed up at Father Little's office door, his first assumption was that you had committed some kind of offense and therefore would inquire if you were visiting blackjack.

A visit with blackjack always meant three lashes on your hand or six lashings on your ass. Father Little would start the disciplinary consequences almost ritualistically, by stating: "Keep your hand very still or I could break your fingers or hand, if you move unexpectedly." The first lash on your hand always seemed to send you into shock and you were never too sure how much pain you were experiencing and if this was, your first time being disciplined in this manner, you would have believed that the lashings were not so bad. However, the administration of the second lashing seemed to incite a severe pain reaction, which cleared up any confusion you had about the severity of the kind of pain you were experiencing. At this point, your hand would be swelling up before your eyes. Every nerve ending on your hand felt as if it was on fire. I never met a boy who was willing to take the third strapping without pleading for mercy and failing this, asking to switch hands. However, the rules were very clear, only the left hand; in case Father Little broke your hand, it was essential to him that you still continued your school work.

In this particular dream, Father Little and I were having a disagreement, and to keep me submissive and subservient, he said, "Watch your manners or else," and from his tone, I understood that I was being threatened with blackjack. But, in this dream, instead of being fearful, I challenged father to explain, what good manners he meant, as I was not sure if they meant anything for my African context or if he was immersing me into colonial servitude? The audacity of my challenge sent a shock wave of silence among the other orphanage boys, because it was uncustomary for anyone to publicly challenge Father Little.

Without saying anything, Father Little got up and reached into a locker for a car crowbar. It was unmistakable to me that he intended to kill me with the crowbar, but as he swung at me, I managed to move out of the way and lessen the blow against my back. Angered by his vicious attack on me, I wrench the car crowbar out of his hand and as I held the car crowbar in my hands, contemplating my next move, it turned into 3 meters of heavy-duty work chain. Vengefully, I subdued and restrained him, but I would be lying if I did not tell you that I squeezed those chains until he struggled with fear and humiliation. As he grasped for air, he pleaded for me to release him. As I released him, I looked into his eyes with a smug sense of justice, but when he looked up at me, I was he and he was I. I woke up in a cold sweat, screaming, "No I am nothing like you." I could not figure out what this dream meant until reading the work of Leela Fernandes (2003). I am now aware why this dream has haunted me for so long. This dream shows how I wanted to create binaries between Indigenous social injustice and colonial exploitative actions in order to justify my own actions of retribution as justified social justice. Yet if we see the dream as spirit, talking to me, then another lesson emerges. For me, the spirit wants me to remember that abuse, injustice and colonialism occur at the intersection of patriarchal accumulative power, which calls to me every single day. As differently as father Little and I were called to perform colonial patriarchy, we both did perform colonial patriarchy and yes, I have a right to be angry about the injustice I suffered but I inflict the same level if not more of suffering on others through my participation in capitalistic accumulation. Hence, my everyday actions of resistance and transformative learning must be grounded in everyday acts of resistance and resurgence (Corntassel, 2012), while being grounded in relational spiritual Ubuntu practice.

My second dream, interesting enough, is also set in the orphanage. It starts with Zimbabwean armed soldiers coming into the orphanage and asking us if we would like to help them hunt down the White colonial killers of our parents and families. Again, like in the first dream, the excitement of vengeance for the disintegration of my family by White people makes me extend my arms, so that I can receive my death bringer gift. The coolness of the weapon stirs up the uncaring emotions in me. I think to myself: "Let them all fucking die, let them taste death like we have, let them feel our pain." I start to fire my weapon and my other orphaned brothers respond in kind. As I look at us, I am aware that we are all Black boys ready to kill the White enemy. The Black soldiers order us to halt firing our weapons and we stop. The songbird drops dead at my feet. Its beautiful head has been shot off. Sadness and vengeance oppose each other in my mind.

Even despite this bad luck omen of the dead bird, the commander uses it to his advantage by yelling: "You have blood on your hands, there is no going back." In my vengeful violent outrage, I have killed the songbird, I have silenced the love song, and its body lies dead at my feet. I start crying because I did not mean for the songbird to die. Again for me, this is the spirit not allowing me to be fooled by token talk of decolonizing. The Ubuntu spirit does not allow for false binaries to be created, the spirit seeks the truth, social justice, relational love and above all seeks to make us all responsible and accountable to our actions. Even when whole institutions support our actions, the Ubuntu spirit guides us to relational accountability and responsibility. So, when one of the soldiers yells at me to stop crying like a baby (boxing me into a specific masculinity), I know we are disposable to them. I know that our Black skin does not bind us to a fraternity of relational love. So, for survival we cooperate with them and to show that we are ready for the task, I yell to the other boys: "Let us go and kill the White man."

The response from my orphanage brothers to my call of action is weak so I repeat my call until it is clear to us and the soldiers that we will hunt down and kill the White man. The commander informs us that the White devils are in the woods ahead of us, so our job is to flash them out by combing the woods from our end to the other end. The commander also informs us that his soldiers will take up two position, half will sweep behind us and the other half will wait for us at the other end of the woods. We start to sweep the woods while firing our weapons into the air, and within a few minutes, it is clear to us that we are driving out mostly old White people, young children and women. I am disgusted that we are herding defenseless people toward death. As we emerge on the other side of the woods, it is clear that we have been used by the soldiers to root out unarmed White people. I start to run to the commander to express my outrage, when I hear gunfire from behind. I turn and find that the rear soldiers are indiscriminately killing all of us. As this is happening, the commander is yelling, "drop your weapons if you want to live." I throw my weapon away and drop to the ground. The chaos of people being herded to army trucks is now my shield against being seen. In my path is a brick BBQ pit. I crawl into it and start to cover myself with the ashes. An old White man says in Shona: "I see you have eaten from the tree of knowledge." This phrase is connected to other sacred dreams I have had and because of that, I am angry and want to question why he (the old colonizer) uses our language. Have his people not taken enough from us already.

But I remain silent because I want to live and to ensure that no one sees me. The old White man starts to help cover me, but he does it in a manner that makes him look senile so that he does not draw attention to me. As if he is just rambling to himself, he says to me to, "Tell my kinfolk how I died." I whisper, to the old White man, "who are your people?" But as these words leave my mouth, I want to take them back because from the angle of my hiding place I can see his tattoos on his arms. He is one of those old retired colonial settler soldiers. On his arms are the symbolic marks that represent his kill tally NUMBER. He is a killer of Black people. I awake and question the teaching point of this dream.

These spiritual dreams remind me that our need for social justice should never be grounded in colonial realities because within a colonial context, colonialism reproduces itself. Yes, it is true that we may affect the ways that colonial structures function, but we are talking about degrees of colonial variations, but in the end, we still reproduce colonialism. If we do not transform the colonial structures that we live under, colonial structures will only keep mutating and reproducing themselves. To stop the mutating of colonialism, bell hooks (1994) and Leela Fernandes' (2003) work on transformative learning and engagement is grounded in responsible and accountable relational connections, which for me is spiritual love without the restrictiveness of religious practice. I, therefore, agree with Leela Fernandes (2003) that retribution cannot be used as a form of social justice by the oppressed because without the spiritual guidance of Ubuntu worldsense, we enact colonial vengeance and violence on others or ourselves as a way of getting even. This being said, I believe retribution has an important place in the healing process of those that have experienced injustice. I see retribution as not an effort to get even with the perpetrators of violence and oppression. I see retribution as acknowledging a deed by the perpetrator, which has caused injustice and is, therefore, an offering or a symbolic gesture to show a willingness to mend the damaged relationship. This shows a willingness to create resolution. Restitution and retribution are for me the precondition for creating a lasting resolution grounded in healing and truth, which can lead to forgiveness. To bypass this approach is to risk igniting the issue at a later date because unresolved injustice resides in our hearts and in the unchanged governmental institutions of colonialism. Until these injustices stop and some effort is made to mend the damage done to the relationship, there cannot be justice, and forgiveness becomes an empty word. I am not also saying that we should only be spiritual and nonviolent when whole institutional governance structures are stacked against us. Especially, when the objective of the aggressor is total genocide and annihilation, how are you going to be nonviolent? I believe violence cannot be justified in most situations but I believe it can be justified in self-defense. Self-defense is a natural response, corner a rat, a snake, a rabbit or a bird and you will see what happens. I do not believe pre-emptive strikes are self-defense. I do not believe the threat of violence warrants a military attack. For me self-defense is the act of preserving lives in the face of annihilation. These actions can range from verbal interventions to migrating and finally military action. Yet, the act of killing is always a regrettable one and its consequence is that we have to live with the haunting spirit of the dead.

## Conclusion

As a way of concluding, I want to restate that I am connected to my ancestors through our naming of geographical and social memories as conveyed in our stories. We tell our orature as our efforts of reaching out to our spiritual ancestors and to each other in the living realm. The names of our traditional geography location let me know how my ancestors experienced these spaces and locations. How my ancestors named these places speaks to how these places spoke to them in specific ways. Meaning the spirits of these lands spoke to the spirits of my ancestors, who used the symbols of art and language to convey this relationship, which is grounded in respect for the land as part of the sacred elements for human survival on this earth. Another connection is that the land and human being are all a part of the same creative energy force that makes all possible. Hence, in spirit form, the land and our ancestors can communicate because they are of the same energy, the eternal Black creative energy flow. We know this because our ancestors taught us to honor our Ubuntu spirits by meditating within our sacred locations but how do we do this when we are on the territories of other Indigenous peoples? As an Ubuntu, I was taught at a young age to always introduce myself to the people of the new territories I was on. I was taught that it was my responsibility to inquire about how to honor and respect the people, their ancestors and their territories. Yet, when I came to Turtle Island, my desire for colonial acceptance had made me forget these Indigenous ways of being. Just when I was accepting my marginal place in the colonial project of Canada, the spirits steered me into dialogue with Indigenous folks from these territories. With each day, all my relationships are getting stronger because my spirit could not be colonized when I had willingly signed up to be colonized. I am also learning that it is never too late to do the right thing. Trust the spirits and they will guide you to relational connection and real decolonizing actions.

## Note

1. Khomba is a Swahili word for Bushbaby and Isinkwe or Nhlathini Umntwana is the equivalent in Zulu.

## References

Burnham, O. (2000). *African wisdom*. London: Judy Piatkus.

Corntassel, J. (2012). Re-envisioning resurgence: Indigenous pathways to decolonization and sustainable self-determination. *Decolonization: Indigeneity, Education & Society, 1*(1), 86–101.

Creation in African thought. (n.d.). http://www.afrikaworld.net/afrel/creation-in-atr.htm.

Fernandes, L. (2003). *Transforming feminist practice: Non-violence, social justice and the possibility of spiritualized feminism*. San Francisco: Aunt Lute Books.

Hall, S. (1997). *Representation: Cultural representations and signifying practices*. Thousand Oaks, CA: Sage.

hooks, b. (1994). *Teaching to transgress: Education as the practice of freedom*. New York: Routledge/Taylor & Francis Group.

Mathabane, M. (1986). *Kaffir boy: The true story of a black youth's coming of age in apartheid South Africa*. New York: Macmillan.

Mucina, D. D. (2013). Ubuntu orality as a living philosophy. *The Journal of Pan African Studies, 6*(4), 18–35.

Mutwa, C. V. (1969). *My people, my Africa* (1st American ed.). New York: John Day.

Okri, B. (2002). *A way of being free*. London: Phoenix House.

Oyěwùmí, O. (1997). *The invention of women: Making an African sense of Western gender discourses*. Minneapolis: University of Minnesota Press.

Somé, M. P. (1994). *Of water and the spirit: Ritual, magic, and initiation in the life of an African shaman*. New York: Putnam.

Thiong'o, N. W. (2008). *Moving the centre: The struggle for cultural freedoms*. London: James Currey.

Wane, N. N. (2000). Reflections on the mutuality of mothering: Women, children, and othermothering. *Journal of the Association for Research on Mothering, 2*(2), 105–116.

CHAPTER 11

# Shedding of the Colonial Skin: The Decolonial Potentialities of Dreaming

*Kimberly L. Todd*

## Dream Narrative: The Cannibal and the Waterfall

I want to begin by sharing a powerful dream that I had not long ago. Before beginning I would like to mention I am grateful to Elder Renee Thomas-Hill for her wisdom and insight she shared with me about this and other dreams and to traditional teacher and prolific author Lee Maracle, for her assistance, wisdom and guidance in seeking help with the unfolding of this dream.

The dream begins in a lush forest that is warm and dense with vegetation. It is raining heavily and increasing the humidity in the air. The only part of me present in the dream is my consciousness and it resides in the mind of a man. I know in the dream that I am in Rwanda despite the fact that I have never visited this country in waking life. The man in whose head I am residing is an older white man and he is moving through the forest quickly. Because I am in his mind, I can observe his thoughts, and he is ravenous for food—the hunger insatiable. His thoughts swirl obsessively

K. L. Todd (✉)
University of Toronto, Toronto, ON, Canada
e-mail: k.todd@mail.utoronto.ca





N. N. Wane et al. (eds.), *Decolonizing the Spirit in Education and Beyond*, Spirituality, Religion, and Education,
https://doi.org/10.1007/978-3-030-25320-2_11

over his hunger, again and again. He locates another white man in the distance, a younger man with shaggy brown hair and he sets his sights on him. Suddenly the old man rushes up behind him, grabs him and sinks his teeth into the left side of the brunette's neck and begins to devour him at the bank of a river. Blood flows everywhere and begins to turn the water red and the only thought in the mind of the cannibal is to continue satiating his unending hunger. At this point in the dream my consciousness is observing his and there is no repulsion or reaction because there is no differentiating between myself and the cannibal. As the cannibal eats, he looks up because he senses something deeply powerful close by. It is a thunderous and gushing waterfall and now he becomes filled with abject terror. He shrinks away from the waterfall, trying to hide from it because he knows it has the power to destroy him. I, however, am drawn to the waterfall and it is as if my consciousness or soul is pulled toward it, as if my soul is free to move about as desired and I materialize, in my own body a few feet away from the waterfall. The cannibal then leaves my own consciousness because the waterfall encompasses all of my awareness and is summoning me. The waterfall is the most beautiful vision that I have ever laid my eyes upon. There is immense energy pulsating and reverberating outwardly. It is cleansing, healing and life-giving. It has a profound affect on me, enlivening me with a deep-seated sense of awe, wonder and peace, and the only thing I could do is move towards it.

Then I immediately jerk awake because of a disruptive alarm from my cell phone and I am overcome by the power of the dream wanting to desperately reenter the dreamscape. Upon waking, I realize that I was able to navigate the enfolded sacred dimensions of Earth and it was amazingly a glimpse behind the veil. The cannibal speaks to me of many destructive and embedded ways of being during this time and in times past colonialism, capitalism, extraction, the continual burning of fossil fuels in the wake of climate change and the unending consumption and destruction of life on this planet. The cannibal as an enfolded symbol encapsulates aspects of our broken, fragmented selves, our destructive colonial systems and structures and our deep-seated lack of connection to ourselves, our own indwelling spirit, our wider community, our home the Earth. I knew that the waterfall had the power to destroy the cannibal, transforming him back into a man, a man with a soul, a conscience and the capacity to love. Now I know that waterfall was pure love, a love that I could physically, emotionally and spiritually feel. This dream demonstrated to me the Earth's love for all of us. A love that literally flows from Her to us, and for us—because we are all Her children and love is our life-giving source.

I am extremely grateful for the many ways in which the spirit of the Earth has visited me; however, this dream was not for me alone. It is a dream for you too, dear reader and all of her creation. The Earth's love has the capacity to transform us all in Her image. As such, what follows is an epistemological theorizing of the decolonial potentialities of dreaming so that collectively we might all reawaken to our belonging and begin healing our fragmented selves, moving toward a collective dream of a thriving planet for all life forms. The Earth is summoning us through the beauty that surrounds us, through our intuitions and through our dreams that visit us in the night and we have an individual and collective responsibility to answer Her call.

## Locating the Self

Dreaming has taught me the language of spirit. It has taught me to read dreams. It literally initiated me into the realm of spirit through the unfolding of a recurring dream. Over the course of a year I had an initial dream of a sea turtle, and a week later I saw a sea turtle while snorkeling in Oman, and then continued to dream and see sea turtles everywhere in my waking life. Something clearly was trying to tell me something; but I did not know what it was. This process culminated in a year to the day from when the first dream occurred. It occurred while sitting on a bus reading a book entitled *Dancing on Our Turtle's Back* (2011) by Leanne Simpson where she describes the inherent power of dreams and visions and how they can help us to bring new worlds into being (pp. 70 and 149). The Sea Turtle brought me to the realization that She embodies spirit of Earth, She came to me to remind me of my belonging to Her. Through this year of the Sea Turtle, I was birthed anew and it took me the full year to determine the meaning behind Her symbolism. I can now in hindsight understand that this process was actually the beginning of the shedding of my colonial conditioning and is still continually decolonizing me. After that year I could no longer adhere to the worldview I had been born into. The dreaming process completely ruptured that worldview; it was as if I had undergone a radical re-membering of who I was. Perhaps, not unlike a soul retrieval, I experienced the great power inherent in dreaming and realized that it should be valued because it provides a gateway into the sacred that can help initiate and facilitate the decolonizing process. This chapter is my attempt to examine two seemingly separate bodies of literature surrounding dreaming and decolonization in an effort to understand the decolonial potentialities of dreaming to help elevate the value of dreaming so that we can begin the collective soul retrieval toward healing and empowerment that the colonial project has attempted to shatter.

## Introduction

Dreaming is universal; it occurs nightly while we sleep, a process that is essential for our survival. The imprints of these dreams have varying affects on the dreamer. Often, the dreamer awakens with loose and fleeting fragments of the dream, but as time passes, they dissipate from awakened memory. Sometimes, a single dream can be an emotionally charged experience, following the dreamer like an unbidden haunting throughout the day. Other times, dreams appear to bring visitations from those who have passed on. Some dreamers have dreams which alter the course of their lives. *But what are dreams really? What are their inherent potentials? What do they do for us and what are they capable of doing for us?*

This chapter seeks to investigate an epistemological theorizing of the decolonial potentialities of dreaming. I will attempt this task by exploring the inherent value in cultivating a relationship with dreaming. I will also examine the Western world's failure to value dreaming by examining the Cartesian Split and colonialism. Subsequently, I will briefly outline decolonization and how cultivating a relationship with dreaming can contribute to a shedding of the colonial skin and provide a personal gateway into the sacred.

Dreaming is a powerful process that everyone engages in, whether or not they remember their dreams and thus, the mystery of dreams has attracted much speculation and study (Tedlock, 1992). Consequently, it is necessary before moving on to be clear about what exactly is meant by dreaming. Barbara Tedlock in her book *The Woman in the Shaman's Body: Reclaiming the Feminine in Religion and Medicine* beautifully defines dreaming:

> Dreaming is a universal experience, one that we may attempt to induce or avoid, remember or forget. It can occur while we are awake or asleep. The waking path consists of guided fantasies known as omens, waking dreams, and visions. On the sleeping side are personal dreams (based on everyday events or wishes of the soul), prophetic dreams, archetypal dreams, nightmares, and lucid dreams. (Tedlock, 2005, p. 103)

The above definition is all inclusive of dreaming. I refer primarily to dreams while sleeping; however, the understanding of dreaming can spill out into the visionary episteme (Irwin, 1994) and the imaginative. When speaking about the definition of dreaming, it is also necessary to grasp the various cultural associations attached to dreaming as dreaming is understood in different ways depending on the cultural influences of the dreamer, and there is great fluidity in all aspects of dreaming. Perhaps, it is this fluidity that contributes to some of the enigmatic principles of dreaming. Carl Jung, in his book *Dreams*, describes the unconscious aspect of the mind as autonomous, which can contribute to the mysterious nature of the dreaming psyche (2011). Jung writes:

> The conscious mind allows itself to be trained like a parrot, but the unconscious does not-which is why St. Augustine thanked God for not making him responsible for his dreams. The unconscious is an autonomous psychic entity; any efforts to drill it are only apparently successful, and moreover are harmful to consciousness. It is and remains beyond the reach of subjective arbitrary control, in a realm where nature and her secrets can be neither improved upon nor perverted, where we can listen but not meddle. (2011, p. 120)

The autonomous nature of the subconscious is for me one of its most fascinating components of the mind and has fuelled my curiosity. Dreams can touch a wide array of fields and that may be why there are many possible ways in which to examine the role of dreams. I want to begin this chapter by discussing the importance of cultivating a relationship with dreams.

## Cultivating a Relationship with Dreaming

Dreams tap into feelings and emotions that are generally unprocessed and help in the mediating process (Jaenke, 2001; Quattrocchi, 2005). They provide tools to begin thinking differently and more creatively about the problems that plague the dreamer's life. Cultivating a relationship with dreaming is exceedingly valuable because dreams are wonderful teachers. Leanne Simpson in *Dancing on Our Turtle's Back* writes the following about dreams: "Dreamtime has always been a great teacher for me. I see my dreams as guides or mentors, as the Grandfathers and Grandmothers giving me direction in my life. Dreams are how my own spirit guides me through my life" (2011, pp. 35–36). Dreams open the dreamer to a multitude of layers of the self by tapping into the unconscious and exposing the dreamer to fears, desires, intentions and possibilities. Valuable knowledge about the self can be extracted, absorbed and understood. However, the dreamer has to engage with the dreaming process which entails that the dreamer cultivates a relationship with dreaming.

What does cultivating a relationship with dreaming involve? As a starting point, it requires an ability to recall dreams upon waking. This can be fragments or snippets of the dream and any accompanying emotions that are residually left with the dreamer upon waking. At times, recalling dreams can be a difficult process due to morning routines, a lack of sleep and additionally sociocultural dismissal of the dreaming process as is the case in the West. Cultivating a relationship with dreaming also requires a sense of curiosity and open-mindedness directed toward the meaning inherent in the dream. Additionally, a curious desire to seek answers is critical to facilitate this relationship process (Simpson, 2011) and a sense of perseverance due to the symbolic and imagistic nature of dreams. There are a variety of strategies to help dreamers remember their dreams, such as repeating the dream aloud upon waking, jotting down notes in the middle of the night and discussing dreams within trusting relationships such as with family and friends can also be helpful in deriving meaning from the dream and help with recalling dreams (Quattrocchi, 2005). Marina Quattrocchi in her book *Dreamwork Uncovered: How Dreams Can Create Inner Harmony, Peace and Joy* (2005) writes about strategies to help dreamers remember their dreams. Keeping a journal of dreams is additionally a helpful process, particularly for pulling out common themes over time, and as a tool for remembering the dreams (Quattrocchi, 2005). Utilizing a trusted dream dictionary is an exceedingly helpful tool when it comes to decoding the symbols inherent in dreams. Determining the meaning of dreams relies heavily on resonance and intuition as they both help the dreamer to locate the correct meanings symbolically embedded in the dreams.

Ultimately, cultivating a relationship with dreaming is a dialogical process and it is through the process of continual seeking that the relationship is cultivated. Dreams, whether they are valued or not, will continue to come and with them the seeds of new possibilities. They come despite the patriarchal and colonial histories that have tried to repress them; dreams come because perhaps they have something of value to teach us about our belonging. Therefore, the next two sections will delve into the Cartesian Split and colonialism in order to explain how the split between matter and spirit came to be, and how this sense of human disconnection was spread throughout the world.

## The Cartesian Split

The separation of matter and spirit has its connection in the Cartesian Split which began in the seventeenth century (Tedlock, 1992). René Descartes was instrumental in this regard, in terms of stripping philosophy of its inherent connection to soul via Artistotelean and Christian ideals (Colman, 2017, p.33). Which over time created a schism between matter and spirit rendering matter dead and lifeless and hollowing out the understanding of spirit that is inherent in matter (Colman, 2017). Thus, science began to revolve around, and explain in some manner or fashion, how to try to bring nature under control, as if it were something separate from humanity. As such, the Earth became something to be exploited for human consumption and desires and, with it, followed a loss of life. I will utilize Tedlock's summation of the Cartesian Split and how it served to invalidate dreaming. She writes:

> But, as Carl O'Nell (1976) observed, while dreaming was already depressed in value within the West by the time of the emergence of naturalistic or scientific thought, it was not until the development of Cartesian mechanistic dualism in the seventeenth century that dreams were finally placed totally within the realm of fantasy or irrational experience. It must be remembered, however, that the Cartesian irreducible dualism of 'spirit' and 'matter,' which denies the common principle from which the terms of this duality proceeded by a process of polarization, was an historical development within Western philosophy. (Tedlock, 1992, p. 2)

The Cartesian Split with its schism between matter and spirit has left residual impressions on the Western psyche to the point where dreams are rendered nonsensical, if not useless. Tracing the origins of how the Cartesian Split emerged throughout Western history is useful in understanding what work needs to be done to heal the split and elevate the inherent value of dreaming.

Warren Colman in his essay entitled, *Soul in the World: Symbolic Culture as Medium for Psyche* (2017), discusses the Cartesian Split. Colman also writes, "The aim of this deanimation was to clear the way for science to explore the world in terms of purely physical mechanisms" (Colman, 2017, p. 33). In order for science to be able to understand the mechanisms of life, they had to open up, dissect and sever the very connections that made life possible, and through this process, matter was perceived as inert, lifeless and lacking any imbued sense of spirit. Colman writes about both the benefits and losses of the residual affects of Cartesianism:

> The scientific method developed in the 17th century has been spectacularly successful as a means of understanding the natural world and harnessing its forces for industrial and technological transformation. Yet this has come at a high price, often described in terms of the desacralization and pillaging of the natural world, together with the alienation, isolation and loss of meaning that characterize Western societies. (Colman, 2017, p. 33)

However, the Western world still holds hard and fast to a Cartesian worldview, invalidating a multitude of ways of communing the world and leading to severe disconnection from self, community and ultimately the planet. The human capacity for revelation, intuition and connection has become invalidated; these qualities have shaped so much of collective human history, but in the Western context it has been hauled out of the bodies, minds and souls. Dreaming, in this instance, is only one of many examples of what has been lost with the Cartesian Split's mechanistic worldview. In the next section, an examination of colonialism will demonstrate the need for decolonization and an understanding of dreaming as one potential vehicle for decolonization.

## Colonialism

It is necessary to unveil the destructive nature of the colonial logics and how the intergenerational affects seep into all aspects of body, mind and soul for humanity at large. Colonization has sought to sever bodies from land, history, ancestries, languages and spiritualities. It has sought to take the myriad ways in which people commune, connect and participate in the world and to dismember them. Colonization is an ongoing process that continually recreates itself utilizing the four pillars of the colonial matrix of power (Mignolo, 2011).

I will begin by discussing the structures of the colonial matrix of power in Walter Mignolo's book *The Darker Side of Western Modernity* (2011) and subsequently delve into the relationship between the colonizer and the colonized (Memmi, 1965) examining how this has impacted cognition and an understanding of the self.

The colonial matrix of power is a framework that exposes the pervasive affects of colonialism throughout time, place and space (Mignolo,

2011). The term was first outlined by Anibal Quijano and Mignolo further explored its depths and implications in his book (2011). Mignolo premises that "that the colonial matrix of power is the very foundational structure of Western civilization" (2011, p. 16). Mignolo unveils the colonial logics by locating the four pillars on which colonialism operates through constructs of power and control (2011). The first pillar is comprised of knowledge and subjectivity, the second pillar is racism, gender and sexuality, the third pillar is economy and the fourth is authority (Mignolo, 2011, pp. 8–9).

The first pillar of the colonial matrix of power is knowledge and subjectivity (Mignolo, 2011, pp. 8–9). Mignolo writes "Knowledge in the colonial matrix of power was a double-edged sword: on the one hand, it was the mediation to the ontology of the world as well as a way of being in the world (subjectivity)" (2011, p. 13). Thus, colonialism generates knowledge and in so doing alters the subjectivity of others by degrading knowledge forms produced by colonized bodies. This move to erasure by colonialism causes severe intergenerational trauma that cascades through time distorting and fragmenting colonized people's sense of place, languages, knowledges and spiritualities by attempting to replace their ontologies, languages, epistemologies and worldviews.

The second pillar of the colonial matrix of power is racism, gender and sexuality (Mignolo, 2011, pp. 8–9). Control is enacted by the colonial powers through the dehumanization of human beings on the basis of their race, gender and sexuality. This provides a means of signaling out people, invalidating their person and oppressing them for the benefit of the colonizer. Memmi discusses how racism is one of the primary weapons of the colonizers:

> Racism appears then, not as an incidental detail, but as a consubstantial part of colonialism. It is the highest expression of the colonial system and one of the most significant features of the colonialist. Not only does it establish a fundamental discrimination between colonizer and colonized, a *sine qua non* of colonial life, but it also lays the foundation for the immutability of this life. (Memmi, 1965, p. 74)

Through this dehumanizing process, the colonized body internalizes the degradation of the colonizer (Memmi, 1965). Patriarchy which preceded colonialism, but also deeply influences colonialism attacks colonized bodies through gender and sexuality (Sjöö & Mor, 1991). Further dehumanizing people on the basis of their gender and sexuality, thus from a colonial standpoint a white male who is heterosexual is considered "fully human" and anyone who deviated from this, whether by race, gender or sexuality, is perceived "as less than human" or "not human at all." Therefore, gender, sexuality and racism are the basis from which the colonial project enacts its oppression. When all that the colonized body encounters is everything that they are not, in addition to a continual erosion of anything that can give them a sense of self, identity and pride, a cycle of hatred for the self emerges within the psyche. This can result in what Anne Anlin Cheng refers to as racial melancholy, which she outlines in her book *The Melancholy of Race* (2001). "On the one hand, anyone who has been confronted by racism face to face understands the complicated, vexing web of feelings that ensues: shock mixed with expectation, anger with shame, and yet again shame for feeling shame" (Cheng, 2001, p. x). Racial Melancholy is characterized by the internalization of racism that results in a deep melancholia that is both gripping and pervasive (Cheng, 2001). The subject yearns for a sense of completeness in their being, which is other than what they are and, at the same time, are confronted with the impossibility, namely that one cannot change their skin colour and so experience deep-seated grief (Cheng, 2001, p. xi). Ultimately, for the colonized body, it is not wholeness that they perceive but a fragmented self that is forever failing at being the colonizer (Memmi, 1965). This second pillar of the colonial matrix of power is insidious and effective in its means of dehumanizing colonized bodies (Mignolo, 2011).

The third pillar of the colonial matrix of power is economy (Mignolo, 2011, pp. 8–9). The economy generates and grows wealth and resources, sustaining the ongoing colonial structures. Mignolo utilizes the analysis of Karen Armstrong's understanding of the shift in the economy in Europe and its colonies that enabled the West to "*reproduce its resources indefinitely*" and this was achieved through "...reinvesting the surplus in order to increase production" (Mignolo, 2011, p. 6). However, the crux of the matter is that the economy which sustains the colonial matrix of power was birthed, and is in fact continually generated through the expendability of colonized bodies (Mignolo, 2011). The economy upholds the colonial matrix of power through the degradation of colonized bodies and generates wealth by means of their exploitation. This third pillar has helped to co-construct Western modernity via the degradation of colored bodies under ongoing colonialism continues to reproduce itself in new and created forms, but with same colonial structures (Mignolo, 2011).

The fourth pillar of the colonial matrix of power is authority (Mignolo, 2011, pp. 8–9). Authority that is achieved and maintained through force, domination, violence and genocide. Land, wealth, resources and greed have always been at the core of colonial violence and it was sought out by any means necessary. In relation to North America, this took place under the guise of "terra nullius" which invalidated the humanity of Indigenous people living on Turtle Island. Authority is maintained through systems that can enact violence at will and under the protection of "law" and/or governmental structures, which is always determined by power. The military and the police are examples of how authority is maintained in a colonial settler state. Authority also dictates epistemologies and ontologies and particular versions of history that are disseminated. Therefore, authority is a pillar that upholds the colonial matrix of power and it reverberates throughout systems and structures creating everything in its own likeness and degrading other ways of knowing and being in the world.

What are the costs of colonial violence? How to encapsulate the loss of life, human life, plant life and animal life? Ultimately, what better metaphor to use than a collective soul loss? How to begin calling back the pieces of our collective soul? What songs do we sing to do this? What rituals do we enact? What ceremonies? This fragmentation has been caused by colonialism continually and incessantly on colonized bodies. Moreover, in order to enact and perpetuate such violence, a severing of connection and love had to occur in the colonizers as well causing its own brand of intergenerational trauma for such dehumanization and fragmentation to disseminate. Perhaps the cannibal in my opening dream narrative aptly conveys and illustrates this deep internal disconnection and the need to acknowledge this loss of connection as a first step toward decolonial transformation. Eduardo Duran, a psychologist who works with patients on healing ongoing colonial trauma, writes the following in his book *Healing the Soul Wound*:

> It is important to note that decolonizing does not apply only to Native People or other people of color who have been colonized. So-called mainstream Westerners also may want to decolonize from the collective consumer colonization process that has been imposed on them. Colonization processes affect human beings, at a deep soul level… (2006, p. 14)

I hope to demonstrate this point onward and how the decolonial potentialities inherent in dreaming can begin to heal the fragmentation that the colonial project has enacted across the world. Perhaps, it is in dreaming that the ceremonies, the rituals and the songs lay dormant, waiting for us to reawaken to their power, a power potentially great enough to enact a collective soul retrieval through each and every one of us, calling back the pieces of our dismembered selves so that we can begin healing and transforming our destructive systems and structures.

## Dreaming and Shedding the Colonial Skin

The imperative behind this work is that decolonization is a process in which everyone should engage. Decolonization is for everyone, because it works to reconnect humanity to all facets of their being. Since colonialism has attempted to sever the means of communing with the world through dehumanization, dispossession and erasures, returning to relational ways of connecting is an act of renunciation of colonialism and, more importantly, an act of renewal. Decolonizing needs to begin first internally in the mind, the body and the spirit and then move outward to transform existing colonial structures. The fact that we are currently living in the age of climate change speaks to deep inherent disconnection from any sense of belonging with the Earth. Now, more than ever, we need to awaken to our potentials and possible answers that lie embedded within the dreaming process. Reconnection is essential for everyone and decolonization provides that pathway; it can be accessible through the process of cultivating a relationship with dreaming. Political, social and economic action is necessary for decolonization at all levels of society. In no way am I saying that dreaming provides a quick cure for all of colonialism's dehumanizations. However, what I am saying is that it is a useful transformative and spiritual faculty that humanity possesses and, as such, it should be valued and used appropriately to help support and facilitate the decolonial process which is absolutely inclusive of political, social and economic action.

Dreaming contains, within its unfolded potential, the capacity to decolonize. Dreaming and decolonization have been viewed as different bodies of literature. However, dreaming can aid in the decolonizing process, by tapping into ancestral memory, reconnecting the dreamer to Earth and reminding the dreamer that her origins lie within an ensouled cosmos. In the words of Audre Lorde:

> For within living structures defined by profits, by linear power, by institutional dehumanization, our feelings were not meant to survive...feelings were expected to kneel to thought as women were expected to kneel to men. But

> women have survived. As poets... We have felt them all already. We have hidden the fact in the same place where we have hidden our power. They surface in our dreams, and it is our dreams that point the way to freedom. (Lorde, 2007, p. 39)

Dreaming can potentially heal the Cartesian Split by reconnecting with land and ancestry and potentially help initiate other forms of revelatory knowledges (Castellano, 2000, p. 24). Thus, dreaming orients the dreamer to a home within the self, stripping the colonial conditioning layer by layer and setting the dreamer on a pathway toward transformation. Through this process, the dreamer becomes more attuned in body, mind and soul enabling the dreamer to understand what colonialism has robbed from humanity; with this knowledge, new pathways can be charted, solutions sought and communities forged together by working collectively toward potential decolonial futurities.

In order to properly unfold the potential inherent in the decolonial capacity of dreaming, I will rely on the unpublished thesis of Karen Jaenke (2001), entitled *Personal Dreamscape as Ancestral Landscape* and the work of Eduardo Duran (2006) and the story of Jessie Little Doe Baird (2016). One reason Karen Jaenke's thesis is so powerful is that she is of European ancestry and through her work evocatively demonstrates the shedding of colonial conditioning. Irrespective of the extent of the disconnection and the damage, dreams can provide a means of bridging one back to the self. Jaenke suggests that the main component that enables dreaming to facilitate a transformative process is its link to memory, memory that stretches beyond the individual dreamer's lifetime (2001). The first of Jaenke's dreams that shall be discussed are those related to family, largely because our first experience of the world takes place within a family.

## Dreams Reconnect the Dreamer to Their Ancestry

### *Dreams About Family and Ancestry*

Family is central to our sense of belonging. However, there can be many reasons why one feels disconnected to family. Oftentimes, communication gets shut down, there are conversations that we fail to have with our family members and there are underlying dynamics that we fail to grasp. There can be many reasons for this including individual shame and family history, or they can be tied to sociocultural and political reasons. Jaenke, in her thesis, discusses a few dreams that she had about her grandmother who passed away (2001). Jaenke had one dream in particular, in which she managed to connect with her grandmother lifting the veil between the living and the dead.

> *(December 1,1996, 4hrs, PT) In the most recent dream of her, my Grandma Jaenke comes to me not only alive, but with all her vital faculties restored. In her prime, poised at full maturity, vitality alive, it is an apparition of her revitalized presence*...The day following this dream. December 1,1996. I found myself sharing it with an acquaintance. As I started to recount the background around my grandmother's death, flipping my mind backward through the catalog of years. I recalled she had died on December 2, 1986. The dream appeared on the eve of the tenth anniversary of her death!... Then the dream repositioned itself in my understanding, becoming instead a visitation. (Jaenke, 2001, pp. 84–85)

There ensues a conversation about the dream with Jaenke's father—her grandmother's son (Jaenke, 2001). During this process, her father tells her that her grandmother also had a strong connection with her dreams and had dreamt of the passing of her own mother on the night it happened (Jaenke, 2001, p. 86). Up to this point, Jaenke was unaware of this inheritance that had been passed down to her (2001). She writes:

> But now for the first time I saw the lines of *psychic inheritance* to which I was attached. I was amazed and overjoyed to learn of my grandmother's attentiveness to her dreams, now understanding in a new way that, across the generations, her fascination had been bequeathed to me...A temperamental disposition to embrace the realm of dreams had been passed down to me along with a certain genetic disposition and physical resemblance. (Jaenke, 2001, p. 85)

Through this dream, and the dream sharing process, Jaenke learns about her "*psychic inheritance*" and how she is connected to her grandmother in a synchronistic moment that maps on to her grandmother's death anniversary (Jaenke, 2001). This knowledge of psychic inheritance is gifted to her by her grandmother through the cultivation of a relationship with her dreams and a medium of connection, namely dreaming. It strengthens both her connection to her grandmother, despite her death, and her understanding of herself, her family and of her own role in the world. Jaenke writes about this ancestral lineage:

> With this realization, I experience myself woven into an ancestral lineage of women dreamers stretching back in time. I witness to the capacity of dreams to bridge the generations, weaving between this world and the next. "Dreams are the umbilical cord to one's ancestors." I hear my native teacher say, and finding one's ancestors is at the heart of "indigenous dreaming." (Jaenke, 2001, p. 86)

This dream, and its reverberations, is inherently decolonial in that it ruptures any notions of what is conceived as possible under an inherited Western colonial worldview. Riyad Shahjahan in his article, *Spirituality in the academy: reclaiming from the margins and evoking a transformative way of knowing the world*, writes the following: "Colonialism, as noted by Fanon (1963), 'by a kind of perverted logic…turns to the past of the oppressed people, and distorts, disfigures, and destroys it' (p. 210)" (2005, p. 693). Colonialism, as the above quotation indicates, "distorts, disfigures and destroys," yet as Jaenke's dream indicates a recovery of a fragmented past is possible through the cultivation of a relationship with dreaming (Jaenke, 2001) as a reclamation of spiritual knowledges that can rebuild the self (Shahjahan, 2005, p. 694). This dream demonstrates a direct ancestral connection that delinks from the colonial matrix of power (Mignolo, 2011). Mignolo refers to Anibal Quijano where he writes:

> In this respect Anibal Quijano redefined decolonization in terms of decoloniality when he affirmed: 'It is necessary to extricate oneself from the linkages between rationality/modernity and *coloniality*, first of all, and definitely from all power which is not constituted by free decisions made by free people.' (Mignolo, 2011, pp. 52–53)

Visitations, psychic inheritances and ancestral connections granted by means of the dreaming process fall outside the realm of an empirical, rational, logical and colonial ontology. Jaenke's dream is inherently decolonial and helps to empower her, anchor her in her own place in the world and re-establish ancestral connections that work toward a personal resurgence by providing a means of breaking her out of her colonial epistemic barriers through the power of dreaming.

Dreams can be utilized as a decolonial tool to help dreamers remember their origins despite years of disconnection from place, ancestry and language. Duran describes a project that he has his students (learning about clinical practice in therapy) undertake (2006). The purpose of the project was to find their connection to their own ancestry and when they struggled with this task, he had them utilize their dreams (2006). In order to set his students along this path, he has them answer the following questions for an assignment that would span the entire year "They would be asked to do a project in which they would find their tribe, the name of their tribal God, and their tribal creation story" (Duran, 2006, pp. 44–45). These questions propel students to look beyond the surface of their own perceived limitations and to participate in the act of deep remembering that can be inherently decolonial:

> ...I referred them to their dreams and asked them to be mindful of synchronistic events. By the second month or so, students were engaged in a process that had become quite interesting to them, both individually and collectively as a class. They began the process of identifying themselves as people standing in the center of the world and thus healing their own alienation. This understanding of being at the center provided the students with an identity that surpassed the identity that they previously had and allowed them to become acquainted with a way of relating to entities versus pathologizing patients. The rationale of this assignment lies in the question, "How can you guide someone who is alienated if you are alienated yourself?" (Duran, 2006, p. 45)

Duran concludes this matter by discussing the transformative nature of this assignment where some students even went so far as to visit places that connected them in deep and meaningful ways to their ancestry (2006, p. 46). What is so thought provoking about Duran's teaching methodology is the means by which his students were able to rupture their colonial mentalities and to utilize their dreams as a way of healing their own sense of disconnection, a disconnection they were not even cognizant of, by reconnecting to their ancestral origins. Duran clearly demonstrates the decolonial potentials of dreaming as well as the deep value it has in bringing about healing, transformation and belonging.

One of the most incredible stories of dreams and ancestry is the story of Jessie Little Doe Baird and her story of Wopanaak Language Reclamation Project (2016). She is a Native American Wampanoag woman and her story follows a prophecy that her people received wherein they would have a thriving language and then it would be lost, and after some time and when they were ready to receive the language once again, it would return (Baird, 2016). Little Doe Baird had a series of visions for a number of consecutive nights where she found herself in a room with the ancestors from her tribe (Baird, 2016). In the vision, they asked her if the people were ready to receive the language once again and she was given specific instructions in the vision to seek out Elder Helen Manning from a nearby tribe to ask her this question (Baird, 2016). Elder Helen Manning agreed that it was time to bring the language back to the people and from this point onward, they utilized resources such as documents, deeds and a Bible used by former missionaries (that was written in Wampanoag to initially convert people to Christianity) in an effort to begin reviving the Wampanoag language (Baird, 2016). Additionally, Little Doe Baird sought out community elders from tribes in the region, with the help of a linguist Professor from MIT named Kenneth Hale, and sought out a number of grants and thus started Wopanaak Language Reclamation Project (Baird, 2016; Beck, 2018). From this project, after years of work came the creation of curricular resources in Wampanoag, a dictionary with over 12,000 words, and they opened Mukayuhsak Weekuw Immersion School where children are now immersed in the Wampanoag language (Baird, 2016). This story speaks volumes about the role of dreams in regard to our ancestral, cultural, spiritual and political revival. It was through the language that Baird was able to validate the Wampanoag people's claim to land via linguistics and place names inherent in the Wampanoag language that mapped out the boundaries of their territory and was subsequently granted "land in trust" by the U.S. government (Baird, 2016). Jessie Little Doe Baird's inspirational story speaks volumes about the intersections of dreaming, decolonization and political action.

## Dreams Reconnect the Dreamer with the Earth

Perhaps the most powerful aspect of dreaming, particularly in relation to its decolonial potentialities, is its ability to remind the dreamer of their belonging, a belonging to the Earth. Dreamers often awake having dreamt of animals, landscapes and various aspects of the natural world. These visionary moments during the encounter dissipate the distance between the self and the planet. Thus, the continual damage wrought by ongoing colonialism such as the dispossessions of people from the land, degradation of other knowledges and severing of ancestral connections can potentially begin to reconnect the dreamer to healing pathways of belonging. This can provide the dreamer with the tools, the visionary perceptions and the skills necessary to begin de-linking from the colonial matrix of power, opening new pathways that bridge toward new decolonial futures. Duran writes about our ability to commune and heal with the Earth in the following quotation:

> Over the years, a lot of patients have expressed this sense of loss of culture. My purpose here is to guide the patient to realizing that the essence of the cultural "ways" are still here on the very Earth that gave them birth in the first place. Also, the insight that the ways are not static but are fluid and alive is important. The ways need to be fresh and new if they are to be viable in our present-day life-world. Of course, access to the Earth's consciousness emerges through our earth body, which can act as a translator for earth consciousness through the dreamtime and the dreams that dream the patient. (Duran, 2006, p. 101)

The means by which dreams connect the dreamer to the Earth is through love. Love is center of Earth dreams since love can transcend all barriers. In such dreams, the Earth demonstrates Her love for the dreamer by dissipating the distance between herself and dreamer, so that the experience of the dreamer is one of existing in a pulsating, vibrating, field of interconnection that is supreme love. My dream narrative at the beginning of this chapter provides an example of the reciprocity inherent in the flow of love between the Earth and myself. The waterfall in my dream is beckoning to me, and I am inextricably drawn to it and overcome with peace, love and awe. This is unfurled in the imagistic and symbol contents of the dreamscape, and the dreamer awakens with their previous worldview ruptured. Upon waking and through years of unpacking the dream, I continually find more layers to its meaning and it does that work of rupturing my old beliefs. However, this chapter would not be complete without an understanding of the sacred, the numinous and the mysterious by outlining the transformative capacities of dreaming and *how* they work with the dreamer in a dialogical relationship. Therefore, the next section hopes to swim in the waters of the sacred and, in so doing, illuminate the very depths that dreaming can take us through.

## Dreams Sew Back the Seam of the Cartesian Split

### *Dreaming a Gateway into the Sacred*

Dreams can provide a means of communing with the implicate order of the cosmos. It can be assumed that dreaming was perhaps humanity's first glimpse into the sacred and by extension dreaming can be viewed also as humanity's first gateway into the sacred (Deloria, 2006). Lee Irwin expands on this notion in his book *The Dream Seekers: Native American Visionary Traditions of the Great Plains* writes the following: "Dreams and visions are one of the most fundamental means for discovering the 'living' quality of the natural world, and this quality frequently leads to a conscious shaping of objects that are intended to communicate power to others" (1994, p. 31). In many accounts of dreaming, people have reported prophetic dreams, dreams that contain mythical and supernatural qualities, visitations with the dead and the sensation of spirit traveling during dreams (Jung, 2011; Tedlock 1992). In his book, *The World We Used to Live in: Remembering the Powers of the Medicine Men*, Vine Deloria Jr. writes the following:

> Initial and unexpected contact with the Great Mysterious power must have come prior to the development of ceremonies and rituals for seeking a relationship with the spirits. We can imagine the surprise of the first person having an unusual, and perhaps prophetic, dream and then discovering that it accurately described an event that came to pass in his or her daily life. Surely, here was reliable information, but from an unknown source that could not be summoned at one's pleasure. (2006, p. 1)

The dreamscape is built around the dreamer, so that all things coalesce with the dreamer, beginning and ending with them. The gift of knowledge and power noted above is enacted through the centering of the dreamer at the heart of the dream totality. This personal component of dreaming is what makes it so powerful. The sacred, through the dreaming process, is not something untouchable nor inaccessible, but completely experiential. The personal component of the dream pulls the dreamer in, evoking emotions at a core level, whereby the separation between matter and spirit dissipates. Jung expands on the personal nature of the dream experience: "The self is not only the centre, but also the whole circumference which embraces both conscious and unconscious; it is the centre of this totality, just as the ego is the centre of consciousness" (2011, p. 115). The experience of the sacred in the dreamscape is entirely personal, in a way that perhaps no other mediums can provide and, as such, dreaming provides a *personal* gateway into the sacred that can be highly empowering.

> The individual's experience of the world is not limited to ordinary motor action or to the five physical senses. It is possible to experience flights into the sky or penetration into the earth or mountains; it is possible to know the future or the distant past or events occurring in faraway places. The collapse of physical boundaries is a consistent feature of the visionary topology. Thus, the world constitutes itself as permeable, transformative, mysterious, and powerful. (Irwin, 1994, p. 27)

As the above quotation explains, knowledge, abilities and understandings, whether they be psychic, prophetic or intuitive and can bring about real change in the waking world of the dreamer. Empowering them and, potentially strengthening their worldview or perhaps rupturing it.

Rupturing a world order that was previously held opens a vast array of new capacities to the dreamer especially if the former worldview was deeply influenced by Cartesian logics. The dreamer upon waking is able, as in the dreamscape, to merge matter and spirit in the living world. The faculty to see the cosmos as ensouled is transferred when the dream is valued in the proper manner. Leanne Simpson, in *Dancing on Our Turtle's Back*, expands on the responsibility that comes hand in hand with the dream:

> Because dreams and visions for Nishnaabeg people are spiritual in nature, if one is living in a good way then one becomes open to receiving Pauwauwaewin. But once one has received an important dream, he or she has a responsibility to act on that vision. That responsibility is in essence a treaty we make with the spiritual world when we place our tobacco down and ask for help. Pauwauwaein is an awakening, a vision that gives understanding to matters. (Simpson, 2011, pp. 146–147)

The visionary episteme (Irwin, 1994) provides access to an understanding of an interconnected and interdependent cosmos that entails the reciprocity of living the dream. Or to put it more simply, to live in a way that utilizes the knowledge of an ensouled cosmos in a good way. Joe Sheridan and Dan Longboat poetically describe the living cosmos in their article *The Imagination of the Haudenosaunee and the Ecology of the Sacred*:

> *Imagination* will be initially replaced with the term *animist realism* to portray a planet where everything is alive and sentient… Animist realism attempts to mirror Creation's temporal and material totality by accounting for the unseen and the dreamt in a complex implicature that intersects with and provides passage to other domains of knowledge and understanding. (Sheridan & Roronhiakewen "He Clears the Sky" Longboat, 2006, p. 368)

Dreams can provide a glimpse into all that is seen and unseen and this glimpse has the power to shift worldviews or enhance an understanding of them on an ontological level. This experience with the numinous is completely personal but can have implications for the dreamer in the wider context of the community they live in, or their life's purpose. The dreamer may have to continually seek for the meaning of the dream which can be an intensive process (Simpson, 2011). Leanne Simpson writes "It may take months, years or even decades of searching and learning to fully understand the meaning of one's visions and to chart a course of action" (2011, p. 147). Thus, dreaming is a revelatory capacity that humans are born with, but simultaneously, comes with a responsibility. These are deeply powerful and potent dreaming encounters that have the ability to propel the dreamer out of their epistemic and ontological cages, rupturing the framework of their previous held worldviews. However, these dreams also come hand in hand with a responsibility to uncover the enfolded meaning and to live it out in the daily life of the dreamer (Simpson, 2011).

## Conclusion

In closing, this chapter sought answers to the following questions: What are dreams? What are the inherent potentials of dreams? What do they do for us and what are they capable of? Ultimately, this chapter sought to perform an epistemological theorizing of the decolonial potentialities of dreaming. It is my hope that the value of dreaming has shifted, in the mind's eye of the reader. Moreover, my hope is that this chapter has demonstrated that dreaming can breathe new life into the ongoing process of decolonization. As Eric Ritskes in his chapter entitled *Connected: Indigenous spirituality as resistance in the classroom* in the *spirituality, education & society* writes "Fanon (1963) examines how colonization attempts to distort and misrepresent the past, divorcing people from their histories." Linda Smith (1999) argues that a vital part of the decolonization process is "about recovering our own stories of the past" (Ritskes, 2011, p. 25). Culture, language, ancestors and spirituality are all paths helpful in rebuilding a bridge to oneself and can aid the beginning of the healing process that is inherently decolonizing. Memmi discusses the need to stop co-creating one's identity in the image of the colonizer (1965). One way in which the colonized can stop defining themself in relation to the colonizer is by rebuilding that relationship to self and dreaming can usher in this decolonial pathway home. Eduardo Duran and Bonnie Duran echo this hope in their book, *Native American Postcolonial Psychology* (1995):

> Since the soul wound occurred at the level of myth and dream, it follows that the therapy or transformation of the wound should also occur at the level of myth and dream. The level at which the wound occurred is accessible

> through the vehicle of dreams, since dreams are part of the awareness that emerges from the depths of the unconscious. (p. 45)

Our internal wounds are waiting for the healing that lies within each one of us. Dreaming is a vehicle that can do the work of healing our wounds (Duran & Duran, 1995, p. 45). It is also important to note that dreams can also help ignite a material, innovative and political pathway that can be inherently decolonial. Our pathway through this world does not have to be cannibalistic, we can choose another path and our dreams beckon us to take this alternative path that is forged in love like the waterfall of my dream. Thus, dreams can initiate and/or catalyze the decolonizing process so that we can call back our dismembered selves and begin working toward a world fused with love and the continual regeneration of all life forms on a thriving healthy planet acting in the very likeness of our Mother Earth.

## References

Baird, J. L. D. (2016). Wopanaak language reclamation program: Bringing the language home. *Journal of Global Indigeneity, 2*(2). Available at https://ro.uow.edu.au/jgi/vol2/iss2/7.

Beck, A. (2018, April 19). Native language schools are taking back education. *Yes!* Retrieved May 25, 2019, from https://www.yesmagazine.org/peace-justice/native-language-schools-are-taking-back-education-20180419.

Castellano, M. B. (2000). Updating aboriginal traditions of knowledge. In G. J. Dei, B. L. Hall, & D. G. Rosenberg (Eds.), *Indigenous knowledges in global contexts: Multiple readings of our world*. Toronto: University of Toronto Press.

Cheng, A. A. (2001). *The melancholy of race: Psychoanalysis, assimilation, and hidden grief.* New York: Oxford University Press.

Colman, W. (2017). Soul in the world: Symbolic culture as the medium for psyche. *Journal of Analytic Psychology, 62*(1), 32–49.

Deloria, V., Jr. (2006). *The world we used to live in: Remembering the powers of the medicine men*. Colorado: Fulcrum Publishing Golden.

Duran, E. (2006). *Healing the soul wound: Counseling with American Indians and other native peoples.* New York, NY: Teachers College Press.

Duran, E., & Duran, B. (1995). *Native American postcolonial psychology.* Albany: State University of New York Press.

Fanon, F. (1963). *The wretched of the earth.* New York: Grove Press.

Irwin, L. (1994). *The dream seekers: Native American visionary traditions of the great plains.* Norman: University of Oklahoma Press.

Jaenke, K. A. (2001). *Personal dreamscape as ancestral landscape* (Unpublished doctoral dissertation). California Institute of Integral Studies.

Jung, C. G. (2011). *Dreams*. Princeton: Princeton University Press.
Lorde, A. (2007). *Sister outsider: Essays and speeches*. Berkeley: Crossing Press.
Memmi, A. (1965). *The colonizer and the colonized*. Boston: Beacon Press.
Mignolo, W. D. (2011). *The darker side of western modernity: Global futures, decolonial options*. Durham, NC: Duke University Press.
O'Nell, C. W. (1965). A cross-cultural study of hunger and thirst motivation manifested in dreams. *Human Development, 8*, 181–193; (1976). *Dreams, culture and the individual*. San Francisco, California: Chandler & Sharp.
Quattrocchi, M. (2005). *Dreamwork uncovered: How dreams can create inner harmony, peace and joy*. Toronto: Insomniac Press.
Ritskes, E. J. (2011). Connected: Indigenous spirituality as resistance in the classroom. In N. N. Wane, E. L. Manyimo, & E. J. Ritskes (Eds.), *Spirituality, education & society: An integrated approach*. Rotterdam, The Netherlands: Sense Publishers.
Shahjahan, R. (2005). Spirituality in the academy: Reclaiming from the margins and evoking a transformative way of knowing the world. *International Journal of Qualitative Studies in Education*, 18 (6), 685–711.
Sheridan, J., & Longboat, D., "He Clears the Sky". (2006, November). The Haudenosaunee imagination and the ecology of the sacred. *Space and Culture, 9*(4), 365–381. https://doi.org/10.1177/120633120629250.
Simpson, L. (2011). *Dancing on our turtle's back: Stories of Nishnaabeg re-creation resurgence and a new emergence*. Winnipeg, MB: Arbeiter Ring Publishing.
Sjöö, M., & Mor, B. (1991). *The great cosmic mother: Rediscovering the religion of the earth* (2nd ed.). San Francisco: HarperCollins.
Smith, L. T. (1999). *Decolonizing methodologies: Research and indigenous peoples*. Dunedin: University of Otago Press.
Tedlock, B. (1992). *Dreaming: Anthropological and psychological interpretations*. Santa Fe, NM: School of American Research Press.
Tedlock, B. (2005). *The woman in the shaman's body: Reclaiming the feminine in religion and medicine*. New York: Bantam Dell.

PART IV

# The Re-centering of Spirit

CHAPTER 12

# Critical Spirituality: Decolonizing the Self

*Josue Tario*

At the age of thirteen, I was straddling between being an American, Canadian, and a Latino. Being born in El Salvador, raised as a child in Canada, and living in the United States as an adolescent led me to consistently experience movement, differences, and ambivalence when it came to my identity formation. I lived in the *in-between* state of the three cultures and never felt like I belonged to any one of them. Due to the civil war, my family and I left El Salvador when I was very young so I barely remembered anything about my "home" country. Indelibly, being raised by immigrant parents, the Salvadorian culture was the first culture I encountered and Spanish was the first language I spoke. But things quickly changed when I started going to school in Kitchener, Ontario. My parents opted to put me in Christian schools and I was always one of the few, if not only, racialized student in these settings. It was tough.

At the age of six or seven, I started to learn how to juggle two cultures: one at home and one at school. At home, I was Josue, but at school I

J. Tario (✉)
Department of Social Justice Education, Ontario Institute for Studies in Education, University of Toronto, Toronto, ON, Canada
e-mail: josue.tario@mail.utoronto.ca



N. N. Wane et al. (eds.), *Decolonizing the Spirit in Education and Beyond*, Spirituality, Religion, and Education,
https://doi.org/10.1007/978-3-030-25320-2_12

was Joshua. I remember the ambivalence I felt when my peers would ask me where I was from. I would say something like, "I was born in El Salvador but I am Canadian." I was always trying to prove the former identity to my family and the latter one to my peers and friends. But deep down inside, I felt like I was different, like an outcast. For example, I remember always interpreting between two languages (Spanish and English) at parent teacher conferences. For some reason or another, I started to feel embarrassed about my Salvadorian identity because I felt that people looked down on it. So, I tried extra hard to *perform* a Canadian identity, attempting to convince others and myself that I truly was Canadian. I obsessed over speaking "proper" English, ate Tim Hortons all the time, and even lied about liking hockey. No matter what I did externally, I felt inauthentic on the inside. I mean, I felt Salvadorian when I was at home eating *pupusas* and watching *telenovelas* with my mama, but everything would change as soon I stepped outside. And vice versa, I felt Canadian at school or with my friends but there were always reminders that I was not fully one of them—whether it was the color of my skin, my parent's financial hardships, or the fact that besides my father, mother, and younger brother, I had no extended family or relatives in Canada.

Unexpectedly, at the age of eleven, I was forced to move back to El Salvador with my father. I lived there for a year and along with being separated from my mother and brother; the culture shock of moving back to my "home" country was extremely difficult. Suddenly, I found myself being ridiculed for apparently speaking broken Spanish and for being Canadian or a "gringo." Ironically, I was being ridiculed for an identity that I myself did not fully accept or belong to. Immediately, I found myself trying to *perform* a Salvadorian identity and was frustrated at the fact that no matter what I did, I was yet again seen as an outsider, as different. Everything about El Salvador was different for me. It is an extremely burdening situation when you feel like a foreigner in your "home" country. At the age of twelve, my father and I moved to Kansas in the United States and reunited with my mother and brother. However, yet again, I experienced another cultural shock when I encountered the American/Latino culture. For the first time in my life, I would hear people talking about being "Latino" or "Hispanic." Once more, I was the different one because I was "from Canada" and on top of that I spoke "proper" English which apparently did not sit well with my American/Latino friends. At this point, I was an expert, at least in my mind, at being a social chameleon and started to identify as a Latino. I changed my "proper" Canadian English and perfected an American accent in order to fit in. Whether it was because of my age or the fact I was living in Kansas, I started to encounter pervasive state, cultural, and educational narratives defining and constructing the meaning of "Latino" and "Hispanic."

Within the interviews conducted, Latin American Canadian youth consistently conveyed the feeling of living *in-between* the overlapping and layered spaces of Latin American and Canadian culture. Along with being in state of ambivalence, the participants also expressed "feeling not good enough" because of gendered, raced, and national binaries that enfold Latin American Canadian youth into dominant worldviews and social ways of being. While these psychological and sociological *in-between* realties can be troubling, all the participants expressed finding a transformational peace, or what Barthes (1975) calls "jouissance" (bliss), through *critical spirituality*. Regarding the importance of spirituality, Hooks (2003) states:

> I knew only that despite the troubles of my world, the suffering I witnessed around them and within me, there was always available a spiritual force that could lift me higher, that could give me *transcendent bliss* [emphasis added] wherein I could surrender all thought of the world and know profound peace. (p. 106)

For the Latin American Canadian youth in this chapter, *critical spirituality* was found to have the potential to create new forms of *becoming* that temporarily transcend both the constraint and contestation of Latinidad's cultural performativity. According to Anzaldúa (1987), *Nepantla* is a space of in-betweenness that becomes a space of meaning-making and creativity. By inhabiting the space of *nepantla*, border-dwellers (*los atravesados)*, such as the Latin American Canadian youth in this chapter, are more prone to develop a critically reflective stance. The critical reflection that emerges from this "in-between place becomes a turning point initiating psychological and spiritual transformation" (Anzaldúa & Keating, 2002, p. 569).

The fusion of critical self-reflection and spirituality, or what Wane (2014) theorizes as *critical spirituality*, is what propels our agency to activate new meanings. When discussing the importance of spiritually based curriculum, Wane (2014) emphasizes the importance of critical reflection to cultivate in youth a "sense of belonging, connectivity, responsibility, respect, and self-worth" (p. 133). In *Experience and Education*, Dewey (1938) explains that while we cannot be taught how to think, we must learn how to achieve the practice of critical reflection. A component of critical reflection is taking a holistic approach to the experiences one faces throughout our lifetime. This requires taking a deeper look into our past and present experiences while reflecting on how these experiences may influence our attitudes and decisions.

When it comes to spirituality, many scholars have discussed the ambiguity surrounding how to define it (Palmer, 2003; Smith, 1999; Wane, 2014). In our current modern world, and especially in the West, spirituality is separated from the material validation of science. Thus, spirituality is many times undermined and undervalued since it cannot be objectively measured or theorized as a "valid" phenomena (Collins, 1998). In addition, many repudiate spirituality because it is typically conflated with religion and "dismissed as an apolitical, ahistorical form of escapism that inadvertently reinforces the status quo" (Anzaldúa, 2000, p. 8). Furthermore, within academia, spirituality is not considered a credible knowledge since academic epistemologies are typically grounded on rationality, logic, and objectivity (Ellerby, 2000). As Anzaldúa (2000) succinctly puts it, "this whole society is premised on the reality described by the scientific mode of observable phenomenon, while whatever is imagined or subjectively lived doesn't have any credence. Spirituality is subjective experience" (p. 282). Nonetheless, feminists of color have made great strides to challenge the notion that subjective experiences and the knowledges acquired through these experiences are not as important or valid as objective/observable phenomena (Alcoff, 2001; Anzaldúa, 1990; Collins, 2008).

While having different interpretations and definitions regarding spirituality, the youth in this chapter expressed how their subjective experiences of spirituality enable them to not only resist hegemonic discourses and the performative aspects of their gaze, but *temporarily* transcend them. By emphasizing the temporality of this transcendence, I wish to discard the notion that spirituality alone allows us to fully or permanently overcome structural impositions such as discursive constructions (race, gender, etc.) as well as material impediments (socioeconomic status). But for many, including all the participants in this study and myself, spirituality is the most powerful and authentic form of agency. Consider the following *testimonios* from Diana and Bria:

> Honestly, it's hard. It is a hard question. Like I question myself all the time and sometimes it stresses me out because I question myself so much. I question my authenticity, my performativity, and I call myself out on it and it's

> almost like you're not living at the point because of all this. I think my spirituality gets me by. My faith. Like my beliefs. I think what gets me by is addressing what kind of energy I have. I have a thing for like energy crystals and checking in with my *feelings*, checking in with my body. I see that more as a spiritual thing instead of a performativity thing. Like, why do I *feel* the way I *feel*? Why is my body reacting the way it's reacting? Kinda like connecting with myself...mind, body, and soul. Instead of what is imposed on me. And more than just simply resisting, spirituality is the space where I *feel* [emphasis added] the most authentic. (Diana, personal communication, October 14, 2016)

> My spirituality as a Latina is just as complex and full of seemingly contrasting dichotomies, similar to my cultural and racial identity. I believe that I am a very spiritual person because I have to be...it grounds me. I've *felt* and seen supernatural things so much around me that I'm convinced that there is more to life than which we experience as humans. For the longest time, I *felt* that everywhere I went, I was trying to do too much. Because I wasn't embracing all of me, it was hard to fit in. And I think when I let that go, that's when I *felt* most at peace with myself and all of my racial backgrounds Spiritual grounding has been the only consistent source of peace and rest for me as I fight through bouts of depression. I know that whatever inner strength that I possess when I completely drained is God given and somehow I'm able to push through. Who I am as a Latina is deeply rooted in my spiritual walk. Spiritual healing is necessary for my personal authenticity on this planet. (Bria, personal communication, October 15, 2016)

Diana expresses dealing with performativity and the constant internal questioning that living in the *nepantla* (in-between) precipitates. Bria also reveals she was "trying to do too much" and the sentiment of not fitting in. Spirituality counters this as it is not a "performativity thing" and provides a space of authenticity for both. There are many elements that comprise spirituality. However, there are two specific elements articulated by the individuals in these interviews which I would like to focus on. The first element has to do with how Diana and Bria interpret their spirituality as a feeling or a set of feelings. Diana conveys the importance of having a critical spirituality which enables her to "check in with my feelings" while critically asking, "why do I feel the way I feel?" Bria expresses the same attitude when she talks about "feeling supernatural things" and "feeling at peace" when she lets go of trying to put up an act. In many ways, Diana's and Bria's spirituality of feelings entails the "passionate rationality" that Collins (1998) correlates with African American women's spirituality. According to Collins (1998), "this type of passionate rationality flies in the face of Western epistemology that sees emotions and rationality as different and competing concerns... deep feelings that arouse people to action constitute a critical source of power" (p. 243).

Hence, the deep feelings that individuals experience are a powerful source of agency that enables us to not "simply resist," as Diana puts it, the hegemonic discourses of Latinidad but it provides a "consistent source of peace." Critical spirituality becomes a catalyst for the awareness we need to tap into our deepest feelings or what Audre Lorde (1984) refers to as the "erotic." She elaborates on this critical power and writes, "the erotic is a resource within each of us that lies in a deeply female and spiritual plane, firmly rooted in the power of our unexpressed or unrecognized feeling" (p. 53). Consequently, our deepest feelings or the erotic is a key component to critical spirituality because it "becomes a lens through which we scrutinize all aspects of our existence, forcing us to evaluate those aspects honestly in terms of their relative meaning within our lives" (Lorde, 1984, p. 57).

The other element of critical spirituality that was discussed is a sense of interconnectedness. This entails the "I" feeling interconnected with not only herself, such as Diana "connecting with myself...mind, body, and soul," but with all aspects of the universe. It is the belief or feeling that we are all connected both physically and metaphysically through a spiritual force that embodies itself in material and nonmaterial forms. By advocating for a holistic spirituality, we are interconnected with humans, animals, plants, and the intangible world that creates an invisible harmony in the cosmos (Mazama, 2002). As Anzaldúa (2000) explains in an interview, "everything is interconnected. To me, spirituality and being spiritual means to be aware of the interconnections between things" (p. 9). To "be aware" of this interconnection is to practice a critical spirituality. What this means for me is that I am related to everything in one way or another; it speaks to an eternal relationship with the universe, even when I stop living. Both Ana Maria and Stu share this feeling:

> Spirituality is a constant search, identification and revision for me. Essentially, it is *feeling* at peace with who I am and with the world around me...even in the chaos. This has led me to search for other spiritual paths and teachings. For example, Indigenous beliefs of creation and the power of pachamama, Afro-Brazilian candomble deities- representative of our brown and black skins but also manifestations of sacred humanity. The belief that we are *connected*

> [emphasis added] to all creation. My spirituality is necessary to not only the ways I construct my Latinx identity, but also how I navigate, deconstruct, and reappropriate the racialized and gendered discourses of Latinidad. (Ana Maria, personal communication, October 30, 2016)

> Spirituality keeps me grounded because it reminds me that my identity is not found in anything else but Jesus. If I didn't have God, the racial tension and questions about my identity would affect me more. However, God helps me to see the bigger picture, which goes beyond racial barriers. When it all boils down, we are all *connected* [emphasis added]. Every human being has a soul, no matter what skin color or background they come from. God helps me to look beyond the physical. It's not about categorizing or putting labels on people. It's about seeing every person as a human being, a human being made in the image of their Creator. (Stu, personal communication, August 25, 2016)

In her *testimonio*, Ana Maria speaks of being "connected to all creation" as part of her critical spirituality. She also speaks to the temporality of this critical spirituality as it is a "constant search," one that entails constant movement and change. But in this "constant search," there is a feeling of peace, "even in the chaos." Likewise, Stu's critical spirituality enables him to be aware that all of us are connected through a common spirit or soul. For both Ana Maria and Stu, as well as the other Latin American Canadian youth interviewed, critical spirituality offers the ability to "navigate, deconstruct, and reappropriate" the racialized and gendered discourses of Latinidad, giving them a special agency in the formation of their identity. Even if it is temporary, critical spirituality allows us to "see the bigger picture" that goes beyond discursive or structural barriers. Many times, the narratives that are imposed on us can be painful and confusing, making us feel like we don't belong or fit in; nevertheless, critical spirituality engenders a powerful form of agency that replenishes with authenticity, peace, and love.

Thus far, the two elements of critical spirituality that have been discussed are enigmatic feelings and a sense of interconnectedness. Moreover, the combination of both these elements manifests itself and takes form through something we all discuss but rarely fully understand. There is no greater feeling that breeds connection than love. For the youth in this chapter, love emerged as the integral source of their critical spirituality. Love, as the ultimate source of agency, is remarkably liberating, not necessarily because of its capacity to resist dominant narratives (which ultimately is a power struggle), but more so for its ability to *let go* of struggling all together. Consider Andrea's and Diana's concluding *testimonios*:

> I think being able to name what you are feeling is powerful. I think love in and of itself is the most powerful. We're not supposed to love each other, we're not supposed to have self-love, so that, in itself, is contrary to the dominant narratives. They don't want us to love each other. As a direct action, we are going to love. Like, that's actually our revolutionary action. A revolution based on loving more than resisting. (Andrea, personal communication, November 2, 2016)

> Love. I think we forget about that in a lot of the theories and all these conversations about agency and authenticity and identity. It's like you feel things at the end of the day. I don't think feelings are necessarily a performance. I tie that to my spirituality, like what is my body feeling? What is my soul feeling? What am I thinking? Doing things with love is really important because it allows you to let go. (Diana, personal communication, October 14, 2016)

What does Andrea mean when she talks about a "revolution based on love not resisting"? Or when Diana discusses how love "allows you to let go"? When discussing the liberating effects of a differential consciousness and revolutionary love, Chela Sandoval writes,

> love provides one kind of entry to a form of being that breaks subject free from the ties that bind being, to thus enter the differential mode of consciousness, or to enter what Barthes perhaps better describes as "the gentleness of the abyss". In this unlimited space, ties to any responsibility are broken such that, Barthes writes, even "the act of dying is not up to me: I entrust myself, I transmit myself (to whom? To God, to Nature, to everything. (Barthes, 1978, pp. 11–12; Sandoval, 2000, p. 141)

Love provides access to a different consciousness that allows one to let go of control. In this "abyss" or *nepantla* (in-between), adherence to narratives must be let go, and a "third meaning" surface that releases one from the binaries of meaning and signification. Barthes (1977) describes the "third meaning" as always present in this "abyss" but not searchable because it is that which "outplays meaning" altogether; it "subverts not the content, but the whole practice of meaning" (p. 62). As seen through the experiences of the Latin American Canadian youth interviewed, the passage into this "in-between abyss" is a painful crossing which produces ambivalence and a lack of authenticity (feeling not good enough). But this pain or what

Barthes (1978) defines as a "punctum" is what enables us to break free from the meanings of hegemonic discourses and the performative aspects of their gaze. Consequently, even though the meanings transmitted by, for instance, the racialized and gendered discourses of Latinidad do not magically disappear, Latin American Canadian youth can temporarily transcend their significations.

While hegemonic meanings and significations generate internal turmoil, critical spirituality can provide a sense of stillness, creating a space for new imaginations. But this is only possible through the abandonment—albeit temporary, of meaning and one's ego. Palmer (2003) reminds us that "spirituality is the eternal human yearning to be connected with something larger than one's own ego" (p. 377). Thus, critical spirituality and the revolutionary love that it nurtures make it possible to "entrust myself…to everything," a place where the binaries of being oppressed/resisting oppression are interconnected, not opposed. Ironically, through the critical awareness of this interconnection, we are able to, at times, disconnect from the binaries of living and the "act of dying" as well as everything in-between.

This chapter began with the schism of my own cultural identities. At school, I was Joshua, while outside of school, I was Josue. I was stuck in this arresting dichotomy of either being a validated student within an educational space or being a vindicated Latino within the cultural space of Latinidad. I have come to realize that throughout these stages of my identity formation, there was always a constant scrutiny or *gaze* that influenced who I thought I was and how I performed my identity as a Latino male. Holland, Lachicotte, Skinner, and Cain (1998) social practice theory of self and identity comes to mind when they explain, "people tell others who they are, but even more important, they tell themselves and then try to *act* [emphasis added] as though they are who they say they are" (p. 3). The *gaze* or judgment of educators, peers, and even family made me feel like the only way to be validated was by *performing* certain narratives. In the end, no matter how well I performed, I still felt like I was not good enough and that I didn't belong.

Living in a state of *in-betweenness* produces insecurity, feelings of not being good enough, and the overall difficulties of fitting in. These experiences and feelings emerge from the struggles of maneuvering both multiple cultures and realities. It is a fragmented feeling that constantly searches for wholeness. Truth be told, it is a feeling that all humans deal with at some point in their lives and it's something that never completely goes away. Many times, it is hard to find this wholeness or peace in such a divisive world full of dominant narratives telling us who we are or what we are supposed to be. Nevertheless, this state of *in-betweenness* engenders a spiritual and intangible "*conocimiento*" (knowledge) that many have encountered which makes *us* feel whole—albeit temporarily, in a fragmented world (Anzaldúa & Keating, 2002, p. 542).

Critical spirituality has the potential to release us from the constraints of narratives, oppression, and even resistance. Through *critical spirituality*, a meaning of self that goes beyond the dichotomy of oppression/resistance is possible. Anzaldúa describes the potential of a self that rejects binaries and that does not form self-understandings based on external forms of identification such as race, sex, and gender, but instead imagines "a different story enabling you to rethink yourself in more *global-spiritual* [emphasis added] terms instead of conventional categories of color, class, career" (Anzaldúa & Keating, 2002, p. 561). Furthermore, Barthes (1978) speaks about a "third" or "zero" meaning that functions as a "punctum" which breaks social narratives and creates a "gentle hemorrhage" of being that can go beyond the dualisms of meanings/narratives (pp. 12 and 19). When speaking of this transcendental state, Barthes (1975) refuses to be "driven about my language's illusions, seductions, and intimidations. I remove myself from narrative" (p. 18).

Critical spirituality consists of letting go of one's ego to disarm the arresting components that social narratives have on our *being*. This is where the holistic component of critical spirituality is powerful. It engenders collectiveness, community, and relationships. The participants in this study spoke about how critical spirituality induces self-love and love for the other. This dialectical relationship between self-love and love for the other enables you "to rethink yourself in more *global-spiritual* terms" because critical spirituality is not just about the self, it is interconnected to other human beings, animals, the environment, and so on (Anzaldúa & Keating, 2002). The practice of critical spirituality seeks not only an inner transformation but a collective one as well. Unfortunately, due to neoliberalism and the meritocratic culture of achievement, individualism is rewarded over community, rights over responsibilities, and objectivity over subjectivity (Dei, 2008).

We need to understand that critical spirituality is subjectively understood and enacted; thus, differences should not only be tolerated but be allowed to flourish. At the same time, there are many commonalties such as the need for community, relationships, and love that can incite both individual and collective liberation. For Anzaldua, "spiritual activism is spirituality for social change, spirituality that recognizes the many differences among us yet insists on our commonalities and uses these commonalities as a catalyst for transformation" (quoted in Keating, 2006, p. 11). Critical spirituality is much more than simply meditating our way into a better world or having an out-of-body experience. Again, it involves a dialectical relationship between decolonizing imagination(s) and action(s) or what Freire (1972) theorizes as praxis. The imaginative component of critical spirituality empowers and gives us the energy to act upon our reality. I believe praxis, the act of applying new possibilities, is what distinguishes humans from non-humans. According to Freire (1972) and others, praxis is the ontological process of becoming human. Critical spirituality allows us to imagine a revolutionary praxis that rejects oppression, while dialectically creating new forms of social, educational, and political relationships.

Critical spirituality is a powerful source of liberation and reinvention. The reason for this is because it is a source of *becoming* as opposed of *being*. The hegemonic narratives regarding our identity will always be constraining because it limits the possibilities of *becoming* and instead seeks to impose a fixed state of *being*. Critical spirituality enables us to be at peace with the perpetual movement of meaning, identity, and social reality. It enables a critical understanding that nothing can be permanent, whether it be the constraining effects of social narratives on our identity or the transcendence from them. This is the beauty of living in the in-between state; it teaches us that nothing is stable or permanent.

Movement, uncertainty, and vulnerability can become tools that generate new meanings, new imaginations, and new forms of becoming human. Critical spirituality fully embraces feelings like "I don't completely belong in one or the other" because it embraces the unpredictability of becoming human. It embraces the perpetual suspension between the past (being) and the future (non-being). It thrives in learning to abide in the present moment, in the possibility of becoming something, someone new. I share Freire's (1998) sentiment when he writes, "I like to be human because in my unfinishedness I know that I am conditioned. Yet, conscious of such conditioning, I know that I can go beyond it" (p. 54). Based on my life experiences and the participants in this study, the journey or process of "unfinishedness" is at times contradicting and painful but can also be blissfully peaceful. To be human is to experience and embrace this dialectical relationship between pain and joy, self-love and love for others, difference and commonality, and, as much as we don't like to talk about it, life and death. La belleza de esta vida es que todo es temporal.

## Conclusion

Is there a difference between decolonizing the self and decolonizing the spirit? Can the spirit really be colonized in the first place? In order to think about these questions, I would like to expand on the three driving components of critical spirituality: love, interconnectedness, and temporality. As discussed earlier, love is critical for the process of *becoming* because it is ultimately about surrendering to the unknown. According to Greek philosophy, there are four different kinds of loves. When I speak of the love engendered by critical spirituality, I do not mean romantic love (eros) or the love we have for our friends (philia), or even familial love (storge), but a selfless love (agape). Agape love is an unconditional love that transcends circumstances as well as the self. It is the idea that *becoming* human always points and is directed to something or someone else, whether it's a meaning to fulfill or the relationship we have with the universe (humans, animals, nature, etc.). This is what true interconnectedness is—a dialectical relationship where I cannot exist without being part of something bigger. Therefore, I believe that the disconnected self can be colonized/decolonized, but the spirit can never be. The self is an individual state of *being* that can be bounded by colonial histories, discourses, and realities while the spirit is a collective process of *becoming* that transcends ideologies, materiality, and time. I wrote earlier that the beauty of life is that everything is temporal. What I mean by this is that the self and everything the self perceives are temporal, including the state of *being*. On the other hand, the spirit is always *becoming*, thus eternal, because it cannot be restricted by time, space, or perception. For instance, both Buddhism and Hinduism share the doctrine of *Annica* or *Anitya*. The doctrine basically asserts that nothing lasts and that everything is in a constant state of change (Harvey, 2013). This speaks to the temporality of the self. It tells us that as long we are attached to things that are changing and impermanent, we will suffer. Similarly, the book of Ecclesiastes says that "there is a time for everything and a season for every activity under the heavens. A time to be born and a time to die" (Ecclesiastes 3:1, New International Version). Indigenous African spiritualties also speak to this temporality and inevitable fluctuation. Consider the following Yoruba proverb: "igba o lo bi orere, aye o lo bi opa ibon (no life span extends ad infinitum; a life time is not as straight as the barrel of a gun" (Kazeem, 2016).

Nevertheless, the doctrine of *Annica*, for example, distinguishes between the temporal (self/being) and the eternal (spirit/becoming).

All conditioned existence, both mental and physical, is subject to impermanence and, consequently, destruction. This contrasts with *nirvana* (spirit/becoming), the ultimate state of enlightenment and complete liberation of the self (Harvey, 2013). Furthermore, many people believe that heaven represents a similar place of enlightenment and eternal peace. Could Ecclesiastes be saying that everything *under the heavens* (spirit) is temporal? Lastly, in Yoruba belief, death is a transition from one form of existence to another (Kazeem, 2016). Could the transition be from a temporal existence (self/being) to an eternal one (spirit/becoming)?

Some argue that this higher level of existence is not possible while being in our mortal bodies, while others argue that full transcendence can be reached on earth. All I can say is that I do not know. But what I do know is that many, such as the Latin American Canadian youth interviewed, as well as myself, have experienced what you may paradoxically call a temporal transcendence. And the process for these moments of peace, joy, and acceptance always includes letting go of our egos, allowing us to feel truly interconnected with the universe, which in turn, produces deeper manifestations of love and newer imaginations of meaning. Is there an ultimate meaning to life? Is there a collective or ultimate meaning that was here before us and will be here after us? Again, I do not know. Maybe life is like a movie. Every movie is full of scenes. Every scene has a meaning. These are our subjective meanings that arise from the temporal self. But maybe the ultimate meaning cannot be found until the end of the movie. As such, is it possible that only death reveals the ultimate meaning because it is the complete detachment to self and the eternal attachment to the universe?

I believe that death to the self/ego is the closest thing to nirvana/heaven/higher form of existence. The temporality of life will always include movement, uncertainty, fear, insecurity, and pain. The best way to deal with this is to try to surrender the ego, realize the interconnectedness of the universe, and love. I would like to conclude by recognizing the amount of privilege I have writing about the decolonization of the self and spiritual transcendence when many of our Indigenous and African descendant brothers and sisters are fighting for material decolonization of the land. Decolonization cannot only be about theory or pontifications, it must be about praxis and tangible action. Many are literally fighting to survive and dying daily because of colonization. However, I do believe that decolonization of both the land and the self must be done for true decolonization to take place one day. The self has colonized this earth and is rapidly destroying it. I pray that the spirit of humanity intervenes before it is too late. I remain hopeful that we can achieve a higher form of existence while on this beautiful earth. It would be, without a doubt, the most meaningful thing we can do.

## References


Alcoff, L. (2001). Phenomenology, poststructuralism, and feminist theory on the concept of experience. In L. Fisher & L. Embree (Eds.), *Feminist phenomenology* (pp. 39–56). Dordrecht, The Netherlands: Kluwer Academic.

Anzaldúa, G. (1987). *Borderlands/La Frontera: The New Mestiza.* San Francisco, CA: Aunt Lute.

Anzaldúa, G. (1990). *Making face, making Soul/Haciendo Caras: Creative and critical perspectives by feminists of color.* San Francisco, CA: Aunt Lute.

Anzaldúa, G. (2000). *Interviews/entrevistas* (A. L. Keating, Ed.). New York, NY: Routledge.

Anzaldúa, G., & Keating, A. L. (Eds.). (2002). *This bridge we call home: Radical visions for transformation.* New York, NY: Routledge.

Barthes, R. (1975). *Pleasure of the text* (R. Howard, Trans.). New York, NY: Noonday Press.

Barthes, R. (1977). *Image/music/text* (S. Heath, Trans.). New York, NY: Hill and Wang.

Barthes, R. (1978). *A lover's discourse: Fragments* (R. Howard, Trans.). New York, NY: Hill and Wang.

Collins, P. H. (1998). *Fighting words: Black women and the search for justice.* Minneapolis: University of Minnesota Press.

Collins, P. H. (2008). *Black feminist thought: Knowledge, consciousness, and the politics of empowerment.* New York, NY: Routledge.

Dei, G. J. S. (2008). Indigenous knowledge studies and the next generation: Pedagogical possibilities for anti-colonial education. *Australian Journal of Indigenous Education, 37*(5), 5–13.

Dewey, J. (1938). *Experience and education.* New York, NY: Touchstone.

Ellerby, J. H. (2000). *Spirituality, holism and healing among the Lakota Sioux: Towards an understanding of indigenous medicine* (Unpublished Master of Arts Dissertation). University of Manitoba, Manitoba, Winnipeg.

Freire, P. (1972). *Pedagogy of the oppressed.* New York, NY: Herder and Herder.

Freire, P. (1998). *Pedagogy of freedom: Ethics, democracy, and civic courage.* Boulder, CO: Rowman & Littlefield.

Harvey, P. (2013). *An introduction to Buddhism: Teachings, history and practices.*

Holland, D., Lachicotte, W., Jr., Skinner, D., & Cain, C. (1998). *Identity and agency in cultural worlds.* Cambridge, MA: Harvard University Press.

hooks, b. (2003). *Teaching community: A pedagogy of hope.* New York, NY: Routledge.

Kazeem, F. A. (2016). Time in Yorùbá Culture. *Al-Hikmat, 36*, 27–41.

Keating, A. L. (2006). From Borderlands and New Mestizas to Nepantlas and Nepantleras: Anzaldúan theories for social change. *Human Architecture: Journal of Sociology of Selfknowledge, 4*, 5–16.

Lorde, A. (1984). *Sister outsider: Essays and speeches*. Berkeley, CA: Crossing Press.

Mazama, M. A. (2002). Afrocentricity and African Spirituality. *Journal of Black Studies, 33*(2), 218–234.

Palmer, P. J. (2003). Teaching with heart and Soul: Reflections on spirituality in teacher education. *Journal of Teacher Education, 54*(5), 376–385.

Sandoval, C. (2000). *The methodology of the oppressed*. Minneapolis: University of Minnesota Press.

Smith, L. T. (1999). *Decolonizing methodologies: Research and indigenous peoples*. London, UK: Zed Books.

Wane, N. (2014). Student's spiritual selves: Implications for classroom practices. In N. Wane, F. Adyanga, & A. Ilmi (Eds.), *Spiritual discourse in the academy: A globalized indigenous perspective* (pp. 127–139). New York, NY: Peter Lang.

CHAPTER 13

# A Landscape of Sacred Regeneration and Resilience

*Kaylynn Sullivan TwoTrees and Sayra Pinto*

From Kaylynn Sullivan TwoTrees (KTT)

> I am forged out of the womb of experience in which words are sounds that are moved through our bodies from the expanse of the Sacred. My elders, education and human encounters have given me words in many languages. Some of them Sacred. Some of them ordinary. Some useful and some of them useless. My non-human kin and ancestors gave me the Sacred Teachings, wordless guidance that carries me along as food for the journey of life. When I heard the words of Kabir, my soul burst open into the memory of the vastness of the Sacred that is present everywhere, in every detail of life and living and in my own heart. This is the bedrock/base note/backdrop for the road of my life filled with Sacred encounter, loved ones, children, grandchildren, great grandchildren. The power of this foundation is clear and present in the midst of the continuing project of domination and colonization, which diminishes none of it.

K. Sullivan TwoTrees (✉) · S. Pinto
University of Vermont, Burlington, VT, USA
e-mail: ktt@ktwotrees.com



N. N. Wane et al. (eds.), *Decolonizing the Spirit in Education and Beyond*, Spirituality, Religion, and Education,
https://doi.org/10.1007/978-3-030-25320-2_13

## From Sayra Pinto (SP)

> I come from a people and a place carved out from the ancient into the present moment through a process of erasure that has failed. That which is right outside our skins renders us invisible and yet our suns shine into this place of nothingness with every smile and kind gesture. Our hearts beat without apology and pump life into every emotion, action, yearning, and desire. We accept that which we cannot control and squeeze every bit of joy from those moments when we are at choice. We relish in our children's first words, steps, and deeds and affirm their full humanity before they can utter a word. We understand that we are born Sacred out of our mothers' wombs, blessed by their efforts to make sure to give us life. We do forget about ourselves under the vast silence that meets our expectation of well-being. Yet we also remember. Our bodies are faithful guides into the memory of the place before words, where we are met in an eternal ancestral embrace.

This chapter seeks to invite you into a reflection about our collective relationship to the Sacred. Our focus on the Sacred does not obscure the facts of colonization and oppression. We both carry the signature impacts of colonization and oppression in our bodies and psyches. We both have been tasked with carving our lives out of the spoils of Western imposition over our peoples, land, languages, community practices, and ways to access the Sacred. Not much in our lives has been left intact from the immense impact of such violence. Our voices are not emanating from a place of disconnection from this embodied trauma. On the contrary, we have been passionate about affirming our humanity and experiences of joy, abundance, and well-being, as a direct result of the multiple ways in which intense and sustained failed attempts have been made to deny us these fundamentally human experiences.

TwoTrees has been in Higher Ed for the past 28 years working always at the edge of curriculum development to challenge and expand the Academy in the field of non-dominant perspective curriculum in education, environment, business, and the arts. In addition to that, as an artist and activist since 1972, TwoTrees has done work in multiple sectors across three continents as a way to serve as a catalyst to bring forth transformative dialogue and cultural exchange. Sayra has been managing community-based programs to create long-term systems change since she was fifteen years old in Chelsea, Massachusetts. Thirty years later, she has worked in higher education, domestic violence, gang intervention, youth development, and leadership development. In addition to that, as an artist and scholar, Sayra focuses her creative work in art and theory building to the process of the re-indigenization of Black and Brown communities.

Twelve years ago, we met on the hillside of Knoll Farm in Vermont, charged with bringing together a group of very diverse leaders from multiple sectors to connect the issue of race through a land conservation lens with two White male facilitators. The participants came with various levels of preparation for this conversation. Having just met each other for the first time, the four of us had to dig deep into our bodies of experience to facilitate this weeklong retreat. The challenges of that week forged a bond between all four of us. Our work has endured and deepened throughout the past twelve years.

The heart of our bond is the Sacred fire of our love and our connection to the Sacred, which has allowed us to hold moments of great tension in our move toward transformation for ourselves and for those we love and work with. Based on our individual journeys, our collective voice is grounded on a bond that spans the decades of age difference. Our voice here is the enactment of our decision to listen to the oral traditions and connection to spirit of our ancestors—not as informants but as mentors and collaborators in this work. The validity of their voices, lives, and dreams as manifest in our presence is unquestionable. Who is it that would try to convince us otherwise? For what purpose?

Our individual journeys have guided us to choose to expend our energy dreaming into the future from a foundation of the Sacred. We will not attempt to define the Sacred since we see denying the Sacred in itself as a reductive act and a replay of colonization. At best, we can attempt to point toward the Sacred, an act that is never to be mistaken for the Sacred itself. Although we will not offer a definition, we affirm that when one encounters the Sacred, one knows one has done so. The Sacred has many names and faces all over the world. All of these point to the ineffable, the Great Mystery, and all the names given to the Sacred Source. The turn toward the Sacred means the turn toward faith even in the heart of rationality. We affirm that faith is driving the car, not rationality. Faith is an expression of our intimate, dynamic relationship with the Unknown and Unknowable.

In order to choose to dream into the future from a foundation of the Sacred, our life journeys have been forged through paying exquisite attention to the spiritual preservation of relationship to the Sacred. We carry this awareness with us through practices and Teachings such as *surrender*, a deep understanding of *radical reciprocity* in a non-human centered world, and *sovereign logic*. Due to the weight of the continuing project of colonization, it is essential for us to be mindful of how we use our resources. This includes the words on our breath, life force, connections in our community, how we love, who we love, the memories we carry in our DNA, and careful discernment of ideas and theories that can lead away from the Sacred while claiming to bring us closer to ourselves. We must bring rigor and discernment to our participation in institutional and institutionalized arrangements that demand that we decenter ourselves and that which we consider Sacred in our daily lives. Our focus on the Sacred cannot be separated from the embodied experience of our indigeneity.

Our indigeneity operates beyond the particular cultural contexts into which we have been born and from which we have emerged. It cannot be stripped from us by oppression, erasure, genocide, forced migration, or the politics of authenticity. It is centered in the core of the Teachings we have received from our elders as well as from the cosmos and the Earth itself. Beyond the Teachings that have been carefully conserved for our benefit by our elders and gifted to us accordingly, our indigeneity is constantly emergent from our connection and our experience of the Sacred and the wisdom of the Earth. As an emergent condition of our lives, it is mutable and a perpetual source of our creative impulse. It keeps us in appropriate relationship as humans with all of the rest of life. The Sacred cannot be colonized. Any separation we feel from the Sacred is the expression of colonization.

Through our discernment, we believe that centering decolonization as the core conversation of indigenous peoples re-centers colonization and expands our separation from our individual and collective experience of the Sacred. We wish to decenter decolonization as a primary construct and move our energies to that which allows us to dream into a future beyond a dystopic or utopic set of ideas based on our reaction to colonization and its ensuing ingrained obsession with the establishment of dichotomies. Decolonization sets up colonization as a primary force. When we do this, we diminish the power of our own indigeneity. This is at its essence a defensive posture. At this juncture, after the hundreds of years of colonization we have endured, we need more than defensive or offensive postures. We need to re-center our ability to become generative through our experience of the Sacred. By being generative, we shape our future. We do not abdicate responsibility for continued intervention. We want our interventions to emerge from this generative place, to be driven by our intent to assert and access the Sacred.

Let us clarify that our turn toward the Sacred is critical thinking that has been put in service to the role of the Sacred in our lives. This turn has helped us discern what does not serve our spiritual welfare. We have become more rigorous in our inquiry and are clear about our need to exercise courage even when deeply uncomfortable and afraid.

We are going back to the root of the word *courage*, which means that it is centered in the heart and is not an act of will. Here are two stories that illustrate why we believe turning our intent and action toward the experience of the Sacred is an important next step in our daily enactment of our indigeneity. These have to do with the inevitable disorientation and flattening of the idea and emulative practice of indigeneity that occurs when we think of our own indigeneity through the eyes of culture and even through the gaze of the oppressor.

*KTT*: A class I taught recently on indigenous and Western concepts of identity and place offered students a chance to examine the places that are close to their hearts and identities. We also explored historical facts that complicate that attachment. Their work for the term included deep research into that with a focus on uncovering the first person narratives of the First Peoples of that place. Then, they were to develop a creative single narrative that integrated all of the conflicting, contradictory, and incommensurate histories they discovered without privileging one over the other. They could use multiple artistic mediums including painting, collage, sculpture, photography, storytelling, music, dance, and performance.

The demographic of the class included mostly White students and one indigenous student. Many of the White students chose places where their families owned land for several generations. They came to understand one identity of that land as stolen land. This prompted deep personal work and research in the archives and in their own family traditions. The indigenous student was a graduate student in the mist of rediscovering and claiming her own roots. We began this work together based on a series of Sacred agreements intended to create an ecology of learning supported by rigor and compassion and the strength of our *ancestors*.

We worked mostly outdoors so nature could be a collaborator in our work. There were nature awareness practices as well as research, which gave them access to insights and understandings that would not be available through any kind of structured curriculum and intellectual pursuit.

We used circle as our primary means of discourse and spent a good portion of our time articulating the struggle to find the voices of First Peoples rather than representations and stereotypes. When it was time to review the projects before presentation, one of the students presented a cartoonish drawing of an indigenous stereotype as a visual representation with romanticized text propagandizing the noble savage idea. When it was delivered in class, there were multiple reactions. The indigenous student left the room; some White students were in tears and there was an expectation of a harsh reprimand. What really seemed called for was a return to the Sacred agreements we had made coming in, which were to center love, well-being, and learning in our circle while attending to impact. As an Indigenous person, I was deeply hurt by the presentation and did not feel capable or willing to tend to the student's explanation of why they had done this. I chose rather to focus my energy on holding the original intention of our class. I asked the student who had delivered this presentation to not return to our circle but to use the remaining classes (there were only 2 left) and consider how to address the impact they had on both me and their peers. I asked other White students to assist them in this process so they would not feel isolated.

Given our learning community's strengths, we addressed the presentation collectively. Three White students stepped up to support the student who made the presentation process the incident and consider the impacts. I reached out to the indigenous student and explained all the ways I responded to the situation. In addition, I offered to process the experience with them. It was the first time I had an indigenous student in this class and was committed to creating a space for her journey of discovery as well as offer the experience of learning in an indigenous centered learning environment. What I encountered saddened me more than the impact of the presentation. What was evident is that although they had begun to discover their cultural indigeneity, this experience existed within the context of the academy and made it difficult if not impossible for them to engage and understand the indigenous ethics and the underlying ideas of community we were trying to embody. This student seemed focused on making sure the White student was punished. I focused on making sure our learning community was strengthened as a result of the event. Despite my efforts to connect, the student separated themselves from any deep connection around the incident and instead shared her ideas about exclusion of the White student and asking why the other students did not leave with them. By centering their personal experience, the student operated in contrast to what was actually happening for the entire group and interpreted my commitment to the well-being of the group as either betrayal or poor pedagogy. By drawing heavily on the academic historical understanding and analysis, the student was limited in their understanding of community, of how we can and do repair harm, how we do not throw anyone away by virtue of their actions.

When rooted in the Sacred, we have the capacity to be in relationship and to witness multiplicity of experience, expression, and being in the natural world that transcends our human centered understanding of the world we live in. As this student begins the process of unlearning Western ideologies and relearning indigenous ontologies, it is my hope that they will one day understand that a foundational difference between the West and indigeneity is the ability to be in expanded awareness of the multiple realities we inhabit at the same time. I also offer that this capacity is deepened through our experience of the Sacred.

Without access to and the practice of connecting to the Sacred, our spiritual, emotional, intellectual, and physical development is limited. By experiencing the Sacred, we deepen our relationship to ourselves, other loved ones, and the non-human world we live in. The cultural framework of our relationship to the Sacred is only the beginning of our journey back to the Sacred, which culminates beyond the practices that have been mapped out for us in our cultures through language and practice.

*SP*: Until recently, I was a tenant at a POC-owned land cooperative in Durham, NC. I was invited into that community by one of the cooperative's founders. My experience there is illustrative of the ways in which the languaging of indigeneity is being appropriated by people of color, both Black and Brown, without much reflection or connection to actual community, elders, ceremony, and most importantly, the type of world view that can center the Sacred. When I think of my time there, what happened at the dinner table when I decided to make chimol and offer it to that community comes up in high relief. Chimol is a Central American topping made of green peppers, onions, tomatoes, lime, and salt and pepper.

We were meeting to make peace about what was clearly the mistreatment of an indigenous elder there. I had called the cooperative to task on their attempt to monitor a ceremony this elder was intending on holding at the fire pit there. Recently, there had been a major shake up with the founding member that invited me to live on the land with her. She had been asked to leave the land and the cooperative was reassessing the activities and programming this person had been bringing on to their property. Due to their lack of self-awareness and fundamental understanding of the roles of elders, cooperative members began to assert their authority over their land and to try to ascertain time limits on the ceremonies being held there by native people. As a response, I wrote an email holding them to account for this behavior and also in protective response of the elder, who was experiencing intense psychological distress from this treatment. Their response was to ask to come together.

I hosted the meal we agreed to have at the place on their land that I was renting from them at that time in the hope that the situation would be worked out. Some cooperative members resented my email because they did not see me as an indigenous person and yet no one told me directly about this response. When we came together, and all the food everyone had brought was on the table, someone asked about the chimol. They asked what it was. I explained. Someone else said something like, "Oooh it's authentic Honduran." That worked my last nerve. So I said, "Actually, my aunties would have a fit because I used a food processor and three different kinds of peppers." I had added yellow and orange peppers to my chimol. Then that person said, "Oh." And fell silent. I then said, "You know that thing about being Honduran, is that I will be Honduran whether my chimol has one or three kinds of peppers. My chimol will always be Honduran whether I choose to innovate or not."

Those of us who are learning our ancient ways must remember that to an extent we cannot recover what we have lost. We can enact and embody but we cannot erase the loss. In the effort to erase the loss at times, we become tyrannical and mandate a type of fictitious authenticity. That group of folks, who so clearly struggled with standing in disciplined integrity and alignment with their intentions, kept adhering to ideas of purity, excellence, and the finality of culture which are all traits deeply embedded in Western culture in order to try to enact and embody their ideas of indigeneity. These ideas do not match, thankfully. If they matched, the project of our genocide would be complete. It is not. The deepest most transformative ceremonial experiences I've had have occur when highly disciplined ceremonialists use the tools and protocols at their hard earned disposal and surrender them to the call of the heart. By following our heart, we open up access to the Sacred. My chimol was a Sacred offering, met with the objectifying eye of a set of Western observers who had yet to learn that indigeneity is a process of surrendering form on behalf of the enactment and experience of substance when in the presence of the Sacred.

We are responding to an ancestral mandate to excavate our way back to our Source, which is the Sacred: indomitable, mutable, and undefinable. We have observed the replication of colonizing dynamics that affect our communities in ways we want to illuminate, identify, and name. We offer these observances in gratitude and in service to the possibility of a Great Migration Home to the Sacred. These dynamics show up in all kinds of ways and in all kinds of contexts related to both the enactment of oppression and the enactment of so-called liberatory behaviors, analyses, strategies, and ways of building community. We have seen and experienced oppressive enactments and identify them here. We offer this in the belief that we also need to discern more effectively how these dynamics pervade our discourse around liberation.

We have observed a propensity toward the elevation of grief and rage as primary legitimate reactions to oppression. They then infuse our outward political strategies and collective action while also presenting us with an intoxicating way to cope with the devastation which oppression creates within us. Rage and grief are important responses to the experiences of oppression; however, they can also blind us to and distract us from our deeper connection to our source of resilience and regeneration. Untended rage and grief often lead to separation, amnesia, perpetration of violence and trauma, and accommodation.

Untended rage and grief often serve as a justification for our separation from healthy connected interdependent relationships in community. Those tools born out of untended rage and grief are the most easily co-opted by the oppressor and continue to create separation. For example, one of the tools often glorified is resistance. Yet, resistance often turns us into mirror images of the very same oppressive system we are trying to resist while also replicating separation. Resistance uses up the resources that could otherwise be used to remember and embody our own spiritual foundations because it becomes an end in itself. There are numerous historical examples of the perpetration of separation as a direct result of resistance and revolution. We are not purporting that no one intervenes where harm is happening. Our intervention is essential in the current reality we live in. Centering the Sacred is not a zero sum game. We are willing and capable of centering the Sacred while living in this current situation without relying on separation and its tool, resistance. Our connection to the Sacred enhances our responses to the current situation and enables the longest-term intervention possible for any one of us with a view toward the next Seven Generations.

Amnesia is another feature of effective colonization. When we center grief and rage, along with a conversation on decolonization, we in fact put at the center of our lives a narrative where the oppressor is the protagonist in our lives. Centering the oppressor as a protagonist in our narratives about who we are as a people, who we have been, what we have accomplished, how we have failed, how we have lost the power to name and count ourselves, is the ultimate victory of colonization. We refuse to concede a victory. We are attempting to reveal amnesia as a necessary tool of colonization. Our participation in this is our complicity in our own devastation. In following our mandate of excavation, we are accountable to illuminating what we excavate along the way and we offer our own experiences of uncovering our complicity in order to correct our course as a guide for those who may want to follow. We have no interest in sounding righteous or like we know something. We are sharing our lived experience and the guidance of our Teachings through the lens of decades of living and self-work.

Untended rage and grief often transform into violent behavior of multiple sorts: physical, emotional, and psychological. Privileging rage and grief as the primary legitimate responses to oppression endangers our internal condition, our intimate relationships, and the type of quality of life that actually connects us to our source of renewal and healing. It diminishes our capacity to see beyond rage and grief and to understand our need to operate from a place of abundance, well-being, love, and courage.

Our ancestors' act of survivance was to dream us into being. Their dreaming of us was the enactment of courage. We discount the power of that dreaming when we allow ourselves to privilege rage and grief. We are all miracles of survivance. Many of us who have experienced poverty and violence also know the deep wells of love and generosity to be found among people who are the most impacted and who have the least.

Untended grief and rage give way to the normalization of these unfinished experiences in our daily lives. Our hearts become dampened. We internalize hopelessness and then normalize it in our relationships, our organizations, and our outlook on the world. We begin to objectify love, to denounce the Sacred, to make these trifling unnecessary endeavors in our lives in favor of more concrete, practical, immediate, justifiable, and sensible pursuits. We accommodate the endless presence of grief and rage in our lives and shape our lives around them in order to justify their perpetual place in the landscape of our hearts. We begin to live lives we cannot imagine being free from the stifling pain of rage and grief. Our hearts, love, intellects, imaginations, generosity, kindness, mercy, and courage shrink when we accommodate. And we say that when we accommodate grief and anger at the core of our lives, we assimilate. And when we assimilate, our path to the Sacred also shrinks.

One of the more recent and increasing dynamics we have experienced in our work in the world is the use of intellectualization to normalize our internal separation from ourselves in order to leverage more power, access, legitimacy, and even standing in the eyes of institutions, individuals, and other systems of power in the West. This has caused us to come so far from our center as a people. Intellectualization leads us to develop narratives about ourselves from the third person and these narratives then are framed to meet the demands and requirements of the oppressor. The tragedy and tyranny of this are that we then believe these narratives to truly be our own. We then replace our actual stories about our connection to ourselves, our cultures, the land, and our spiritual foundations, with these pseudo-narratives.

It took much prayer, thought, and discernment to decide to write these things. It made our hearts heavy to do so. We could not, however, describe a landscape of regeneration and resilience without talking about the challenges to those very things. We have chosen to spend the bulk of our energy focused on that landscape but we would be remiss had we not done both. All reactions to oppression are legitimate. We also have multiple ways to transform those reactions into generative, hopeful, and inspirational acts of remembrance that can bring us closer to the Sacred. From that place of connection can emerge innumerable possibilities for our futures that make us free, powerful, whole, and able to dream for the Seven Generations coming after us. The turn from our reaction to oppression to a generative stance looking to the future is what we pray and live for.

The passport to the land of the Sacred is the continual practice of surrender. We are not talking about surrender in human terms. Rather in terms of offering our will and strength to the service of the Sacred. The nature of surrender is not a passive giving over. It is allowing oneself to be in open collaboration with the divine flow of grace. Our physical bodies are actually designed for surrender because we breathe automatically and our breath puts us in connection with the one breath that connects everything. Our consciousness needs to be brought into that kind of intimate automatic act of collaboration with the continued reality we want to be in the world. We call that *surrender* to acknowledge our appropriate place in that collaboration, and to understand ourselves as a detail in the cosmos. Surrender is a practice that allows us to be mutable. To grow, to unlearn, to relearn, to remember, to change, to innovate, to respond to divine impulses, to ensure our ongoing survival.

Without surrender, we become static and are eroded by the continuing change in the world, so we will eventually disappear. Given this, in relation to our cultural practices, these too can become static and limit our ability to respond to the world of which we are a part and which is continually changing and evolving. Although we have struggled to rescue, remember, and maintain culture including language, ceremonies, and social structures, we are also called to surrender them on behalf of a vibrant and connected future.

Thus, we are called to turn to substance from form. From the performance of ideas of ceremony to the enactment of ceremonial practices that give us unmediated access to the Sacred. The gift we have been given as humans is that we are able to renegotiate the contracts that hold our reality in place. Ceremony is a process through which we renegotiate these contracts in right relationship horizontally in the human and natural world, and vertically with the spiritual world. This power requires that we have apprenticed to, practiced, and become masterful in that reality before we make attempts at innovation. The type of command and mastery we are talking about is the result of deep practice and deep relationship. We are called back to the source of our cosmologies.

The enactment of deep practice and deep relationship are *radical reciprocity*. Deep practice and deep relationship is possible when we understand ourselves as beings embedded in deeply layered webs of relationships that are interdependent. Our actions, words, thoughts, prayers, all affect these webs in conscious and unconscious ways. When we live in the world in this way, we are aware of ripples of impact from all interactions we have with any other beings and with the whole of nature. We want all of those interactions to benefit these interdependent webs. We stop behaving as if our individual actions are isolated from these webs. This is the place where we move far beyond self-interest and mutual benefit, to an understanding of ourselves as a point in the whole that is connected to everything else. Our well-being then is dependent upon the health and well-being of the whole.

Radical reciprocity depends on our ability to be aware and in command of our *sovereign logic*. By sovereign logic, we mean the ways in which we make sense and intuit the present moment and the emergent future based on our relationship to place, lineage, experience, and the learning we have done based on our life path. Each of us embodies a sovereign logic that is unique. We need to be in relationship with both our own sovereign logic and others'. As humans we all have our sovereign logic and we are also in relationship with nature in which individuated species have their own sovereign logic. We also live in nested systems, and each of those systems also have their own coherence, which we must take into account in the process of knowing, commanding, and enacting our sovereign logic. To welcome each encounter with other beings with a full expectation and appreciation of their sovereign logic enables radical reciprocity.

We have talked about *surrender, radical reciprocity* and *sovereign logic* in the effort to unveil the entry to the landscape of Sacred regeneration and resilience and to point to the practices for embodying and co-creating this landscape. Dreaming a regenerative and resilient future is a communal activity conducted in connection with our ancestors through our experience of the Sacred. Each of us comes to that dreaming in our own unique way along the pathways of our own sovereign logic. There is no one path to the future and yet we will dream it into being together. We hope to continue this dreaming with all of you.

CHAPTER 14

# Dialogue on Decolonizing the Spirit with Dr. Njoki Nathani Wane and Kimberly L. Todd

*Njoki Nathani Wane and Kimberly L. Todd*

January 18th, 2018

*Kimberly*: Hello my name is Kimberly Todd and I am going to be interviewing Dr. Njoki Wane about our anthology Decolonizing the Spirit.

*Njoki*: Thank you, Kim for this opportunity to talk about our anthology Decolonizing the Spirit. It is a good project and I have enjoyed working on it and I am looking forward to this interview. My name is Njoki Wane and Njoki means come back.

*Kimberly*: For our first question Dr. Wane how did the concept that the spirit could never be colonized come to you?

*Njoki*: It is interesting you ask that question, because a lot of people have asked me how did the idea that the spirit could never be colonized come about. The way it came about was a reflection, a look at history, a look at

N. N. Wane (✉) · K. L. Todd
University of Toronto, Toronto, ON, Canada
e-mail: njoki.wane@utoronto.ca

K. L. Todd
e-mail: k.todd@mail.utoronto.ca



N. N. Wane et al. (eds.), *Decolonizing the Spirit in Education and Beyond*, Spirituality, Religion, and Education,
https://doi.org/10.1007/978-3-030-25320-2_14

the resiliency of the people who had been subjected to so much suffering. Yet those people held on together. Yet those people had succumbed to so many oppressions, so many…I can't even give a name to that and I thought in terms of what made these people stand under such dehumanizing circumstances? It is the Spirit, the Spirit that you cannot touch, that you cannot see, but the Spirit that is always there. The Spirit that people may assume that you don't have.

*Kimberly*: Wow, that is profound. Do you think that during times of oppression that it [the Spirit] sort of initiates a spiritual awakening?

*Njoki*: The conversation on spiritual awakening is a different type of conversation because you can have spiritual awakening even when you are not suffering. So, it doesn't mean that spiritual awakening comes because you are subjugated to pain or challenging moments in your life. It can come at any point. But for the Spirit- in relation to the Spirit cannot be colonized—the awakening comes in when you least expect…. and you look at the oppressor, or you look at the situation you are in, then you go inward. You go inside yourself, you hold that breath, then you look at the in breath, that is the in breath and you hold it and the breath holds you. That in breath is the Spirit. At that particular moment it is the awakening for you, that is inner you- an inner person, something that we have no name for that we refer to as the Spirit.

*Kimberly*: What propelled you along this personal journey to come to this understanding, in your own life, would you say?

*Njoki*: Coming to school in North America, you know the desire to acquire a western education was high. I wanted so much to have the colonial education from the source... Reflecting on that now, unconsciously, I was longing to be colonized—I don't think I have ever even used that word/term-the desire to be colonized. But we do it unconsciously because you feel that if I go to a Western country, going through the Western Education system I will be like White people, I will be like them, I will be a white woman, in a Black skin (Fanon, 1965). So, without us realizing, we are desiring to be colonized-but we are. It's the coming here and the let down, that awakens you. You start questioning, you doubt yourself; I have acquired the western education, I dress like them, eat their food, why have I not been accepted and invited into their circle. When I got here I was like 'Oh my God, this is not what I was looking for'. I was looking for something that reflected on the whole world. The things I had been learning in Kenya about the Western world. So, I thought wait a minute there is something missing here. That is when I started reflecting on the teachings of my parents. My mom would chant, we call it prayer. We would reflect and ask our Creator for our needs, we would ask for guidance from Creator, and ask for blessings and for the whole family and our neighbours. Then in the evening again, instead of my mom doing it, my dad would do it.

If I did not go back to that. I would have packed my bags and gone back to Kenya. My spirit needed to awaken to survive in this country. The Spirit in me that had been dormant. It was submerged under the colonial yoke. How did I navigate that going back in. I do remember putting up my hand and asking, one of the professors-why my African ways of knowing were not included in his course—I remember saying, I thought the West included everyone and all their knowledges. And the professor said maybe not for his class. I do not know why I thought that I should write about African Indigenous knowledges. I was however, determined to write about African Indigenous knowledges. So, I went back to Kenya, and I looked up where Indigenous Ways of knowing were being taught or even African spirituality, interestingly at that time-there was no space for Indigenous knowledge within the Kenyan system. So I interviewed students in urban dwellings and in the rural settings about Indigenous education, Indigenous ways of knowing; I was yearning and seeking. I talked to students about the inclusion of Indigenous knowledges. The students had no knowledge about what Indigenous knowledges were. I thought I probably should to talk to the Elders. So, I talked to the Elders and it was the Elders that taught me. They said to me young lady you need to go back to the source; you need to know your own culture; your own Indigenous knowledges. You need to pay attention to the generation of your mom, like we used to say to you when you were growing up.

*Kimberly*: How has the theme of this book "Decolonizing the Spirit" shaped your scholarship and pedagogy?

*Njoki*: It has shaped my scholarship in different ways. Number one, to realize that I am not the only one who is interested in this topic is refreshing. There are other people who are privileging the Spirit. Number two; it has confirmed to me that when we talk about spirituality and notions of decolonization.... there are different theories to that....it can be a practice; it can be a tool and that has energized my being. Spirituality can be a theoretical tool, spiritual tool, a tool for decolonizing, spirituality can be a tool for activating your inner self. To see other people picking up those aspects and writing about them, is amazing. It has truly awakened the second Spirit, there are several Spirits in me, the second spirit. Number three, to create the resources for doing this work was not easy, but it was a project I enjoyed doing. So that we don't have to constantly be running around saying we don't have these resources. The book itself will be a great resource for many people. It has given me great pleasure going over all the chapters. Because its a whole book on spirituality... different aspects of it; and going through the various chapters, the sincerity with which the people are connecting to themselves, that inner Spirit, that sincerity and that inner strength.... .... that is awakening the spirit in itself. I believe in the whole book there is some presence, some force that we cannot see.

*Kimberly*: I would really agree with that because even reading all the chapters ...there is so much rawness and vulnerability in it. There really is so much Spirit [in the chapters], you can really see that sort of evoking of the authors' internal Spirit. That you don't see often, that it gives you so much hope for what can be...

*Njoki*: Can I ask you a question?

*Kimberly*: Sure.

*Njoki*: Going through the chapters, because you are also part of this book, how did it speak to you?

*Kimberly*: To be honest after reading them, even for my own chapter I thought there needs to be more of my Spirit in there. So, I included a dream narrative that I had never shared publicly before, only after reading the other ones-because it was so inspiring. The personal narratives, I think they provide avenues for people to see their own stories and transformations reflected in the writing. Even afterwards after reading the chapters, there are pieces that stay with you and they help you formulate your own understanding. I think the book itself is transformative. Even in the way it is put together. There is a process there, a spiritual process that ah, that it has come together, I am going to say, that there is a...synchronicity to it. It is so, its been incredible. It gives me a lot of hope because there is a pathway that is being charted, that we are collectively charting, I think.

*Njoki*: The other thing I find with the book is within the Academy there is so much focus on the abstract, the book provides an entry point to look beyond the abstract, to look beyond the invisible. I don't know whether you noticed that when you were reading.

*Kimberly*: What really comes out at me in the reading of the book, is love. The pervasiveness of love, and our interconnection and our interdependence. Even despite, despite so much ongoing continual oppression. Even myself I have been thinking about this idea of wounding and healing. If maybe in there, there is a sense that we are all humanity, you know, I am not sure though where that it is going yet, yeah.

*Njoki*: The interesting thing about wounding and woundedness. The Spirit can never be wounded. You cannot take a spear and put it through a Spirit. You cannot wound the Spirit. That's what gives me hope because when everything else is crumbling, when everything else is falling by the wayside the Spirit stands and that is the hope we are talking about. Different ways of healing emanate from the Spirit. From the Spirit that is how people are led. Because it is coming from somewhere pure, that's my understanding. Of course, there is the element of bad spirits. I guess this is not the place for this, but people might say that for this book-I am mentioning just in case that somebody might say that we do have that bad spirit—but that is for a different conversation.

*Kimberly*: But I also feel like even when we heal ourselves, that healing can transfer outwards. It can be contagious in a way. Even for those people who are not far enough along their journey, it can help, it can be healing because we are interconnected.

*Njoki*: Yes, because we are energy, if you are healing, if you are emanating positive energy. That positive energy is very contagious, and if you multiply it—it will get to the next person. That's why the wholeness of the Spirit gives us hope.

*Kimberly*: It is so true. I completely agree with you and that's what so powerful about it. Okay, so my next question is why do you think it is valuable for people to be aware of the resiliency of the Spirit. I know it seems like a very obvious question, but I want to hear your views on that.

*Njoki*: Many times, we despair ... we despair and we think there is nothing we can do. It is so hopeless. Without knowing that we should not despair. We have something within us that we can tap into. That we have something inside us that we can tap into it [softly].

*Kimberly*: I love that. That sometimes we do not know we have it. Especially with my work on dreaming. Everybody dreams, but it is something we can, but don't tap into. You are right about that.

*Njoki*: Let's think of the analogy of a child. What makes the child think they can walk.

*Kimberly*: [Laughs].

*Njoki*: Something propels them to walk. If you have been to a safari.... sometimes you see an elephant or zebra give birth and within minutes the calf starts walking-how on earth? The calf will come out of their mother's womb and start walking. What is it that make them walk? I think we have that, and we can tap into it. We can move forward.

*Kimberly*: Even when you think about the seed of a tree. What is contained in that seed? The potential. The seed has the audacity to drop into the ground and a giant tree emerges and all the possibilities that it offers.

*Njoki*: The interesting thing you bring about the analogy of the seed. When the seed falls down. There is the interdependency of seed, the soil, water, the surroundings. It gets fed with all that. It dies and what emerges out of that is a new plant, it is a rebirth.

*Kimberly*: Yes, a rebirth.

*Njoki*: How does that happen? It drops and changes... it dies, and in death it gives birth to something new... not sure how to explain it. Humans, the way we look at a seed when we are planting it; we never think of it dying or even say oh it is dying. We just assume, it will sprout and grow... But something emerges out of that. No, it does not die, it grows into a big tree.

*Kimberly*: In relation to that tree, all that the tree provides for all the animals and people.

*Njoki*: The resiliency of that seed in itself.

*Kimberly*: In terms of the human spirit with that rebirth of the Spirit, when you realize that, that is within you. There is also so much giving and healing that can be given to others.

*Njoki*: The rebirth is very important that's where the healing comes in, the energizing of the Spirit. The awakening of the Spirit.

*Kimberly*: Can you speak to the concept of the spirit becoming dormant in times of violence and oppression?

*Njoki*: That's a good question. For instance, when I talk of the Spirit becoming dormant. We see it in colonization, through colonization, different colonial machineries. Somebody accepts to behave in different ways from their own, you accept a language that is not your own, you accept to be subjected to an education that is different from your own education. I am talking about non-Western people-you are subjected to a religion and worshiping that is completely different from what you were taught to do or taught to believe in. Remember at the center of all that, there is your Spirit. So, the Spirit, this is my analysis, the Spirit says do I fight or do I go dormant? If I fight, I will not go far the Spirit says I will wait till I have people who are on the same wavelength and then we can start the awakening of Spirit, bringing it out of dormancy state. If you do it alone then you are subject to the *death* of the physical body, the Spirit does not die, but then you will be gone. The Spirit knows the time to sleep, it is time to grow the base, grow the roots, it is again like the seed, like food itself, if the seed opens too early before it is ready it dies, if it opens on a rock it dies, it was not in the right space at the right time for it to give birth, it is the same thing with the Spirit.

*Kimberly*: I have even heard that there are certain animals so when they give birth, say in times of drought, when they are pregnant, they will wait, that they can wait to give birth. So, the Spirit knows when…

*Njoki*: This is the mystery, that we need to find out as humans, why the Spirit decides to wait to fold the hands and wait for the moment, that's what I think.

*Kimberly*: Wow that is so profound. I think that when the Spirit has emerged, then people start coming. It's like a, I don't know it is like a calling.

*Njoki*: It's like a calling, the Spirit does not come out of that dormancy unless it is ready.

*Kimberly*: Wow!

*Njoki*: Because for instance for you; dreaming, there was a right moment for you to start saying I am going to write on this I am going to base my academic degree on this particular topic which is so controversial. That is very central to our educational system, yet people do not see currency in dreaming. But there came a moment when you said I want to show that there is currency in dreaming. It is part of who we are, its part of our knowledge production, it is part of our dissemination and so on and so forth.

*Kimberly*: Because I have been thinking about, my year of the Sea Turtle, that' what I call it, when I had all these dreams about the Sea Turtle. I was in a place where I was away from home and I was struggling a lot, so much, for so many reasons. Why then? And so that's so interesting your concept of the Spirit being dormant. But knowing when to emerge. It was the right moment for me. But being able to understanding the why—at that time, I don't know it hasn't come yet. I don't know.

*Njoki*: There is no reason for the why. The Spirit just knows. There is no reason to ask Why now? Why me?

*Kimberly*: Then it reoriented my whole life since then.

*Njoki*: I can give the example of teaching the class Spirituality and Schooling. Why on Earth would I teach a class on spirituality and schooling and not emphasize on religion? I don't know and I never asked why. It's a moment.

*Kimberly*: I guess there is like a resonance of spirit and I guess you are drawn to certain things because there is recognition in yourself-that this is right-intuition you can say.

*Njoki*: And when people try to make sense of what you are doing, they can completely misunderstand you. They do not know why you are doing what you are doing. And the notion that Spirituality is not scholarship that it is too soft, that it does not have a place in the academy. But from the book we have seen that spirituality is really central in the Academy, as a topic, as a theory, as a tool.

*Kimberly*: Yes, it is so true. It gives me a lot to think about. (Laughs)

*Kimberly*: How do you envision decolonial healing, resurgence, and resistance in light of the emergence of Spirit?

*Njoki*: That's a whole book!

*Kimberly*: Sorry!

*Njoki*: (Laughs) We have to take into consideration before colonization, during the colonial period, after the colonizers "left", when technically they did not leave. A lot of scholars got into the postcolonial. But a lot of the marginalized people got involved in Anti-colonial work and decolonial work. That negated the notion of wait a minute, we did have scholarship before colonization came, we had everything. It is not a question of decolonizing. It is a question of letting go of the colonial. Distancing yourself from that and literally paying attention to what was. And not in relation to how it has been placed on a continuum and how it is classified. It has its own merit. The Latin American scholars started saying we need to start thinking about the decolonial. We have gotten so consumed with -we had this and we have that. It is us responding to and continually reacting to colonization -causing confusion. In regards to decolonial healing, it is about now. If we can sit still (colonial subjects) and start thinking about who we are, who you are, and what you have-you will be in a position to start healing. You don't have to start looking for the external to heal you. The healing is within you. It has always been within you. The ancestors provided you with that. Your ancestral society has given you that, generation after generation you have been given the tools for healing. But with the colonization there was confusion. There was reprimanding, you can't use this that form of healing, you can't use this form of healing. That created confusion and chaos. But if you can sit still and listen to the now, then decolonial healing will start.

*Kimberly*: Ah so that talks about the re-emergence of spirit.

*Njoki*: Exactly. It is a form of restitution. Because when we are constantly at the fore-front fighting we don't have the time for now. Our whole energy is consumed by fighting. But If we have that stillness which is a form of resistance, because we are telling whoever is subjecting you to a particular mode of pain and suffering. You are saying I am going to use the now as my resistance-the stillness of the now as my resistance. Because out of that comes the resurgency of the new me.

*Kimberly*: Wow I love that. You capture the re-mergence of Spirit so beautifully.

*Njoki*: What do you think about what I have just said? Does that speak to you?

*Kimberly*: It really does. What I have been noticing in my own work with dreaming in my own experience is that ah even in terms of your ancestry. When it has been so degraded by colonization for so long. That subconsciously your dreaming can help you find your answers too, even to your own ancestry. It can actually do that work-of stretching. And when you wake up and look into that-there are real truths embedded in it. It can be really incredible. So, I think that it is very powerful that somehow the Spirit it even has the capacity to trace your origins even if you don't even-if you don't even know them and then bring them to you through spiritual tools-whether they be visioning or dreaming or journeying. It can actually do that for you. So, there is that, you can really tap into all that you are despite colonization.

*Njoki*: It is interesting you talk about dreaming. I started writing down my dreams. Of course, all my life when I dream the majority of the scenes of my dreams are my ancestral home. Next to my ancestral home there was a river. So invariably in all the dreams there is a river. Either I am trying to cross it, or I am swimming in the river or I am fetching water from the river. The last dream I had with the river my daughter and my husband were with me. My husband because of his condition could not come out of the river and we were thinking how to bring him out of the river. So, I tried to come out of the river-and this is very interesting-I always try to go to the dry land on the side where my house was. So, I tried to climb out-but the whole bank is lined with sweet cakes. It is lined up with red cakes and white cakes with a lot of cream. I thought it was interesting and I put out my hand. Somehow, I did not eat those cakes, I just try to create a space so I can hold on to get out. So, when we are talking about colonization-those cakes are colonization. Because we are brought up thinking if you can eat cakes, bread-all things that are not our things-then we are educated -we are Westernized.

*Kimberly*: Even in terms of the water. Water is one of the most powerful symbols in dreaming. It speaks to us about our origins. Even the body is made up of such a huge percentage of water. Even when you think of us in the womb. Water tends to be a symbol that speaks to us about being in contact with the collective unconscious. So even you being emerged in the water itself, you are tapped in. So, at home you are in your ancestral waters. So even in the dream-maybe in the dream the river is where you should be. You carry that with you in your dreams. Your ancestral waters are always with you. There are so many layers to the dream.

*Njoki*: Even thinking about those cakes. They have no nutritional value. Very Interesting.

*Kimberly*: If you were to envision- the reason I am asking you this question is because I think we need start to envisioning different futures-different futures from where we are now so we can begin to chart our path there. If you were to envision a future where the revival and re-emergence of spirit is valued and cultivated what would that future look like?

*Njoki*: It brings tears to me. What that means is we will be conscious of each other. Our humanity would have emerged. We will stop thinking this person is better than me. We will stop gaping to the outside for our own satisfaction. Because we start defining what we have and what we need from the parameters that we occupy. As a human being you don't occupy a lot of parameters. When there is that clarity of what you need, there is clarity of intention, that clarity of where you want to go. Then when you emerge and step out of that particular space that you occupy and you go outside and meet with people who will tell you-that is not good for you-you shouldn't do that. You have the courage to look into their eyes and say no that is not good for me-I think I know what is good for me-this is the path I want. Come with me as I journey on this particular path. If you want to assist me on my path then come with me. Then help me, and come with me as I journey on this particular path. But if you had not at that moment – been present to the spirit having that inward conversation with the self. Then you emerge out of that space into the chaos of the world. Then what will happen is the first person you meet will say this is the path and you will say yes and you will run and it will lead you to nowhere. Because somebody else has mapped out a path for you. That is how the world has been run, that is how the political system has been structured and that is how the education system has been structured [with paths that other people have mapped for you]. That is how the economic systems has been structured. Because you are always thinking about how you can manoeuvre and control the people who are emerging from their spaces having not thought out their path.

*Kimberly*: That is so true. I really believe that your Spirit knows the trajectory you need to take. Because-I don't know how (laughs). And even when you are in touch with that-you look back and you think wow there was a pathway. I have found a pathway just based on resonance and intuition. Being true to yourself and doing that helps bridge a pathways for others to begin bridging also, but it takes a lot of courage. You don't necessarily have the same accolades or you don't get the same respect even in society because your path doesn't look like other peoples. You have to have so much inner strength because you are usually charting new territory in terms of your own path.

*Njoki*: The interesting thing is, as you journey on that path. People will recognize you, people who have had that awakening.

*Kimberly*: Or even an inkling of an awakening.

*Njoki*: Yes, even an inkling of the awakening. They will look at you and recognize you, because they recognize the spirit in you. How do you do that? How do you manage to be calm? How do you manage to do what you want to do? Those are your comrades.

*Kimberly*: Oh woah…

*Njoki*: However, you get another group of people. They will say she has no scholarship, she doesn't know what she is doing, she is soft. They haven't been in touch with their own reality. Their reality is being controlled by external forces.

*Kimberly*: That is so true.

*Njoki*: If we can create a mass of people, like minded people who start envisioning the world you are talking about, I think there will be a lot of hope in the world you are talking about. I think we will not see so many wars, starvation, flooding all kinds of things.

*Kimberly*: What about the Earth?

*Njoki*: I know. That's a good one. The Earth is part of who we are. Approximately 70% of the Earth is water. Human beings are, approximately 70% water. When we think we can exploit the Earth we are actually exploiting ourselves. We are part of the cosmos, we are part of the Earth. I know we are a really really a tiny speck on the surface of the Earth. Our space is part of the Earth. With our lack of knowing we think we can control the Earth-but the Earth is in charge.

*Kimberly*: I actually think the Earth is actively ushering us in through this awakening because Her destruction is so horrific at this time. That in us, she is speaking to us. She is speaking to us through our dreams, our visions. She can communicate I think through the medium of our spirit. So, She is ushering us into the next phase of our awakening.

*Njoki*: I agree with you.

*Kimberly*: Can you speak to your work with the Decolonizing the Spirit Conference. This has been over ten years and this is why this book is coming out at this time.

*Njoki*: You know our conversations have indicated that sometimes you don't know the path you are taking or you don't know the moment you do things.

*Kimberly*: It is true.

*Njoki*: When I think back to the ten years of running the Decolonizing the Spirit Conference it takes me back to the first year that we did it. It was like we were talking about the spirit in the class. It was very clear from the conversations and the readings-and I have to tell you when I thought of teaching this class, I had no idea where I was going to get the readings and the materials from. Just how I am working with you now. I had a student and his name was Riyad who worked with me then.

*Kimberly*: Riyad Shahjahan?

*Njoki*: Yes. I remember his suggestion was we should do spirituality and education-but I chose schooling. I have no idea why I chose schooling. Because education is more tangible, education depends on the culture, the context. But schooling is very broad and when you think about it, it is meaningless. So, after teaching that course for two sessions-two semesters if I can be more specific, this is bigger than the class. This is bigger than OISE {Ontario Institute for Studies in Education}. I think it is important for me to open spaces to hear from people who have never been to the academy to have a conversation about the academy -to talk about spirituality-because spirituality had been shut off from the academy. And I saw that there is a need-to have conversations, to have dialogues within the academy and to ask questions -to have conversations about the various modes of spirituality within the academy. That is when I thought about Decolonizing the Spirit. Because we had talked about decolonizing the land, decolonizing politics so I thought why not Decolonizing the Spirit? And that is how it came about- boom! I am so happy because throughout the years we started with a very small group and it grew to two hundred, three hundred. And the last one we had over 800 people.

*Kimberly*: I was at the last one (conference), and during my time there, it felt like there was something opening up in my chest. It felt like hope was residing there. Like it was expanding. When you see so many people you get a glimpse that we are working together and that is so powerful and so hopeful. And literally I spent that time at that conference with this opening feeling in my chest. It was so beautiful and it was almost overwhelming. You need to do this work in community.

*Njoki*: My first class I had maybe ten students and then it grew to twenty and then thirty. Now look, the conversations have gone in different directions. During the second year TwoTrees was our keynote speaker.

*Kimberly*: Look TwoTrees is writing our foreword another {with Sayra Pinto} and another before this dialogue. Incredible.

*Njoki*: Yes. Thank you so much. As I close this chapter, for me, and release. It is no longer mine, it is no longer mine, or my conference, it has taken its own path. I do not know where my path will lead now [laughs].

*Kimberly*: Thank you!

*Njoki*: Thank you so much for this.

CHAPTER 15

# Conclusion: The Politics of Spirituality—A Postsocialist View

*Miglena S. Todorova*

I am neither Indigenous nor racialized in the ways in which the other contributors to this collection have been historically constructed, exploited, marginalized, and displaced as 'African,' 'Aboriginal,' 'Indigenous,' 'Latino,' 'Brown,' and 'Black' subjects. I am from the Balkans: a land ambiguously situated and constructed by outsiders as neither 'White' nor 'racialized' and in the south and east of Europe but not of it. The Balkans is also a land shaped by conquests and empires: Ottoman, Russian/Soviet, and Habsburg empires have all ruled over the region and its peoples over the centuries. In the Western social sciences, the Balkans is referred to as the 'Second World' somewhere between the developed and civilized Western 'First World' and the 'Third World' marked by cultural, racial, and economic deficiencies .

M. S. Todorova (✉)
University of Toronto, Toronto, ON, Canada
e-mail: miglena.todorova@utoronto.ca



N. N. Wane et al. (eds.), *Decolonizing the Spirit in Education and Beyond*, Spirituality, Religion, and Education,
https://doi.org/10.1007/978-3-030-25320-2_15

Here, I do not wish to address the question of spirituality from within the Balkan history of political domination and epistemic and cultural violence that has made the region and shaped my own identities; nor do I wish to enter the discussion about decolonization as an 'ally' of colonized and marginalized communities facing historical oppression. I am aware that political and epistemological alliances and solidarities with colonized peoples do not erase the fact that I have racial and cultural privilege as someone associated with a (darker) shade of Whiteness and Europeanness. Instead, I come to this conversation as a learner and another spiritual person driven by desire for a future that is unlike our past and present marked by violence, exploitation, and suffering. In thinking about such a future I ask: *What political aspects of spirituality are pertinent to making that future?*

In the following discussion, I focus on the political features of the spiritual explorations featured in this collection, especially their relational politics and connection to the struggles of others, radical traditions rooted in the intimate and familial, and links to material systems and structures. I also use a postsocialist lens to address the absence of Indigenous peoples and histories in Soviet Russia, drawing attention to how current geopolitical and epistemological contexts also shape conversations about decolonization, spirituality, social justice, and the future.

## Bridging Time, Places, and Struggles

In his rich discussion of spirituality, Van der Veer (2009) argued that the concept emerged from nineteenth-century Euro-American modernity, specifically the globalization of Western ideas of citizenship, rights, democracy, and nation, which spread through the pathways of European colonialisms, dovetailing with the expansion and integration of capitalist markets and the diffusion of scientific knowledge rooted in rationality and secularism. He argued that spiritualism emerged in Western modern societies as the opposite of secularism, and became a rationalized truth-seeking alternative to religion. By the early twentieth century, Euro-American colonial sciences of religion had developed a concept of 'spirituality' signifying universal morality and the expression of all religions—including Christianity, Islam, Judaism, Buddhism, Confucianism, and Daoism—fostering a Western multicultural liberal view of religious tolerance and spiritual sharing that served the interests of colonial powers. In the 1940s and 1950s, Western ideas of spirituality penetrated deeply cultural and political conversations in the Global South, anchoring claims to nationhood and civilization among political and economic elites in India, China, and throughout the colonized territories of Africa. Political and intellectual leaders such as Vivekananda, Mohandas Gandhi, and the Bengali poet Rabindranath Tagore asserted an 'Eastern spirituality' professing unity, kindness, and all-embracing views of the world as a countering force and an alternative to European colonial violence, Western capitalist exploitation, and materialistic cultures. African and Eastern spiritual traditions further anchored visions of 'the nation' subsuming the religious, racial, cultural, and linguistic heterogeneity of the liberated postcolonial peoples and territories, thus echoing processes in the imperial metropolis. Indeed, there was no equivalent term for 'spirituality' in Sanskrit or Mandarin Chinese: Hinduism, Buddhism, Daoism, or Confucianism became 'isms' only after European colonizing powers and knowledges conquered the world (ibid.).

The contributors to this collection have extended Gandhi's notions of Indigenous forms of spirituality, articulating it as oppositional consciousness, alternative knowledge, and the site of anti-capitalist political and social praxis amid Western political and economic domination. These twenty-first century postcolonial intellectuals frame pre-colonial spiritual beliefs and practices as tools that can dismantle Eurocentric knowledge production, activate racialized bodies, and inspire the struggles of Indigenous peoples within and across countries. Unlike Gandhi and other anti-colonial leaders from the twentieth century, who utilized spirituality as a force for postcolonial nation-building invested in unity and homogeneity, the writers featured here narrate spirituality as a signifier capturing multiple, distinct, and localized ways of knowing and being in the world. For example, in her chapter, Wane defines spirituality as 'invisible inner strength' and a form of individual sub-consciousness and relation to 'Creator' and a 'higher self' that was never colonized and cannot be colonized because it is a form of knowledge free of temporal and spatial boundaries. In the context of colonization, conquest, and oppression, the spirit is a life force whose awakening and assertion are the very meaning of 'decolonization.'

In Tario's chapter, spirituality is framed as 'critical consciousness' arising within Latina/o and Indigenous peoples in the 'borderlands' between Canada, the United States, Mexico, and El Salvador, transcending the boundaries of identifications, nation-states, and knowledge systems attached to structures of power and oppression. In this way, spirituality is a powerful and authentic agency enabling transcendence amid racism, domination, marginality, and subjugation. Tario's discussion of Latinx ontologies experienced by young people in these regions illustrates the painful ways of being in-between Indigenous and Western/colonial knowledges, and in-between identifications with original land yet citizenship in nation-states. Love for self, family, strangers, and non-human others in the midst of such oppressive realities is the ultimate expression of critical spirituality, acting as the basis of revolutionary praxis that rejects oppression, imagines novel social forms, and gestures to a different future.

The narratives in this collection further connect the spiritual to the material in explicit ways, locating them both on the 'racialized body' whose spiritual yearnings alone cannot sustain anti-racist, anti-Black, and anti-colonial struggles. In his chapter, Doyle-Wood reminds us that the racialized body must endure as well because it is the material presence of that body, despite colonial and murderous state instrumentalities, that grounds 'constant holistic contestation of the colonial structure itself.' Spiritual resurgences also cannot do the work of radical politics if the spiritual is simply an act of self-protection by inner escape, enabling one to cope with oppression. Rather, spiritual healing takes place when the racialized and colonized body also feels anger and pain, igniting shared rage and collective resistance in the face of 'colonial, White supremacist, racializing power.' The sociality and outward direction of such deeply personal and individual feelings and experiences embody the relational aspects of the spiritual narrated by the other authors included in the collection.

For example, Devi Mucina extends in his chapter an Ubuntu greeting originating in his native Zimbabwe to all native peoples of Turtle Island, thus giving voice to the 'relatedness' the author feels with Indigenous and colonized others in North America. Spatial and epistemological tensions, however, underscore this greeting as Mucina acknowledges privileging a particular mode of spirituality originating in Africa and calls himself an 'unwanted settler' on occupied Indigenous land in Canada. Yet, his Ubuntu greeting presents a spiritual path allowing the author to walk toward and connect to the narratives, world-senses, and struggles of Canada's Indigenous peoples, illustrating a spiritual journey of acquiring self-knowledge to understand one's connection and relation to others and the universe. TwoTrees and Pinto's references to 'the Sacred' in their chapter also center on the bonds holding Indigenous, Black, and Brown bodies together across history, time, and space. In their chapter, they frame the Sacred as a meeting point of individual paths merging into a collective voice forged out of tensions, differences, and love. That collective voice recognizes how modes of oppression are connected and calls for radical collectives, political solidarities, and mutual support in forging decolonizing, anti-racist, and anti-capitalist struggles locally and internationally. The social and historical 'martyr' holding these collectives together is made up of acts where individuals take responsibility for the oppression of others who are not like them. Such an act is performed by Mucina, as he describes his awakening from the seduction of Canadian capitalism and his realization that his prosperity as an immigrant from Africa is enabled by colonial and state extractions of Indigenous resources, land, labor, knowledge, and lives. His Afrocentric Ubuntu greeting to Indigenous peoples on Turtle Island is thus a political act of both solidarity and spirituality.

## Spirituality as the Site of Radical Traditions

In his passionate, personal, and empowering articulation of the political nature of culture, Ferguson (2018) located radical anti-racist and anti-colonial political traditions in the United States in the immediate and familiar; he mapped family, kin, neighborhood, and community as sources and carriers of creative and political imaginations upon which important social movements raised and transformed the world. As a young Black queer man in the American South, Ferguson encountered and made sense of racism, imperialism, oppression, patriarchy, and homophobia through the songs sung by his mother, the stories and memories recounted by his grandmother, the labor of his father, the sermons and people meeting at the local church, as well as White, Latino, and immigrant families who lived or crossed the streets of his small town located on land first inhabited by the Cherokees and the Muscogee Creeks. Ferguson found his spiritual and intellectual inspiration in the political energies, cultural creativity, and resilience of the ordinary folks with whom he grew up: energies and creativity constituting radical traditions of struggle and determination that provide hope for contemporary generations and struggles. In Ferguson's words, 'Engaging those sources and powers is our only chance to use the land in the way that the land intended, as the basis for envisioning and activating inter-relatedness… and possibilities' (ibid., 21).

The authors contributing to this collection show us that such radical traditions are present in the vast historical spiritual and cultural reservoirs of knowledge available to all people and communities. The chapters in the collection enact local and global political traditions, drawing strength and inspiration from land, family, and community. For example, Karanja theorizes the land as a site of healing, noting that healing practices in Africa, Australia, and North America are 'gifts' passed down from grandmothers to daughters and granddaughters, thus extending knowledge across time, space, and generations. Expanding on the theme of food growing and food preparation, Demi enacts a powerful critique of capitalist food chains from within the realm of the domestic and the family, where Indigenous traditions related to food and eating survive and thrive, serving as the backbone of Indigenous cultures in Africa. Similarly, in her poem titled 'In my Mother's Kitchen,' Brady depicts food and cooking as everyday events where she seeks and finds spiritual connection to her mother, aunts, and grandmothers, whose struggles against racism inspire Brady's own strength in facing continuous oppression as a Black woman in Canada. In her chapter, Kimberly L. Todd describes night-time dreams and dreaming as connecting to myth, spiritual origins, and historical ways of knowing inspiring generational resistance to oppression and visions of a different future. Night-time dreaming, food preparation, feeling and loving land and the natural world, and other intimate practices recounted by the authors in this book thus serve as conservation efforts. They help build an archive of historical spiritual and political know-how supporting contemporary struggles for social and environmental justice, material and racial equality, and the well-being of human and non-human life, and planet Earth.

## Spirituality, Decolonization, and (Post)Socialism

The contributors to the collection further identify racial Whiteness, Eurocentricity in education and knowledge production, nation-states, global food chains, capitalism and consumerism, Western medicine, and masculine scientific paradigms as major elements of colonial structures and the skeleton of oppression. Across the chapters, decolonization takes the form of displacing and dismantling these structural elements, building in their place spiritual, social, political, cultural, and epistemological forms that support a forest of knowledges. Such rich flora captures multiple and diverse ways of knowing upon which we can imagine, dream of, construct, experiment, and enact social forms marked by kindness, collaboration, love, compassion, and togetherness of a new kind.

Decolonizing acts of displacement, rejection, and renewal are always shaped by place and time. In this context, place serves as an epistemological site from where we can address and practice the spiritual. Place is also a geopolitical location marked by history and power relations that are both the object and context of decolonization and spirituality. Here, we are identifying and articulating the spiritual from within knowledges, practices, memories, and imaginations tied to locality, family, and community. Yet, we also speak to each other and the world from within North American academies and Western nation-states, using our voices and bodies to assert non-Western and Indigenous ways of knowing and being in the world. Our experiences within such places allow us to identify and imagine both (post)colonized subjects and colonizers in certain ways, which may fail to fully appreciate the ideological implications of our place-bound conversations.

For example, academics and activists have engaged extensively in writing about and theorizing the intersections of colonialism, racism, and capitalism—but we have yet to conduct an in-depth examination of the Eurocentric ideologies and philosophies associated with 'the good society.' Marxism, socialism, visions of communism, and other egalitarian ideologies and philosophies grounded in European modernity and ways of life have remained the end goal of revolutions leading to the redistribution of wealth and power, equality, and non-capitalist democracy. These communist, socialist, and Marxist ideals continue to define critical conversations about a better future amid the social, political, moral, and environmental crises societies are experiencing today.

One way to explain the lack of critical and decolonizing engagement with these paradigms is our own location as thinkers, researchers, writers, and activists doing decolonizing and spiritual work from within Western academia in Canada and the United States. In our passion and desire for liberation, we forget that entire lands and peoples are still struggling with the realities of colonization. For example, social sciences and humanities scholars in Western academies have not been particularly interested in the so-called Second World of former socialist states in Central and Eastern Europe, the Balkans, and the former Soviet Union. However, historical evidence suggests that the term 'decolonization' was first used in the English language in the 1930s in relation to the liberation and postcolonial independence of the small Balkan states emerging from the rubbles of the Ottoman, Hapsburg, and Russian empires in the early twentieth century; the term's usage at the time further gestured to the inevitability of similar processes in Africa and Asia (James & Slobodian 2015, p. 2). The success of communist revolutions across the Balkans at the end of World War II imbued decolonizing processes in the region with Marxist and socialist imaginations supporting the establishment of socialist states including

Albania, Bulgaria, Romania, and former Yugoslavia. This history illuminates important linkages between colonization, decolonization, spirituality, and state socialism that have remained understudied, thus obscuring how and why the building of socialist economies and societies based on material justice and social equality in the Balkans was predicated on the eradication of the spiritual lives of these societies.

Classical Marxist and Leninist theories and philosophy construct dualistic notions of material/spiritual and natural/supernatural, framing ideas of religion and spirituality as manifestations of how individuals are alienated from their own world defined by poverty, oppression, and capitalist exploitation. From this perspective, religion and spirituality represent incapable and impotent forces that cannot entice change and sustain human liberation (see Brentlinger, 2000; Surin, 2013). Marxist and communist leaders governing socialist states in Central, Eastern, and Southeastern Europe (the Balkans) considered spiritual life and religion to simply be escapes from human misery: opium for the subjugated masses. Therefore, they considered the secularization of workers and other oppressed classes to be the key to achieving individual and public consciousness, which in turn would ignite a socialist revolution resulting in material equality, collectivism, and social justice. The ensuing economic redistribution, collectivization, and social engineering taking place in these socialist states in the latter half of the twentieth century explicitly targeted religion and spirituality, driving these modes of human expression underground and into darkness. Citizens were not permitted to celebrate religious holidays, marry in a church, or openly explore any form of the mysterious or the occult. I grew up in a socialist state that was not just anti-religious; it was soulless. It reduced centuries-long spiritual beliefs and traditions to state-sanctioned folkloristic presentations that were often performed as tourist attractions to foreigners, especially Western visitors and 'proper Europeans' musing over the cultural primitiveness of Bulgarians, and the Balkans in general. The socialist state persecuted men and women engaging in spiritualistic practices such as healing, reading the future, or even greeting the Sun with physical movements meant to enhance the human inner spirit and connect to the universe.[1] These attacks on religion and spirituality illustrated what the Fourteenth Dalai Lama described as violent communist statecraft failing to grasp the central role of the spiritual in human compassion and capacity for goodness (Dhar, Chakrabarti, & Kayatekin, 2016). Yet, such compassion and love for others presented major tenets of the socialist and communist aspirations in whose name we, who lived in socialist states, endured that violence. Violence was also a central aspect of socialist building in other parts of the world, especially Soviet Russia.

## Colonization, Indigenous Peoples, and Spirituality in Russia

The ongoing struggle of Indigenous peoples in the Russian North serves as an important political and historical site to study and perceive how oppression, land extraction, and the displacement and eradication of entire people, languages, and cultures have been enacted in order to build a socialist state and society. Indigenous (and Muslim peoples) in the Soviet North were imprisoned, resettled, murdered, raped, and put into boarding schools to foster a 'higher social order and consciousness' in socialist and communist nations and subjects. Powerful political Marxist, Leninist, and Stalinist ideologies rationalized these colonial technologies as a necessity and historical stage upon which the Soviet nation would emerge and endure. At the heart of these ideologies was the erasure of Indigenous spirituality and cosmologies.

When the Soviet revolution swept Russia in 1917, Indigenous peoples at the Northern frontiers of the Russian empire—Chukchi, Inuit, Nenets, Evenk, Saami, and more than 30 other societies—comprised the majority of the population inhabiting these remote areas of the empire, alongside missionaries, who were mainly Protestants actively propagating Christian norms and beliefs among the native groups (Leete & Vallikivi, 2011; Petrov, 2008). Prior to the revolution, many of these Protestant missionaries in Russian Chukotka had come from Alaska, bringing with them American modernity in the form of material objects, services, waged employment, and Protestant work ethics. The early Bolshevik government targeted both Protestant missionaries and Indigenous peoples in the Soviet North. In the eyes of the Soviet state, both were deviations from communist and socialist ideals, and hence, these groups had to be managed, controlled, and above all, recruited for the purposes of socialist nation-building. They were also perceived as naturally suited for communist projects because Indigenous peoples in the Soviet North lived in classless societies, practicing collectivist social forms. Similar classless formations were present in Protestant communities in the region, who at the time even borrowed the language of communism and brotherhood to appeal to the masses, including the Indigenous populations they targeted for Christian conversion and baptism.

By the end of 1920, Soviet polices directed at the Northern peoples took a sharp turn under the leadership of Stalin who referred to Christian Orthodox, Protestant, and Indigenous priests and shamans as 'exploiters' of the people. Stalin also proclaimed that the eradication of all religiosity in the Soviet Union would be complete by 1937. As a result, Indigenous shamans were shot or imprisoned; many went into hiding, practicing rituals in full secrecy. Soviet police forces were sent to the North to confiscate Indigenous drums, costumes, regalia, and objects deemed 'religious.' However, ancient stories and myths about the power of the spirits endured, inspiring contemporary cultural and social Indigenous expressions in Siberia. The Nenets people in the Russian North recounted the following story to contemporary anthropologists: A Russian communist came to the reindeer herders' camp and asked to see the image of the female spirit guarding the tent. The communist took his rifle out and shot at the image, but the bullet ricocheted back and killed the Russian communist (Leete & Vallikivi, 2011). Other examples of Indigenous resistance also reveal the role of spirituality under Soviet colonialism. For example, between the 1920s and 1940s, Soviet hegemony and brutality over Indigenous peoples in Siberia led to intensified Indigenous spiritual sacrificing of reindeer and other animals appealing to higher powers to stop the colonizing power. These sacrifices were directly provoked by Soviet collectivization and the repression of native cultures and spiritual beliefs (Leete, 2005). In another example, a new group of Indigenous spiritual leaders emerged, mimicking and performing Christian rituals disguising native spiritual forms (Leete & Vallikivi, 2011).

Soviet policies aiming to acculturate and socialize Indigenous peoples into the ideals of socialism, communism, and Marxism-Leninism explicitly targeted Indigenous spirituality. Colonial pressure on the sacred mobilized strong and persisting Indigenous resistance throughout the Soviet regime all the way to its end in 1992. Attacks on Indigenous spirituality included forced collectivization of the economic means of production sustaining Indigenous societies, centralization of food and other supplies to the remote North, dependence on Soviet state social and health care, and the exploitation of natural resources upon which Indigenous livelihood depended. These forces reorganized Indigenous life and social relations in dramatic ways. They displaced the centrality of the family and the household, creating instead nameless 'collectives' of Indigenous waged workers. By identifying and persecuting Indigenous shamans as exploiters and enemies of the people, the communist regime created 'classes' and 'workers' out of Indigenous social structures, where such divisions did not exist prior to state socialism. These acts of social, cultural, and political engineering of socialist citizens reveal an ideologically driven communist colonial Soviet instrumentality that created class-based human, social, and economic conditions in order to prove the historical necessity of its own existence and capacity to rule.

The collapse of the Soviet Union in 1992 did not liberate Indigenous peoples on its territory. State exploitation of the natural resources in their lands dovetailed with harsh new policies reducing Indigenous populations to 'ethnic groups' with little rights over the political, social, and economic laws governing their lands. Presently, more Russian settlers than natives inhabit the northern territories designated 'Indigenous' by Russian law. Russian settlers also comprise the majority of the urban population in these lands, holding power over local legislature, cultural production, and trade (Petrov, 2008). However, Indigenous groups in the Russian North are currently experiencing a spiritual renaissance and cultural revival, as illustrated by local artistic and political movements that are active internationally. Diverse Indigenous groups in Siberia have formed international alliances and collaborations with Native American organizations in Alaska and other parts of the United States, Indigenous peoples in Greenland, and native groups in Norway and Canada. These international alliances are supporting the Indigenous spiritual and political revival in the Russian North, providing resources to native peoples seeking self-identification, self-governance, and full political rights over Indigenous lands—not just in Russia but globally.

However, spiritual and cultural awakening alone will not and cannot sustain Indigenous well-being in Russia. In the nineteenth century, colonization along with poverty and disease had serious effects on the health and longevity of Indigenous peoples in Russia. That period was followed by Soviet violence and assimilationist policies tied to centralized economy, which failed to sustain even the basic needs of native populations in the North (Diatchkova, 2001). In the post-Soviet period, severe unemployment and scarcity of food staples put more pressure on these populations, leading to a series of health and demographic crisis and prompting discussions about the very survival of Indigenous groups in Russia (Petrov,

2008). Forced assimilation, poverty, poor nutrition, limited access to traditional food resources, and declining health reduced Indigenous population growth by 70% in the 1970s alone, and by 12% in the 1980s (ibid., 274). High mortality rates drove Indigenous life expectancy down to about 60 years creating in turn a tremendous social, cultural, and knowledge gap across the generations (ibid.).

These demographic developments illustrate important linkages between the spiritual and the material. Material resources are key aspects contributing to the sustenance and survival of Indigenous, racialized, and colonized bodies. Policies and material structures supporting spiritual life, cultural revival, the longevity of native languages, health, well-being, education, autonomy, and participation in civic and political life remain central to Indigenous survival in Russia and other colonized lands. Spirituality—that inner strength, life force, and higher self, narrated by the contributions to this collection—is also a political force that affects material life and structures upon which a better and just society could form and thrive. The locality of our decolonizing efforts should not obscure the globality of colonial conquests. Liberation of colonized peoples here and now depends on the liberation of others who are far away and may not be visible to us. Relational, connected, and globalized consciousness is the spiritual soil upon which the material equality and rich flora of knowledges and ways of being embraced by the authors in this collection can and will flourish.

## Note

1. I am referring to the influential spiritual movement in Bulgaria called Danovism after the Bulgarian philosopher and spiritual leader Peter Deunov, who founded it in 1932 (see Kraleva, 2001).

## References

Brentlinger, J. (2000). Revolutionizing spirituality: Reflections on Marxism and religion. *Science & Society, 64*(2), 171–193.

Dhar, A., Chakrabarti, A., & Kayatekin, S. (2016). Crossing materialism and religion: An interview on Marxism and spirituality with the Fourteenth Dalai Lama. *Rethinking Marxism, 28*(3–4), 584–598.

Diatchkova, G. (2001). Indigenous peoples of Russia and political history. *Canadian Journal of Native Studies, 21*(2), 217–233.

Ferguson, R. (2018, November 9). *To catch a light-filled vision: American studies and the activation of radical traditions.* Key note address delivered to at the American Studies Association Annual Meeting, Atlanta, Georgia.
James, M., & Slobodian, Q. (2015). Eastern Europe. In M. Thomas & A. Thompson (Eds.), *The Oxford handbook for the ends of empires* (pp. 1–28). https://doi.org/10.1093/oxforfhb/9780198713197.013.20.
Kraleva, M. (2001). *The master Peter Deunov: His life and teaching.* Bulgaria: Kibea.
Leete, A. (2005). Religious revival as reaction to the hegemonization of power in Siberia in the 1920s to 1940s. *Asian Folklore Studies, 64*(2), 233–245.
Leete, A., & Vallikivi, L. (2011). Adapting Christianity on the Siberian edge during the early Soviet period. *Folklore: Electronic Journal of Folklore, 49*, 131–146.
Petrov, A. (2008). Lost generations? Indigenous population of the Russian North in the post-Soviet era. *Canadian Studies in Population, 35*(2), 269–290.
Surin, K. (2013). Marxism and religion. *Critical Research on Religion, 1*(1), 9–14.
Van Der Veer, P. (2009). Spirituality in modern society. *Social Research: An International Quarterly, 76*(4), 1097–1120.

# Index




N. N. Wane et al. (eds.), *Decolonizing the Spirit in Education and Beyond, Spirituality, Religion, and Education*, https://doi.org/10.1007/978-3-030-25320-2

P



R



S



T



U



W

Printed in the United States
By Bookmasters